EMF 10

EMF: Studies in Early Modern France

Editorial Board
Peter Bayley
Thomas Carr
James Farr
George Hoffmann
David LaGuardia
Sarah Maza
Allan Pasco
Marian Rothstein
Kathleen Wine
Amy Wygant

Founding Editor
David Lee Rubin

Copy Editor
Marie Herizler

Production
Angel Applications

Cover Design
Dallas Pasco

EMF: STUDIES IN EARLY MODERN FRANCE

Edited by Anne L. Birberick and Russell Ganim

Volume 10
Modern Perspectives on the Early Modern:
Temps recherché, temps retrouvé

Rookwood Press
Charlottesville

©2005 by Rookwood Press, Inc.
520 Rookwood Place
Charlottesville, Virginia 22903-4734, USA
All rights reserved. Published 2005.
Printed in the United States of America.

This book is printed on acid-free paper.

ISBN 1-886365-54-7

Address proposals and submissions (in duplicate with return postage) to the Publisher, EMF, Rookwood Press.

CONTENTS

CONTRIBUTORS
vii

RUSSELL GANIM
Introduction
1

DAVID LAGUARDIA
French Renaissance Literature and the Problem of Theory:
Alcofribas's Performance in the Prologue to *Gargantua*
5

KATHERINE ALMQUIST
The Bibliophile and the Archivist on Montaigne
39

WILLIAM CLOONAN
La Barque de Dante: Michelangelo and the Anxiety of Influence
60

STEPHEN SHAPIRO
Roland Joffé's *Vatel*: Refashioning the History
of the Ancien Régime
77

UGO DIONNE
Sans peur, sans reproche et sans perruque: La figure du Philosophe dans le
cinéma français contemporain (1988–2001)
89

SÉVERINE GENIEYS-KIRK
(Ré)visions de la période pré-moderne
dans l'oeuvre de Philippe Sollers
108

JEFFREY N. PETERS AND TODD W. REESER
Between Freedom and Memory:
The Early Modern in Barthes's *Le Degré zéro de l'écriture*
126

JEAN-VINCENT BLANCHARD
The Cyber-Baroque: Walter Ong, The History of Rhetoric,
and an Early Modern Information Mode
150

INDEX
183

Contributors

KATHERINE ALMQUIST is Assistant Professor of French and Coordinator of Liberal Studies at Frostburg State University. Her edition of Montaigne's parliamentary papers will be published by Editions Honoré Champion.

JEAN-VINCENT BLANCHARD, Associate Professor of French at Swarthmore College, is the author of Optique, religion et langage au XVIIe siècle. De la rhétorique des jésuites au style de la raison moderne (Presses de l'Université Laval, 2005).

WILLIAM CLOONAN is Richard Chapple Professor of Modern Languages at Florida State University. His most recent book is The Writing of War: French and German Fiction and World War II (University of Florida Press, 1999).

UGO DIONNE is Professeur d'études françaises at the University of Montreal. His articles have been published in Poétique, Lumen, Dix-septième siècle, and elsewhere.

SÉVERINE GENIEYS-KIRK is a lecturer at University College, Dublin. She has contributed to several collective volumes, notably Lectrices de l'ancien régime (Presses universitaires de Rennes, 2003)

DAVID LAGUARDIA, Associate Professor of French and Comparative Literature at Dartmouth College, is the author of The Iconography of Power: The French Nouvelle at the End of the Middle Ages (University of Delaware Press, 1999).

JEFFREY N. PETERS is Associate Professor of French at the University of Kentucky and author of Mapping Discord: Allegorical Cartography in Early Modern French Writing (University of Delaware Press, 2004).

TODD W. REESER is Assistant Professor of French at the University of Pittsburgh. His book, Moderating Masculinity in Early Modern Culture, is forthcoming at the University of North Carolina Press. He was an NEH Fellow at the National Humanities Center, 2003-2004.

STEPHEN SHAPIRO is Assistant Professor of French at the College of the Holy Cross. His research examines seventeenth-century strategies of dissident historiography.

EMF 10

Introduction[1]

Russell Ganim

Traditionally, early modern scholars have always been skeptical of anything associated with the modern. Part of this skepticism naturally derives from a proprietary feeling about one's discipline. At this same time, it also stems from a somewhat venal but nonetheless inevitable sense that deciphering meaning in texts from a more distant, seemingly less accessible era is somehow more difficult than performing the same task with contemporary works or with those from the relatively recent past. On a psychological level, this false sense of superiority is oddly reinforced by the jealousy many early modernists (not just in French, but in other foreign literatures as well) experience when their undergraduates and graduates consistently show preference for courses and research dealing with the modern or the contemporary because students supposedly find these topics more "relevant" to their concerns.

In a period where the value of literature and of the Humanities in general is constantly called into question, such "turf wars" seem silly at best and are dangerous at worst. Within the last twenty-five years, the move toward cultural and interdisciplinary studies provides a context in which the *rapprochement* between eras continues to provide new kinds of analysis that were impossible given the scholarly trends toward specialization and the political trends (within the academy) toward the balkanism that dominated much of our profession throughout the better part of the twentieth century.

To detail the history and causes behind the real or perceived schism between early modern and modern studies is to go beyond the scope of this introduction and of the volume in general. Neither is the purpose to retrace the Foucauldian epistemological shifts that account in part for this perceived gap. From a somewhat more localized perspective, however, it should be pointed out that every period—from Antiquity, through the Renaissance, neo-Classical, modern, and the post-modern—has undergone its own version of the *Querelle des Anciens et des Modernes.* What invariably results from such discussions is that even those who decry the "Ancient" as irrelevant and the "Modern" as shallow cannot deny the existence of a literary and historical continuum where books generate other books and where the aesthetic standards and practices of one era serve to inform and redefine the other. In terms of generating meaning, the relationship is best defined as reciprocal, if not symbiotic, because just as Proust needs Madame de Sévigné's *Lettres* as a model for the narrative, social, and psychological nuances that help constitute the *Recherche*, Sévigné needs Proust not only to lend a sense of present-day "legitimacy" to her text, but more importantly to enable contemporary critics to ask questions of the *Lettres* and reveal truths about them that were not available before Proust or Proust scholarship. In the realm of theory, the same can be said of Sainte-Beuve (whether one is for or against him) and the sixteenth and seventeenth centuries, of Freud and Shakespeare, and of Bataille and Sade.[2] In the grand "hypertext" that is literary criticism, the past writes the present just as much as the present writes the past.

Accordingly, the current volume seeks to blur the boundaries between eras by tackling the problem of representing the Past in the Present. One could argue that such an attempt is inherently anachronistic and is therefore not worth undertaking. Similarly, any effort to define terms such as "early modern," "modern" or "modernity" seems futile because these expressions are used so indiscriminately as to become devoid of meaning. These counter-arguments are certainly valid to a degree, but to embrace them fully would negate the realities of influence and change that occur within a historical context. More fundamentally, contrarian perspectives of this nature overlook the dialogue, if not the dependence that exists between various periods, genres, and media.

This volume makes no pretense of establishing fixed meanings for the "early modern" and the "modern." It does, however, illustrate that these notions are significant if only because scholars who specialize in both eras constantly appropriate the terms, concepts, and worldviews associated with these epochs in order to lend authority to their work. In addition, the articles presented here highlight the process in which an "early modern" mind-set seeks to free itself from external absolutes in order to evolve into a "modern" one which sees itself as rational and autonomous–despite the inherent dangers of founding what Heidegger calls the "world picture" (Cascardi 1) on reason and individual agency.[3] The "early modern" and "modern" are coterminous, and thus more frequently emphasize commonality of thought and practice rather than difference. Representing the Past in the Present is justified because when seen as conjoined, the two lose part of their temporal distinction. Viewed from this perspective, both are still evolving to produce new ways of interpreting the artistic, scientific, and philosophical inheritance that constitutes present-day intellectual endeavor.

What follows is organized along chronological, generic, and thematic lines. We begin with the Renaissance, where David LaGuardia's study of Rabelais's Prologue to *Gargantua* raises fundamental questions of how to apply forms of contemporary theory while avoiding anachronism. His analysis of Alcofribas's "textual performance of subjectivity" sheds light on Rabelais's narrative strategy and his "interpellation" of the reader by linking Renaissance philology and post-structuralist criticism. Katherine Almquist focuses on that other beacon of the French Renaissance, Montaigne, but not so much in the authorial or literary sense, but for what Montaigne represents as a nineteenth-century movement for government sponsorship of document preservation. Her essay chronicles the efforts of Gustave Brunet, Jules Delpit, and Jean-François Payen among others, to inscribe Montaigne in the national patrimony via institutional means such as periodicals, archives, and academies. The impact of the Florentine Renaissance on the Romantic era resonates in William Cloonan's comparative study of Michelangelo's *The Last Judgment* and Delacroix's *The Barque of Dante*. Analyzing Delacroix's fascination with Michelangelo as detailed in the former's *Journals* as well as articles the artist published, Cloonan revisits Harold Bloom's famous work in part to read the *Barque* as "a pictorial enactment of the anxiety of influence."

The impact of "New" media is necessarily a part of the encounter between eras, with cinema also marking the intersection between the modern and the early modern. Stephen Shapiro's examination of the film *Vatel* views Roland Joffé's work not only as a commentary on the "exploitation, corruption, and decadence of the *Ancien Régime*," but as an indirect indictment of "democratic capitalism" and its "emptiness and immorality." Certain luminaries of the *Ancien Régime* are portrayed in a more favorable light in Ugo Dionne's essay on recent French films which make heroes of Enlightenment figures such as Diderot, Honoré and Cyprien Fragonard, Beaumarchais, and Grégoire de Fronsac. The result is a "mythologization" of the intellectual which reaffirms the place of the *philosophe* in modern French cultural identity. The deconstruction of myths and legends associated with the early modern and its authors becomes a line of inquiry for Séverine Genieys-Kirk as she studies the representation of François Villon and Cyrano de Bergerac, among others, in the work of the contemporary novelist Philippe Sollers. These novels call attention to themselves because of the highly stylized, and sometimes poetic way in which they allude to, if not re-create, the literature of the past. The legacy of literary antecedents and their conflict with modern critical sensibilities become the focus of Jeffrey Peters's and Todd Reeser's analysis of how the memory of preclassical and classical thought and art shapes Roland Barthes's notions of *écriture* and *littérarité*. While the preclassical must ostensibly be effaced in the creation of a modern theory and aesthetic, the authors suggest that "the multiple *écritures* of modernism necessarily remember the past, even a past that is cast as absent." Looking toward the future, Jean-Vincent Blanchard concludes the volume by "examin[ing] the significance of the early modern in regard to pedagogy." Blanchard relies on Walter Ong's noted study of Ramus as a "model of communication" that could be applied to enhance the use of cybernetics in the classroom and in research. As part of a curriculum designed to teach "rhetorical history," technological innovation serves to improve the "critical literacy" of those charged with interpreting the early modern.

NOTES

[1] The editors are indebted to their colleague Larry Riggs for his suggestions on the topics of modernity and early modernity.
[2] See Bataille's *L'histoire de l'érotisme*.
[3] Cascardi specifically refers to p. 130 of "The Age of the World Picture."

Works Cited or Consulted

Bataille, Georges. *Oeuvres complètes*. Paris: Gallimard, 1976.

Berman, Morris. *The Reenchantment of the World*. Ithaca and London: Cornell University Press, 1981.

Cascardi, Anthony. *The Subject of Modernity*. Cambridge: Cambridge University Press, 1992.

Ferguson, Harvie. *Modernity and Subjectivity: Body, Soul, Spirit*. Charlottesville: University Press of Virginia, 2000.

Heidegger, Martin. 'The Age of the World Picture.' *The Question Concerning Technology and Other Essays*. Trans. William Lovitt. New York: Harper and Row, 1977, 115–54.

Matthews, Steven. *Modernism*. London: Arnold, 2004.

Moriarty, Michael. *Early Modern French Thought: The Age of Suspicion*. Oxford: Oxford University Press, 2003.

Rigolot, François. 'Pour Sainte-Beuve (1804–1904–2004): Propos d'un seiziémiste.' *Revue d'Histoire Littéraire de la France* (2004): 3–24.

French Renaissance Literature and the Problem of Theory: Alcofribas's Performance in the Prologue to *Gargantua*

David LaGuardia

At least since the 1950s, the role of "theory" in literary analysis has been a cause of contention among scholars devoted to the study of Renaissance literature.[1] For those of us who concentrate on French literature from the sixteenth century, theory was at the heart of a particularly bitter debate for a very long time. For decades, our field was driven by two seemingly incompatible forms of devotion: the passion for the painstaking work of philology, which has been the core of some of the most exciting and admirable scholarship to be done in sixteenth-century French studies, versus the passion for rereading five-hundred-year-old works from the perspectives of modern, postmodern, and "cutting-edge" theories ranging from poststructuralism to queer theory, gender studies, performance theory, postcolonialism, and beyond. Although major scholars have "applied" theory to French Renaissance literature for decades, theoretical readings are only now beginning to be accepted on a large scale by a generation of scholars educated during and after the "boom" of theory in the American academy in the 1970s, 1980s, and into the 1990s, when theory multiplied into dozens of lines of thought. On one side of this debate, the problem was this: how could one "get rid" of all this theory and return to the serious business of reading Renaissance texts in their historical and intertextual contexts? For the other side of the debate, the problem was this: how could one read Renaissance texts from a theoretical perspective without being accused of anachronism by philologists? This discussion brought into focus the difficulties of defining theory and its application in a domain, that of Renaissance studies in French, in which the term still needs to be interrogated in at least three of its primary aspects. First, we need to examine the extent to which the textual practices that defined the intellectual context of Renaissance writers were "theories" in the modern sense of the word. Second, the notions of history and historical context which are often used as the basis for accusations of critical anachronism need to be examined themselves as theories regarding the conceptual frames that render given texts comprehensible. Finally, the problem of theory in itself needs to be addressed, that is, its current definitions and manifestations, and the justification for their "application" to Renaissance literature. These three concerns might be rephrased as short questions. To what extent did Renaissance writers use "theory" while reading and writing texts? How do our conceptions of these theories as constitutive elements of a given historical context influence our interpretations of texts? What contemporary theories are we authorized to use in our own analyses of these writers and their works?

It could and should be argued that the most productive and cogent readings can be accomplished in our field only if one combines the best of both philology and theory. In the case of Renaissance texts, an understanding of what theory was for writers of the period can be achieved only after a preliminary philological study has been completed. Renaissance texts such as the Prologue to Rabelais's *Gargantua*, which I will use as a privileged example and case study in the following pages, are theoretical inquiries into the concept of interpretation itself, and are based on enormous erudition that included major texts at the foundation of modern philosophy, as well as medieval texts on Biblical exegesis, and Humanist works on the "proper" interpretation of the New Testament, to name just a few sources. If one defines theory essentially as the practice of using abstract models of reading as means of interpreting texts, it could be said that philology, at least in this respect, is itself a theoretical discipline.[2] One might claim, for example, with Gérard Defaux, that a given "theory" of Biblical exegesis, such as that of Nicholas de Lyra, provides a general model for understanding Rabelais's Prologue (Defaux, "D'un problème l'autre," 195-96). Philological evidence to the effect that a Renaissance writer read or knew of given writers (Sextus Empiricus, St. Paul, Erasmus, Nicholas de Lyra, etc.) has often been accepted as proof that these intertexts serve as keys to the interpretation of the text. This belief in the necessity of the historical contemporaneity or contiguity of intertexts that may serve as models of interpretation is a theoretical proclamation: Rabelais knew and read Erasmus, hence the latter's works provide (the only) models that allow for an interpretation of the former text "in its own terms." Establishing this kind of link, however, does not necessarily help one to unravel all of the difficulties of Rabelais's Prologue to *Gargantua*, which requires a theoretical work of interpretation that could be based on the relation between the text and its sources. If, for example, Rabelais's Prologue uses ancient and Renaissance models as the bases of its exposition of the problems involved in interpretation, to what extent can we read the text beyond the privileged meaning that a given intertext seems to authorize? If philology proves that *Gargantua* was written in dialogue with Erasmus and Saint Paul, does this mean that the "design" of the work is inevitably Evangelical, and cannot be read from the more abstract point of view (i.e., Rabelais's work inscribes the aporia of textual undecidability) that some poststructural theorists have ascribed to it? To what extent might theory be used to explain philological evidence?

I will argue here that, if Plato's *Symposium* is one of the major intertexts inscribed in Rabelais's work, it could be that a *Bacchic* mode of reading is as appropriate for interpreting *Gargantua* and the other books as the Evangelical or Erasmian modes that have been the heart and soul of some philological critiques of the Prologue and of all of Rabelais. The definition of what a Bacchic mode of interpretation might be, which has been explored recently by Tristan Dagron in a compelling article, serves as an example of the philological practice of theory as it applies to reading Renaissance texts. Analyzing Rabelais from the perspective of a philologically-grounded interpretation of the theoretical relationship between the writer and Plato, it might be said that the Rabelaisian text inscribes a kind of semantic ecstacy, linked to the ancient practice of contemplation that is described in detail in the *Symposium*, and which Dagron explicates clearly. From this perspective, the letter and the spirit of Rabelais's work are consubstantial, meaning that the often grotesque images of the text have to be understood as material embodiments of the "higher meanings" that have been read as its center and purpose. In other words, the legendary excess of Rabelais's books does not constitute a kind of "burlesque diction," as Edwin Duval phrases it (Duval, "Interpretation," 7), which must be gone beyond in order to understand the Humanist idealism at the core of his thinking; rather, and in an authentically Platonic fashion, one must understand the grotesque features of the work as the necessary and inevitable manifestations of that idealism in the only form that is available to us, in the same way that the Platonic conception of immortal beauty can be attained or achieved only through the contemplation of the beautiful bodies of mortal individuals (Plato, *Symposium*, 210a-212a). In this sense, Rabelais's text inscribes the kind of paradox that was at the heart of Platonic philosophy: it is only in the multiple, the transient, and the base that one may glimpse the universal, the immortal, and the divine. Nevertheless, from this philosophical point of view, which Rabelais adopts "as his own" (as Defaux might say), if the perception of the Forms is the ultimate goal of thought, it is also true that the philosopher must engage in an active contemplation of the transient objects that are the only medium through which the Forms may be revealed to him.[3]

Moreover, once this philological link has been established, Rabelais's Prologue could be read in the latest theoretical terms as a piece of "performance art," in which the narrator defines himself as what one might call, building upon the work of Dagron, a "Bacchic" subject, through the inscription of "felicitous performatives" (in Austin's sense) that appear literally as proclamations and apostrophes in the text. Reading with Judith Butler, in her appropriations of theorists as diverse as Austin, Althusser, and Foucault, we might say that the narrative subject inscribed in Rabelais's Prologue "interpellates" his readers as subjects of a very particular kind: "Buveurs tresillustres, et vous Verolez tresprecieux (car à vous non à aultres sont dediez mes escriptz)" (5). For a certain kind of philological reading, this type of proclamation and apostrophe, with its "grotesque" references to drinking and venereal disease, is part of the "burlesque diction" of the Rabelaisian text, which must be interpreted figuratively as part of an allegorical inscription of an Evangelical or Humanist message. In contrast, from the point of view of contemporary theory, it is precisely this kind of utterance that must be examined carefully in order to understand the subjectivity not of Rabelais himself, but of the narrative subject who appears on the title page of the 1542 edition of the book, bearing the anagrammatic name of Alcofribas Nasier.[4] This second opening gesture of the work, following the poem "Aux Lecteurs," inscribes a curious kind of interpellation that has posed problems for Rabelais scholarship from its inception. In the "classic" form of interpellation described by Althusser, and later expanded by Butler, a given subject is brought into being, so to speak, when s/he is literally called upon by an agent of power, such as a policeman calling out "hey you!" to a suspect, who in turn recognizes, or rejects, or runs away from his/her capture by power as a suspect.[5] In Rabelais's text, the interpellating voice is that of Alcofribas: "hey you, my drunken, syphilitic readers, to whom alone my writings are devoted, do you remember what Alcibiades said about Socrates in *The Symposium*?" From this interpellation, as well as from other indices in the Prologue, it seems clear that the narrative voice identifies the subject it embodies with the drunken and debauched readers to whom the text is dedicated. Far from being an irrelevant or a comic detail, this apostrophe establishes both the inscription of the text and its eventual interpretation by the reader under the aegis of Bacchic thought in the sense that Dagron develops in his article, meaning that all of the details of the work serve as objects of contemplation, upon which the reader is invited to meditate in a certain inspired, if not drunken, state, in order to arrive at an "amplified" understanding of their "higher meaning," which remains, nonetheless, "consubstantial" with the corporeal, at times "grotesque" images in which it is expressed.

Secondly, Alcofribas's performance immediately renders this identification much more problematic by establishing an equivalence between the book he is dedicating and the figure of Socrates that he uses to describe the nature of the work to his readers. If Socrates was a model of sobriety, as Alcibiades notes (Plato, *Symposium*, 214a), how can he possibly be a figure of Bacchic improvisation and interpretation? Reading in the terms described by Dagron, fortified by performance theory, the figure of Socrates is an emblem of reading and interpreting Rabelais, which must be contemplated in all of the varieties of its literal form in order to arrive at a kind of ecstatic or even mystical intuition of what that figure signifies. In this way the ultimate "performance" of the Prologue identifies Alcofribas not only with the interpellated readers, but also with the book he offers to them, as well as with the figure of Socrates who serves as its enigmatic emblem. This series of external identifications also must be understood in the specific intertextual framework of the reference to the *Symposium*, which culminates with Alcibiades' drunken praise of Socrates. In other words, and as Plato implies by ending the dialogue in this way, Socrates as the embodiment of the philosopher cannot be understood without a consideration of the effect that he had on his "disciples," represented here by Alcibiades, who serves as an uncanny mirror-image of the philosopher himself. Socrates made his listeners "dizzy" with his questions, and seemed to place them "under a spell" from which, like Alcibiades, they never were able to recover (Plato, *Symposium*, 216a-c). Similarly, Rabelais's text, through the discursive performance that brings Alcofribas to life as subject, places his readers into a kind of "intoxicated" state, in which, continually off balance, they are faced with the aporia of having to decide between the grotesque surface or "letter" of the text, and its serious lesson or "spirit," while they are never completely able legitimately to give preference to either side of this insoluble dilemma. On the contrary, and as Plato teaches, the "meaning" of the text can be intuited only if one meditates upon all of its material manifestations as objects that are essential to the process of intellection.

This kind of approach to reading Rabelais relies upon a synthesis of philology and theory, since it examines from an abstract point of view a mode of signification that can be understood only after the theory presented in a significant source text has been examined in detail. Furthermore, it makes use of specific contemporary theories regarding performance and interpellation in order to understand the functioning of these processes in Rabelais's work, in the elaboration of a narrative subject who projects his identity into that of his readers. The necessity of this synthesis itself will become clearer after a careful reconsideration and genealogy of the opposition that divided Renaissance scholars for decades over the nature and the interpretation of the Prologue to *Gargantua*. I will continue with my own reading of the Prologue after discussing this debate in detail.

The opposition between philologists and "theorists," which began in a sense in the 1950s, in Leo Spitzer's famous article, "Rabelais et les 'rabelaisants,'" attained its most virulent levels during the heyday of deconstruction and poststructuralism in the American academy. Gérard Defaux's famous attack against the supposed champions of deconstruction included a tactic that is characteristic of a certain kind of philological critique of theoretical readings. This strategy may be formulated as a question that philologists commonly ask: how can a scholar claim that a given author's work is an illustration of certain, possibly anachronistic theoretical principles (the Rabelaisian text as example of *dissémination* and *différance*) when this same scholar has not studied the historical context of the author enough to recognize the intertextual references at work in a given passage, or even to understand the meaning of certain crucial words (e.g., the expression *combien que* in the Prologue to *Gargantua*) in that context? Defaux's exposition of this problem contains perhaps the clearest formulation ever given of a persistent interpretative divide in sixteenth-century French studies that is still in the process of being overcome. This long passage is worth citing in its entirety:

> Nous avons aujourd'hui, à ce qu'il paraît, deux tendances critiques, voire deux écoles qui, si elles ne se querellent pas ouvertement, ne s'entendent à vrai dire sur rien d'essentiel. L'enjeu

n'est plus cette fois entre le texte et le contexte, l'histoire et la poésie—rares étant, en cette fin de siècle assagie, ceux qui, dans le domaine des études rabelaisiennes, contestent encore sérieusement la nécessité de la recherche érudite. Il s'est, cet enjeu, d'une manière très symptomatique, déplacé vers des questions chères aux philosophes et aux critiques de l'ère <<post-structuraliste>>: le langage, la vérité, l'interprétation. Disons, pour fixer le débat, qu'il s'agit ni plus ni moins de savoir si l'exercice qui constitue pourtant notre raison d'être, je veux dire la lecture *critique*, la lecture qui assigne un sens au texte, qui aboutit généralement à une interprétation claire et cohérente de ce dernier, est non seulement possible, mais encore légitime. D'un côté, ceux qui croient, comme Érasme, au langage, au texte et à l'épiphanie possible du sens, et qui sont convaincus que Rabelais voulait non seulement dire quelque chose, mais est encore parvenu à dire ce qu'il voulait, s'emploient, dans un esprit très positiviste et une perspective essentiellement idéologique, à reconstituer la pensée que celui-ci a, de toute évidence, enfermée dans son texte. Pratiquant ce que G. Poulet a fort justement appelé la <<critique d'identification>>, critique d'ailleurs aussi vieille que l'herméneutique des textes sacrés, ils sont, comme le chien de Platon, en quête de la <<substantificque mouelle>> et de l'*altior sensus*. De l'autre, au contraire, ceux qui, pour avoir lu J. Derrida ou P. de Man, ne croient plus au langage, dressent contre ce dernier un réquisitoire accablant. Ils ne cessent d'en souligner l'opacité, la duplicité et la circularité stérile, l'incapacité foncière à représenter, la nature mercurielle, irrémédiablement médiate et déchue. Utilisant avec un rare talent les concepts derridiens de *différance* et de *dissémination*, ils remettent en question le texte lui-même et sa fonction traditionnelle de médiateur de sens. En fin de compte, là où les premiers ne cherchent qu'à tirer du texte la vérité qui y est enfouie, à retrouver, eût dit Nicolas de Lyre, le *sensus* [sic] *mysticum & spiritualem sub littera latentem*, ceux-ci s'emploient, dans une perspective essentiellement anti-logocentrique et réflexive, à recenser tous les obstacles, toutes les stratégies, toutes les apories que le texte de Rabelais interpose nécessairement entre le lecteur et son désir de maîtrise. Spécialistes du soupçon et déconstructeurs systématiques de toute certitude et de tout *altior sensus*, ils sont, dans le texte, en quête de tout ce qui, fragmentation, dislocation, discontinuité, pluralité, leur permet d'en différer *sine die* l'interprétation. ("D'un problème l'autre," 195-96)

Defaux's formulation of the problem contains several elements that are symptomatic of a certain kind of philological rejection of theoretical readings of early modern texts. The first element is the problematic belief that the author's meaning and intention can be reconstituted through a careful reading of the text, which New Critics such as Wimsatt and Beardsley rejected long ago. The second element is the equation of this "positivist" critique and an originary, original mode of reading that is sanctified with a canonical name, which in this case is that of Erasmus ("Like Erasmus, we believe in language, in the text, and in the possible epiphany of meaning…"). The third symptom is the citation of a hermeneutic tradition rooted in ancient and medieval practices of allegorical interpretation. According to Defaux's formulation of the problem, "positivist" critics should accept only readings of at least this specific text that are consistent with exegetical techniques employed throughout the Middle Ages to read the Bible. One of these is the allegoresis described by Nicholas de Lyra, from whom Defaux excises a Latin citation meant to crystallize the object that positivist critics must "unearth" in their readings: *sensus* [*sic*] *mysticum & spiritualem sub littera latentem*. In other words, the "positivist" philological reading of Rabelais wants to be identified with what Defaux calls "l'herméneutique des textes sacrés," which is problematic for a number of reasons, the most serious of which is its perhaps unintentional elevation of *Gargantua* to the level of sacred writing, which Rabelais himself, it has been argued, would have found blasphemous.[6]

A characteristic of many of the readings of Rabelais's Prologue, then, is the idea that it should be read in the same way that an Evangelical Renaissance scholar, such as Erasmus, would have approached the Bible. This view has undoubtedly been carefully grounded in philological research, but it also runs the risk of misrepresenting and misreading elements of the work that are drawn from different intertextual sources. As Alcofribas points out in the Prologue, exegetical readings that attempt to find Christian messages in works that are not sacred scriptures inspired by God almost invariably produce monstrous misinterpretations, like the Christian morals that readers of the "Frère Lubin" type discovered in Ovid and Homer. For example, by claiming that the Prologue invites us exclusively to read and to interpret "en la perfectissime partie," meaning that we as readers are called upon to uncover the Evangelical message buried in the dense soil of this text, Edwin Duval, in his seminal article on the Prologue, dismisses to a certain extent the narrative exuberance, the scatological excess, the misogynist invective, and the sheer bodily mass of a text that certainly is as "carnivalesque" as it is Evangelical, as the persona performed by Alcofribas in the Prologue makes clear. There undoubtedly are apologias for Pauline *caritas*, rational restraint, and the careful reading of Scripture throughout *Gargantua*, but the work also contains poems about defecation, celebrations of codpieces, odes to getting drunk, fake etymologies involving rivers of urine, and parodic interpretations of supposedly prophetic texts. A significant element of Duval's reading of the Prologue, which was commented upon by Cave, Jeanneret, and Rigolot in their commentary and response, is symptomatic of this desire to "look away" when faced with the visceral elements of Rabelais's text. Duval insists that the Prologue instructs the reader to "interpréter dans la perfectissime partie," but he does not quote the parodic elements that follow this injunction: "ayez en révérence le cerveau caseiform qui vous paist de ces belles billes vezées, etc."[7] It is this multiplicity and plurality of meaning that resists a unified or univocal interpretation, such as the Evangelical one, which philologists have been tempted to identify with the author of the text, with his "intention," and with the resultant "design" of the work. A philological reading informed by performance theory would have to concentrate precisely on those elements in which the narrator calls upon his readers, as in the above quotation, as part of his performance of his own textual identity, which is intimately linked to the diverse meanings that the text offers to its readers.

The important question that Defaux addresses throughout his article, as Rabelais did, is of course that of interpretation, the role of the reader in it, and the conception of the author that one may derive from reading. These related concerns are crucial to our activity as scholars, which is perhaps why Rabelais's prologue has provoked so many critiques. Defaux's summary of the state of affairs regarding this question in 1985 provides a clear formulation of a certain kind of philological resistance to various theoretical interpretations of the Prologue. He outlines three positions, associated with illustrious names of scholars: 1) the position of Michael Screech, who rejects the claim of plurality in the prologue, since "Alcofribas ne commencerait pas par proposer l'application à son texte d'un modèle herméneutique connu—celui paulinien et patristique, du <<sens literal>> et du <<plus hault sens>>—, pour en dénoncer ensuite l'absurdité et les errances possibles" (197). In other words, according to this view, Rabelais mentions the possibility of allegorical reading in the exegetical sense only to decry its excesses, especially in the case of his own text; 2) the position of Gray, Rigolot, Charles, and Jeanneret, which "cultivates contradiction," and doubts the validity of allegorical readings: "Remettant radicalement en question la validité de toute interprétation allégorique, subvertissant, par le rire, le sérieux tout apparent de son propos, il se refuse tout subtilement à toute imposition de sens" (198). 3) Finally, Defaux characterizes Terence Cave's position as that of an irreducible plurality, which "s'empare de l'être du texte tout entier, le vouant, en terre d'Aporie, à un éternel exil" (198). From one position to the other, these critics accentuate the difficulties of Rabelais's text, moving from a simple rejection of allegorical readings, to a proclamation of ambiguity, and finally to the aporia of a text that steadfastly refuses any meaning at all. Defaux associates this last position with theory in general, and with deconstruction in particular. As we will see in a moment, this misconstrual of a given theoretical position conflates the affirmation of textual plurality, which was characteristic of deconstruction, with a refusal to interpret, or a relegation of any text to the realm of the undecidable.

Within this contentious scholarly climate, Defaux claimed that the Prologue is a rather simple text that can be read clearly if one pays attention to what it literally says. The basis for this claim is to be found in Biblical hermeneutics and its allegorical practices of reading. After reviewing the numerous, contradictory interpretations of *Gargantua*'s prologue, Defaux suggests an exegetical model of reading that insists upon the primacy of the literal, drawn from Nicholas de Lyra's *Postillae super totam bibliam*. The passage from de Lyra that Defaux cites reads in part as follows:

> Omnes (i.e. sens de l'Écriture) tamen praesupponunt sensum litteralem tanquam fundamentum proter quod sicut aedificium declinans a fundamento disponitur ad ruinam sic expositio mystica discrepans a sensu litterali: reputenda est indecens & inepta vel saltem minus decens caeteris paribus, & minus apta: & ideo volentibus proficere in studio sacrae scripturae, necessarium est incipere ab intellectu sensus litteralis: maxime cum ex solo sensu litterali & non ex mysticis possit argumentum fieri ad probationem vel declarationem alicuius dubij. (199, n. 14)[8]

As I understand him, Lyra attempts to base the certainty of spiritual interpretation on the firm foundation of literal readings, while every element of the spiritual level must correspond strictly to elements that are present on the literal level. Defaux justifies his usage of this text with the following pun, buried at the end of this long footnote: "Quand de Lyre ne délire, le résultat est probant. Érasme dira comme lui" (200, n. 14). There is no doubt that Lyra's insistence upon the necessary link between the literal and spiritual meanings of Scripture represents a certain "orthodox" mode of Biblical interpretation, concerned with the proverbial "four senses" (literal, moral, allegorical, anagogical) of the sacred text.[9] There is also no doubt that Erasmus would have supported this insistence upon making the letter of the sacred text correspond to one's gloss and interpretation of it. Nevertheless, there is no proof whatsoever offered by Defaux that Biblical exegesis serves as a suitable model for the reading of Rabelais's prologue, other than the unexamined assumption that medieval exegetes who foreshadowed the later pronouncements of Erasmus concerning the Bible would provide the correct method for reading the Prologue and the whole of the text. The appeals to Erasmus and to Lyra's practice of reading Scripture are symptoms of a "positivism" that is characteristic of some philological approaches to reading early modern texts, especially those that reject theoretical considerations related to issues of language, truth, and interpretation, which are at the heart of a poststructural philosophical practice that Defaux claims is alien to early-modern hermeneutics.

The important point to stress here as it affects the debate concerning the nature of sixteenth- century scholarship is the justification for a philological as opposed to a theoretical reading of a work. Defaux appeals to texts on allegorical reading that may have been contemporary to Rabelais, which he implicitly claims would have constituted the author's "own terms" for reading and writing, but which belonged to a venerable hermeneutic tradition that is far from adequate to the task of reading Rabelais's works. Based on his reading of Terence Cave, Defaux raises questions regarding the interpretation of Renaissance texts that are crucial to our enterprise: 1) do the language, the discourse, and the rhetoric of the period reflect a presence of meaning, or its deferred absence? 2) In reading these texts, are we concerned with "l'écriture humaniste d'Érasme" as a model of plenitude, or are we justified in using poststructuralist models of absence to describe the resistance to meaning and interpretation of these works?[10] The key to this entire debate thus resides in determining whether or not one is justified in reading early-modern texts in terms of postmodern, or, to use a less loaded term, twentieth- and twenty-first-century philosophical concepts. An important subtext to this concern is whether or not we, as readers, can reconstitute what Defaux calls the proper "terms" in which a given text may be or has to be understood: one must ask oneself "si l'entreprise qui consiste à lire un texte dans des termes qui ne sont pas les siens est ou n'est pas une entreprise légitime," as Defaux formulated this crucial question ("Sur la prétendue pluralité," 719). A prolonged critique of the suppositions that subtend this kind of enquiry is precisely what made Derrida famous. What exactly does one mean by the text's "own terms"? Is it not necessary for Defaux to take some rather spectacular intertextual "detours" (to use Derrida's expression) in order to define what these terms are?[11] If a critic has to look outside of the "text itself" in order to discover what the text's "own terms" are, it seems as though he/she becomes involved in the kind of paradox that was the delight of deconstruction in its heyday. Moreover, it could be that our understanding of "l'herméneutique des textes sacrés," which supposedly served as the basis for our conception of the terms that are necessary to a correct interpretation of Rabelais, is based on assumptions that need to be reexamined from a theoretical perspective. What if supposedly "transparent" works on Biblical interpretation demonstrate a decidedly "postmodern" turn of thought?

To return to Nicholas de Lyra, then, and his *Postillae super totam bibliam*, there are numerous intriguing passages in this work that do not fit so clearly into the paradigm of a simple "belief in language" that Defaux wants to find there. These crucial moments in the text deal with language and signification with a subtlety and sophistication that are often hard to find in contemporary critical texts. For example, in the following passage, Lyra discusses the "mirror" of "speculative intelligence":

> Il faut considérer que le livre a une similitude avec le miroir : en effet, de même que dans le miroir les formes sensibles apparaissent, de même dans le livre, les vérités intelligibles se reflètent. C'est pourquoi la prescience divine, dans laquelle toutes les

> vérités se reflètent, est aussi appelée livre, et c'est dans ce livre que les apôtres et les prophètes ont lu, eux qui nous ont transmis cette science. Et c'est ce que dit la glose d'Isaïe (XXXVIII, 1) : <<Mets de l'ordre à ta maison>>, etc., glose : les prophètes peuvent lire dans le livre même de la prescience de Dieu, où toutes les choses sont écrites. Il ne faut pas toutefois comprendre en ce sens que les prophètes auraient vu l'essence même de Dieu, qui est la même chose que sa prescience, car la part d'énigme que contient la connaissance prophétique serait évacuée dans une telle vision, ainsi que le dit l'apôtre dans I *Corinthiens* (XIII, 9). Mais on dit que les prophètes ont lu dans le livre de la prescience de Dieu pour autant que, grâce aux images imprimées par Dieu dans leur esprit, et grâce à une lumière proportionnée à ces images, ils voyaient à leur manière la vérité qui émanait de la science de Dieu jusqu'à eux par la révélation...
> Ce livre contient toutefois cette particularité, qu'une même lecture contient plusieurs sens. La raison en est que l'auteur premier de ce livre est Dieu lui-même, lequel a le pouvoir non seulement d'user les mots pour signifier quelque chose, ce que les hommes peuvent faire aussi et font, mais encore de se servir des choses signifiées par les mots pour signifier d'autres choses. Tous les livres ont ceci de commun, que les mots y signifient quelque chose; mais ce livre-ci a cette particularité que les choses signifiées par les mots en signifient d'autres. En vertu de la première signification, celle qui tient aux mots, on perçoit le sens littéral ou historique. Mais, en vertu de l'autre signification, celle qui tient aux choses mêmes, on perçoit le sens mystique ou spirituel, lequel est en règle triple. (Delègue, 102-3)[12]

Far from transmitting a "faith in language," in which discourse would be a transparent means of communicating the will of God, Lyra describes a means of signification that is rendered problematic even when it would seem most clear and direct. The prophets themselves are said "to read in the very book of God's prescience," which, Lyra insists, is not the same thing as looking into God's mind itself. Even for those who were inspired by divine intelligence, such as the prophets, there is an enigmatic element present in reading that will never be made clear, the famous "dimming" or "darkening" effect of language as mirror, which St. Paul turned into one of the most quoted axioms of the Christian faith. The metaphors for the inevitably obscure properties of even sacred language are numerous in ancient thinking about signification: in I Corinthiens 13:12 we see "obscurely" or "in enigmas" as in a primitive "mirror" that poorly reflects our faces, while we will see things directly "face to face" in a paradisiac future;[13] for Plato, in Book Seven of the *Republic*, we see only the shadows on the wall of his famous cave, while the philosopher has looked upon the blinding brightness of the sun, and has only language in order to communicate what he sees to those who are chained with their backs to the light when he has returned from his "ascent" to the upper world. In the supposed clarity of exegetical language, the nature of (divinely inspired) discourse includes mirror images, shadows, dim regions, and enigmas that cannot be explained clearly even by the most inspired of prophets.

While it has to be emphasized that Lyra is describing the peculiarities of sacred scripture, which cannot be equated to the particularities of Rabelaisian or Renaissance discourse, his description of language's enigmatic and multiple properties is quite close to a poststructural formulation of how language works. The indirection caused by our imperfect understanding of divine things, which is akin to the unpolished surface of the "mirror" of language, results in the play of difference and the supplemental processes of signification and interpretation that are constitutive of both poststructural thinking, and that of Biblical exegetes such as Lyra, who were working within the context of an ancient skepticism about the abilities of language to communicate the ultimate truths. For this reason, the ancient modes of interpretation that were explicated by Plato and Lyra require the contemplation of enigmatic, incomprehensible, and perhaps even grotesque images, which are understood only when the viewer/reader achieves a state of (mystical) ecstacy that is, in a sense, beyond language. This kind of meditation on the complexity of enigmatic images is, perhaps, characteristic of terms that are particularly well-developed in Rabelais's text, and which Tristan Dagron recently described as part of a "Bacchic" mode of reading. Furthermore, the speaker who presents his enigmatic persona in the Prologue performs a kind of identity and subjectivity that is entirely in keeping with this mode of thought, which is also present in the "performances" of characters such as Alcibiades in the *Symposium*, who is named specifically in the Prologue. A synthesis of theory and philology is necessary to the comprehension of the ways in which Rabelais's work develops diverse discursive strategies simultaneously: that of an ancient exegetical practice that shares some of the signifying characteristics described by poststructural thought; that of Platonic philosophy and its conception of the "consubstantiality" of abstract ideas and their material manifestations; and finally those discursive strategies and techniques by which Rabelais's work presents its narrator as a specific kind of narrative subject, whose identity is constructed precisely upon the abstract foundation of multiple intertextual paradigms.

At the same time that Defaux and his interlocutors were debating the meaning of Rabelais's Prologue, Richard Regosin published another article about this text that performed a much more "authentic" deconstructive reading than those referenced by Defaux. The practice of deconstruction at this time in the American academy analyzed the ways in which binary oppositions were undone by the most provocative of literary texts. Essence versus appearance, presence versus absence, being versus becoming, surface versus depth, inside versus outside: there was seemingly no end to the oppositions that organized what was seen as a kind of archaic, "metaphysical" thinking, which deconstructionists sought to "get beyond" (using the Hegelian *Aufhebung*, which was the answer to all binary aporias)[14] by showing the extent to which essence presupposed appearance and contained appearance in itself, and the ways in which the "outside" was contained within the "inside" of a text, and so on.[15] Derrida cogently described the rupture that separated structuralism from poststructuralism, which was a break in the way of thinking of the "center" of a structure in general. To translate the rather cryptic terms Derrida employed into the Rabelaisian ones that concern me here, it could be said, from Duval's perspective, that Evangelism and Erasmian Biblical hermeneutics constitute the absent "center" that is the organizing principle for the "design" of all of Rabelais's works. And while that center may be literally absent from much of the text, it remains a kind of unmoveable presence beyond the text, which determines the form of all of the substitutions and variations that constitute the text itself. Thus the "center" that is the object of study in Duval's work—i.e., Rabelais's text itself—is in fact *not* the center of meaning, since the interpreter must consult sources beyond the text in order to capture that meaning.

The problem with this mode of binary thinking (the inside versus the outside of the text) from a theoretical point of view is that the presence of the center may be conceived of only within a system of differences. For example, from the philological point of view I have just been describing, the Evangelical or Classical organizing principles that serve as the "transcendental signifiers" of Rabelais's text may be described only by reading other texts, by taking the detour of reference, and by following a "play" of intertextuality that can go on indefinitely. Ironically, then, from the "positivist" point of view, a reading of "the text itself" can only be accomplished by endlessly reading other texts.[16] From the point of view of deconstruction, the network or system of references that constitutes the Rabelaisian text can never be grasped in its totality as a presence; the diverse nature of these references will always be a kind of game of absence, meaning that the text will always paradoxically have to be understood in terms of what it is *not*, and this negation must be seen in pseudo-Hegelian terms as productive of the very *being* of the text. What is more important for my argument than these problematic philosophical meanderings, which have largely been dismissed at this point, is that the deconstructive moment in the history of contemporary theory intersected with other trends in scholarship that interpreted Rabelais's work as the meeting point of multiple modes of discourse in an irreducible "heteroglossia" that was constitutive of Rabelaisian style. In other words, the paradoxical game of presence and absence that constitutes the Evangelical portion of Rabelais's work, which Duval has seen as the principle of its "design," is only one of the discourse registers that operates in the text. A reading of Rabelais's text in its discursive multiplicity conceived of in this way clearly requires a synthesis of theory and philology.

This multiplicity is the main point of Bakhtin's study of Rabelais, and it is also the point of departure for Regosin's deconstructive reading of the Prologue to *Gargantua*. Regosin describes the history of approaches to the text in terms of a binary opposition that has mired criticism in the aporia of either/or thinking:

> In his convolution of language and logic, Alcofribas may appear confused (and may confuse his reader) as to whether to give priority to the hidden interior or to take the surface for the meaning of the text, whether to allegorize or not, but the options remain circumscribed by an inside/outside opposition; the only choice left to the reader seems to be whether to privilege one side or the other of the polarity. The power of this traditional conceptual model has long exerted its influence in Rabelais scholarship in studies which have penetrated (eliminated) a comic surface in order to decipher the "symboles Pythagoricques" promised by the prologue *or* which have taken (ignored) such "symboles" as part of the comic and ironic play which mocks serious interpretation. And in those recent readings which acknowledge ambiguity and indeterminacy and seek to avoid the reductive pitfalls of earlier works, we find the residue of a vocabulary of surface and depth which remains functional, even in the most perceptive and nuanced interpretations among them: [here Regosin quotes Terence Cave] "man [is] exiled on the surface, in a world of comic impropriety which has become his only property; he can designate but never articulate the absent place in which his dislocation would be resolved." (60)

This deconstructive point of view summarizes much of the scholarship devoted to *Gargantua*'s Prologue. The "Rabelaisants" whom Spitzer decried nearly half a century ago were among those who "eliminated" the surface of the text in order to describe the actual historical world to which it referred. On the other hand, Spitzer himself, at least according to Defaux's reading of him, reduced the text to the style of its comic surface. Duval argued powerfully for the existence of a "doctrine plus absconce" beneath the surface of the text, while Cave and others became transfixed by the supposed "ambiguities" that constituted its surface. Regosin provides a two-fold solution to this theoretical aporia. The first is the idea of discursive multiplicity in Rabelais, which leads to a synthesis of the two sides of this opposition in its deconstruction as the operation of the text itself. In contrast to the "positivist" position, Regosin argues that the prologue "is not the uniform place of Alcofribas's exclusive monologue (or the place of Rabelais's exclusive hidden monologue) but the meeting place of complex and multiple discourses and intentions" (63). Similarly, and following in the footsteps of Bakhtin's description of heteroglossia in the work, Regosin states that "Alcofribas's speech discloses the languages of allegorist, exegete, classical scholar, writer, reveler, carnival comic, and fool; into his own context come others that are philosophical, theological, literary, and carnivalesque" (64).

According to Regosin, then, it is precisely in this multiplicity—which, I insist, is not equivalent to the ambiguity so criticized by the "positivists"—that one may find a synthesis (deconstruction, *Aufhebung*) of the binary oppositions that have plagued Rabelais scholarship from its beginnings:

> It would appear that Alcofribas and his author are very much at odds, that the paradigm of outside-inside which wholly circumscribes the narrator's presentation (whether proposing or opposing allegorical reading) is challenged and undermined by the discursive multiplicity which he enacts as the intent of the text. His speech is never absolutely or unequivocally his own, a unique and personal language distinct from that of others but a composite of utterances drawn from others, outsides which are constantly introduced inside. Alcofribas cannot be a unity which univocally proclaims sovereignty or authority, for he is made up indiscriminately of the alien, the outside; his is a fragmented, multi-voiced narrator who always has the words of others in his mouth.... The inside(s) and outside(s) of Rabelais's text are not polar opposites but elements in constant, dynamic interaction and interpenetration which blur boundaries and distinctions. (64)

Here one could hardly be further removed from the point of view of Defaux and Duval.[17] Far from a writer who "believes in language" and in "the possible epiphany of meaning," Rabelais is, from Regosin's perspective, a writer whose text is determined by a Derridean play of difference that locates meaning precisely in the interplay of diverse voices in the text. In this view, the text itself, its very center, is a function of this play, and is far from being a transparent surface through which one may glimpse the intention of the author, the historical period in which he wrote, or the intellectual context that determined the direction of his thinking. For deconstructive thinking, therefore, it makes no sense to speak of a reading of a work that would attempt to interpret it "in its own terms," or according to the "spirit and the letter" of the text itself, since the idea of that which is proper to a work is ineluctably traversed, overdetermined, and saturated by the interplay of the text with its numerous others.

In Derrida's terms, "in the absence of an origin or a center, everything becomes discourse." From this point of view, Rabelais's text is somehow disembodied, while the effects of meaning that it produces are detached from any idea of intention or influence, in the endless play of distinct discourses that crowd into the work. This play of discourse in the absence of intentionality, which is so characteristic of poststructuralist thinking—think of Foucault's definition of power in *La Volonté de savoir*—is perhaps what angers "positivist" critics the most, and motivates their insistence on the idea that Rabelais's Prologue is "a work of literature," as Duval put it.[18] From a certain philological point of view, then, a written work, and above all a "literary" work, cannot be conceived beyond an understanding of its author's intention to communicate meaning, which is the cause of the apparent "design" of the work that it is the task of criticism to describe. In contrast, from the deconstructive perspective, meaning will always escape the intention of any author of any discourse, and the play of *différance* which is constitutive of the very being of language will always already (to use one of Derrida's pet expressions) be beyond the intention of any speaker, writer, or reader. Once again, we arrive at an apparently insoluble dilemma that pits two opposing points of view against one another, with no possibility of synthesis in sight. Yet Regosin's article raises an interesting point that is important to my own reading of the Prologue: the character of Alcofribas appears in the text as an amalgamation of diverse discourses derived from different registers and sources. In terms of contemporary theory, one might say that the figure of Alcofribas is a kind of discursive performance and speech act that relies on the interplay of multiple types of subject positions, or on the self-identification of the narrator within and through diverse discursive forms, most importantly those that are directly addressed to the position of the reader, which is also discursively constructed and "performed" in the Prologue. Moreover, in the light of recent philological work on the text, the "identity" of the narrator may be linked theoretically to a type of subjectivity that was characteristic of one of the most important intertextual sources on which the work draws.

The resolution of this conflict of style versus substance, surface versus depth, discursive play versus authorial intention resides, in other words, in a refusal to dismiss any of the seemingly "burlesque" or "irrelevant" elements of Rabelais's difficult and intractable narrative discourse, especially those that are involved in Alcofribas's performance as a narrative subject. Tristan Dagron's reading of the Prologue attempts to resolve these oppositions by interpreting Rabelais's text not as an apologia of "Evangelical *caritas*," but rather as a transcription of the "Bacchic" philosophical ecstasy that was described in Plato's *Symposium*, which appears as the opening figure of *Gargantua*. From Dagron's point of view, Rabelais's paraphrase of Erasmus in the Prologue has caused most of the text's readers to assume that the opening image of the Sileni is to be interpreted as the Dutch Humanist does, i.e., as a figure that necessitates a Christian, allegorical reading. In contrast, Dagron highlights the fact that in Rabelais, as in Plato, the Bacchic motifs of wine, drinking, and even drunkenness are emphasized, and are associated with a kind of philosophical, unintentional inspiration that leads one to desire and to dedicate oneself to the search for "higher truths," which in Plato are not Christian, but philosophical. In this sense, Rabelais's work could be understood within the context of a Platonism that accepted the flesh in all of its superabundance as the only medium in which abstract knowledge and wisdom could be discerned. From this point of view, Rabelais's text could be read as being as Bacchic as it is Evangelical, but in the ancient sense of religiously inspired, by the ingestion of wine, to become "drunk" on the image of beauty, which is present both within and through the body of the beloved as the necessary first stage in the long process of seeking divine knowledge. In this context, there is no necessary opposition between the "surface" of Rabelais's text, and the "deeper meaning" that it communicates to the reader; rather, the intoxication that the work provokes, often in the form of Bacchic laughter, is a kind of prelude to a more profound ecstasy that is, nevertheless, merely an "amplification," as Dagron terms it, of an initial, physical intoxication that is provoked by the text's narrative exuberance.

Dagron phrases this argument in the following manner, remarking the fact that Rabelais substituted the Silenic statues of the *Symposium* with apothecary jars full of magical drugs:

> A la lumière du *Banquet*, on comprend mieux pourquoi Rabelais substitue aux statuettes sacrées les "fines drogues." On pourrait même aller jusqu'à dire que son erreur philologique ne fait au fond que restituer un point essentiel du platonisme que l'ascétisme érasmien passe sous silence. Le paradigme médical permet d'insister sur la dimention [*sic*] magique et le charme dont Alcibiade énumère longuement les effets physiologiques. S'interrogeant sur la valeur de la drogue qu'il vante, l'auteur du Prologue oppose ainsi deux effets qui correspondent au double niveau évoqué dans le *Banquet*: un effet seulement superficiel, qui risque de se révéler trompeur, "comme au chant des Sirènes," et un effet plus profond dont les vertus sont bien réelles, cet "autre goût" qui révèle la "doctrine plus absconce," et qui n'élimine pas le charme premier, mais l'amplifie pour en manifester le bien fondé. Comme Alcibiade, il montre que la séduction qui pourrait sembler éloigner des préoccupations civiles, enseigne au contraire tout ce qu'il faut pour devenir un "homme accompli": "Les treshaults sacrements & mysteres horrificques, tant en ce qui concerne notre religion, que aussi l'état politique & vie oeconomique." L'énumération développe clairement les différents aspects du "large champs d'application" de l'enseignement de Socrate. (83-84)

The "doctrine plus absconce" that has often been viewed as the "authentic" teaching of Rabelais's work, is thus related to the theme of inspiration that Duval highlighted in his crucial article on the Prologue. The nature of this inspiration, however, may be quite different from that which Duval supposed it to be. The continuous emphasis on the physical attributes of the human body and on its unavoidable excesses throughout Rabelais's work is consistent with a Platonic understanding of the relation between the physical and the spiritual, and between visual and material forms and their interpretation. This conception of the body and the mind being united in a continuum is characteristic not only of ancient thought and of its revival in neo-Platonism, but also of Renaissance medicine, of which Dr. Rabelais was an active practitioner. It is in this idea of the unity of ideas with their material expressions and embodiments that we may find one of the most satisfying syntheses of the two positions that have divided sixteenth-century French scholarship from its beginnings.

From this point of view, it seems as though it would be somewhat inaccurate to claim that a work as complex as that of Rabelais is composed primarily of one type of discourse, for example, in Duval's careful considerations of Erasmian, Evangelical *caritas* as the basis of all of Rabelais's work.[19] It would also be a mistake to claim that Rabelais's text is primarily and exclusively Bacchic in the ancient sense of the word evoked by Dagron. Nevertheless, one could argue that among the astonishing number of discourses that constitute this singular work, the Bacchic strain is one of the most intriguing, in that it provides a way in which the grotesque and the sublime elements of Rabelais's discourse can be understood as a coherent whole, as well as a means of characterizing Alcofribas's performance as narrative subject. Moreover, this conception of a universal whole leading from the basest entrails of the body to the most elevated products of the spirit would be perfectly compatible with the Platonic conception of the human sphere expressed in the *Symposium*, which might be regarded as yet another expression of the terms that were "proper" to Rabelais's thought. In other words, in Rabelais there is something essential and unalterable about the "burlesque diction" in which supposedly "hidden truths" are expressed. According to Dagron's argument, the "grotesque surface" of the Rabelaisian text is a crucial manifestation, in itself, of the supposed higher meanings that the work contains. The Bacchic delirium of the exact words on the page leads to and induces a kind of philosophical delirium that is congeneric with the literal level of the work. The tremendous verbal excess and logorrhea of Alcofribas are, in fact, crucial to the manifold play of meaning that this peculiar form of language generates in us. Either we accept the idea that at least part of Rabelais is Bacchic in the strictest literal sense—the wine of poetry and music leads to physical and intellectual ecstasy for the author who eats and drinks as he writes—or we interpret these Bacchic elements as figurative representations of Evangelical attitudes, as Duval does. From the Platonic point of view that Rabelais revives in the Prologue, however, there is no reason why the most serious and elevated ideas could not be expressed in the strangest and most grotesque kinds of images, which were given these forms precisely because they were meant to remain imprinted on the mind as objects of contemplation. For the ancients, Dagron claims, "la sagesse se révélait toujours sous la forme d'une image," (83) and one which, moreover, provoked a kind of ecstasy, inspiration, and delirium in the viewer. The figure of Socrates is just such an object of contemplation in the *Symposium*, while the identification of Rabelais's book with this figure and its various manifestations and metaphors (the Sileni, the philosophical dog) reveals its importance for the reader, who also becomes a kind of smitten, drunk Alcibiades while chasing after the meaning of the Rabelaisian text.

In light of Dagron's work, then, it could be that Rabelais's oeuvre is concerned as much with exploring philosophical concerns, in a revival of Plato's understanding of philosophy as a practice of ecstatic contemplation, as it is with revealing the "doctrine plus absconce" of religious and spiritual truth in an Erasmian sense. As Dagron remarks, an "emblematic" mode of thinking was an integral part of the Renaissance, meaning that the complex visual expression of an idea that seemed to contain, embody, even *be* the essence of that idea made physical—Dagron uses Aristotle's "entelechy"[20]—often required of the reader the kind of thoughtful contemplation, figurative degustation, and digestion that Rabelais discusses in the Prologue. In other words, while remaining conscious of the opposition between the literal and the figurative, the letter and the spirit of the text, which is characteristic of the exegetical source texts to which Rabelais refers, we should also understand his discourse as embodying the continuity or "consubstantiality" of medium and message, the concept and the form of its expression. And just as Socrates in all of his manifestations—as philosophical ecstatic, walking barefoot in the snow, defending the rear of the army in a retreat, resisting Alcibiades during a long night in bed—is an emblem of philosophical inspiration (by which he is often transfixed, as he is twice in the *Symposium*), the figure of Gargantua, in all of his states, is an emblem of a syncretic, Bacchic, neo-Platonic, greco-Christian, carnivalesque, Evangelical, Erasmian humanism meant to inspire the kind of intellectual ecstasy and confusion in the reader that was often the result of Socrates' interactions with the other Athenians, at least if we are to believe Alcibiades at the end of the *Symposium*.

From this perspective, the most intriguing figure of all in the Prologue is that of Alcofribas, who is presented not in intertextual references, but in literal signs that appear on the pages of Rabelais's text itself. As I mentioned in the introduction to this article, these signs are mostly of the same order, and can be analyzed using a basic version of current critical theories concerning the performance of "fictive" identities.[21] Alcofribas exists on the page through continuous calls to his readers, who are constructed as mirror images of the narrator himself. This interpellation of the readers is involved in a textual performance of subjectivity that requires very little reference beyond itself in order to be interpreted. In our strict adherence to the literal proclamations of the work, with its opening dedication to drunks and syphilitics, we may understand the frequent references to drinking in Rabelais as emblems of the Bacchic process of achieving an ancient form of "enlightenment," as Dagron does. In this sense, and as I have already suggested, Rabelais's readers are placed in the position of Alcibiades at the end of the dialogue: we are called upon by Alcofribas to read in an inspired manner, as Duval notes, but this inspiration is a kind of intoxication that one suffers in the pursuit of "higher wisdom" in the Platonic sense, rather than being exclusively the Evangelical fervor that Duval describes. Alcofribas defines himself as a certain kind of subject by interpellating his readers as "beuveurs tresillustres et vous Verolez tresprecieux," which is undoubtedly the most famous apostrophe in the entire text. The Prologue is full, however, of this kind of sign, which may be interpreted in an intriguing manner by synthesizing Dagron's philological reading of the work with the specific aspect of performance theory that examines processes of interpellation and external identification. On the level of the text itself, this kind of performance takes the form of apostrophes, imperatives, forms of address in the second-person plural, and imprecations directed at the interpellated readers, all of which can be examined in terms of the ways in which they are modified and formulated.

After the all-important dedication of the work to the "beuveurs et verolez," the first paragraph of the Prologue contains two direct addresses to the readers in the second-person plural, which parallel the distinction between the inside and the outside of the Sileni. Referring to the external appearance of the apothecary jars, Rabelais writes: "Tel disoit estre Socrates : par ce que le voyans au dehors, et l'estimans par l'exteriore apparence, n'en eussiez donné un coupeau d'oignon" (5). Similarly, referring to Socrates' interior wealth, the text uses the same tense and formula: "Mais ouvrans ceste boyte : eussiez au dedans trouvé une celeste et impreciable drogue" (5). Alcofribas very subtly interpellates his readers in these brief pronouncements through the usage of significant details, and defines himself rather well in the process. The narrator seems to say to his readers, "I know you well enough: if you had been there to see Socrates, you would have reacted in the way I am describing." The two details of the passage that maintain the readers in the Bacchic register are the onion skin, which continues the alimentary theme developed throughout the Prologue, and the idea of the "celeste et impreciable drogue," which reinforces the notion of intoxication in the face of the "entendement plus que humain" that the reader would have found upon opening Socrates. It should be noted that the image of the apothecary's drugs develops in the alchemical register that is present from the very title page of the work, as Huchon noted in her edition of the text. Aside from being a Bacchic trickster, Alcofribas is also an "abstracteur de quintessence," who is describing "la vie treshorrificque" of Gargantua, the title of which contains a dazzling pun on "horrificque," as Huchon notes: "[ce terme se rapproche de] *aurifica*, <<qui transforme en métal solaire,>> c'est-à-dire qui réalise l'oeuvre" (1059). The text works upon banal and grotesque details, such as onion skins, in the same way that the alchemist works upon lead to transform it into gold, which is why this description of Gargantua's adventures is also sylleptically *aurificque*.

The following paragraph of the Prologue is also full of second-person references that delineate the character of Alcofribas's readers, especially in the first two sentences, which begin the complex process of defining the purpose of the text itself: "A quel propos, en voustre advis, tend ce prelude et coup d'essay? Par autant que vous mes bons disciples, et quelques aultres foulz de sejour lisans les joyeulx titres d'aulcuns livres de nostre invention…jugez trop facilement ne estre au dedans traicté que mocqueries, folateries, et menteries joyeuses" (6). Whether Rabelais's text insists on its outward appearance and literal sense, or its inner message and figurative interpretation, is in fact irrelevant to a certain extent in the performance both of Alcofribas and of his readers as subject types. In details such as "vous mes bons disciples," the work displays the intimate identification of these two textual beings. If Alcofribas is a master who has "disciples," this implies that he has some kind of wisdom, which in this case is a mode of reading and writing, to communicate to others. Furthermore, the form of the question that opens the paragraph, as well as its subsequent development, employs a Socratic method by which the master seeks to elicit a kind of knowledge from that which a disciple (in this case imaginary) already knows, but has not yet examined. This method is confirmed in a later appeal to the reader in the same paragraph: "Car, vous mesmes dictes, que l'habit ne faict point le moine" (6). Like Socrates, Alcofribas elicits the *opinion*—one of the key concepts of Platonic philosophy—of his imaginary interlocutors, combined with an agreement as to shared knowledge, as the basis of the proclamations that will be made in the rest of this opening text. Moreover, this knowledge is proverbial and popular. Throughout the Prologue, the narrator makes appeals to this kind of collective wisdom, in a process of bonding that highlights some of his major characteristics: he is a "man of the people," who knows what his fellow revelers know, how they think, how they would act in diverse circumstances, and above all, the kind of discourse that they would offer in these contexts.

But Alcofribas the alchemist (that is, sorcerer and magician as well) never shows something to his audience without also hiding something else that is perhaps more important. The expression "vous mes bons disciples" in conjunction with "et quelques aultres foulz de sejour" accomplishes exactly this kind of "double coding" that is characteristic of Rabelais's style. Are we to understand from this juxtaposition an identification of the disciples with the "foulz de sejour," and how are we to read the significance of this last formula? In a footnote, Huchon translates the complement "de sejour" as "oisifs," (6, n. D) meaning that these "other" characters who intrude on the text at this moment either were at leisure or "unemployed," in a sense. But if we interpret the expression "foulz de sejour" within the semantic context that Rabelais develops throughout his work, we could read it much more literally as a reference to the rogues, clowns, fools, buffoons, and jesters who are such common figures in these books, and whom Bakhtin examined throughout his study of the carnivalesque, as well as of the "chronotopes" that are typical of this period. Moreover, we might interpret "de sejour" not as "oisifs," but literally as "passing through," or itinerant, meaning that these characters would be of the roving type who went from tavern to tavern, and from marketplace to fairgrounds, looking for opportunities to steal, to eat, to seduce unsuspecting women, or to play tricks on others, as Panurge does shortly after his appearance in *Pantagruel*.[22] In other words, Alcofribas's interpellated audience is, in this instance, exactly the same as the "bons beuveurs" to whom he dedicates the text, and who reappear in chapters four and five ("tous bons beveurs, bons compaignons et beaulx joueurs de quille là" [17]). The consequences of this interpellation for Alcofribas's own identity are evident: he is one of these "bons buveurs" as well, which means that anything that he says or writes has to be taken with a grain of salt, so to speak.

As for the most famous interpellations of the Prologue, which have been debated *ad nauseam*, my remarks will be quite simple. The lengthy proverb of the philosophical dog culminates in the call to the reader to imitate the canine example: "À l'exemple d'icelluy vous convient estre saiges pour fleurer, sentir, et estimer ces beaulx livres de haulte gresse, legiers au prochaz : et hardiz à la rencontre. Puis par curieuse leçon, et meditation frequente rompre l'os, et sugcer la sustantificque mouelle" (7). This most famous of Rabelaisian proclamations operates simultaneously on the two levels of the "fatty" text and the "curious meditation" upon it. Whether the text calls upon its readers to interpret allegorically or to remain at the level of the work's "surface," it is clear that the abstract lesson concerning the "tres haultz sacremens et mysteres horrificques" (7) can only be attained by first devoting a great deal of attention, expressed here using sensorial terms ("fleurer, sentir, estimer"), to the physical and corporeal elements that constitute the text itself. The culmination of the reading process can also hardly be expressed in more concrete terms: the reader must "break" the bone of the text in order to "suck" its marrow. Furthermore, the characterization of the reader is expressed entirely in the canine register, which maintains the consistent depiction of the "bons compagnons" whom Alcofribas calls into being as animals. The extraordinarily physical image of readers who must be "light on their feet while in pursuit" and "courageous in their attack" is that of dogs on the prowl, hunting for prey. As Dagron noted, this mode of description is highly emblematic, which means that whatever "higher meaning" may be derived from the depiction of the reader as an intelligent hunting dog, it can only be an amplification of all of the qualities—courage, tenacity, curiosity, diligence, sensitivity—that are already present in the "primitive" form of the image. The Bacchic interpellation performed by Alcofribas here requires these physical attributes in order to direct its reader toward the amplified spiritual qualities of the text, which can be given priority only in the sense that they are an intensification of that which is already given in the physical description itself.

As for the other "bone of contention" that divided the scholars involved in the debate surrounding the Prologue, the triple interpellation of the reader in the section of the text concerning the nature of allegorical interpretation develops toward the alimentary reference that brings the sequence to its fruition. "Croiez vous en vostre foy qu'oncques Homere escrivent l'*Iliade* et *Odyssée*, pensast es allegories, lesquelles de luy ont calfreté Plutarche, etc…?" (7). This direct address to the readers prepares for Alcofribas's double response, which describes his mode of reading and writing in a way that has given scholars fits for generations. The first part of the response is clear enough:

> Si le croiez : vous n'approchez ne de pieds ne de mains à mon opinion : qui decrete icelles aussi peu avoir esté songées d'Homere, que d'Ovide en ses *Metamorphoses*, les sacremens de l'evangile : lesquelz un frere Lubin vray croquelardon s'est efforcé demonstrer, si d'adventure il rencontroit gens aussi folz que luy : et (comme dict le proverbe) couvercle digne du chaudron. (7)

Alcofribas's rejection of a critique that would assign an authorial *intention* to the allegorical readings that one might derive from these ancient texts has been universally accepted by scholars. In contrast, the corporeal and alimentary terms of this rejection have not been remarked. The narrator's opinion—again we recall the importance of this concept in Plato—has "hands and feet," and, to use a Platonic amplification of this image, it can get up and walk away when it wishes. The notorious "Frère Lubin" who anachronistically finds the Gospel in Ovid, is a "croquelardon," which Huchon translates as "parasite," but which evidently also means literally someone who "nibbles" on fatty meat, once again echoing the "beaulx livres de haulte gresse" of the first injunction to the reader. Finally, this image of the bad reader assumes the form of a stewing pot that would be covered over with a matching "lid" by the foolish readers who would accept the kind of allegoresis in which Frère Lubin engages. As the expression goes, readers of this kind are "cooking up something," and they require confirmation for their "foolish" views. The important element here, however, is the expression of this idea in an alimentary emblem and register which are the stock-in-trade of the festive characters whom Alcofribas interpellates throughout the Prologue.

The second response is much more problematic, and is the passage of the Prologue that has perhaps been the object of the most bitter debates among scholars:

> Si ne le croiez : quelle cause est, pourquoy autant n'en ferez de ces joyeuses et nouvelles chronicques? Combien que les dictans n'y pensasse en plus que vous qui paradventure beviez comme boy. Car à la composition de ce livre seigneurial, je ne perdiz ne emploiay oncques plus ny aultre temps, que celluy qui estoit estably à prendre ma refection corporelle : sçavoir est, beuvant et mangeant. (7)

The opposition between the first and the second parts of this response to the narrator's original question is clear: if you believe that Homer thought of the interpretations that have been attributed to him, you are far from my opinion; if you do not believe that he intended to place these meanings in his text, why don't you do the same thing with this text? What is truly remarkable in this passage is that Rabelais was able to inscribe a textual dilemma that has mystified scholars for such a long time, and that this insoluble problem appears precisely in the form of an inquiry concerning the relationship between "corporeal refection" and the act of interpretation. Alcofribas once again winks at his imaginary interpellated readers in this passage, and bonds with them by referring to the familiar shared experience of drinking wine. If the narrator was imbibing while writing these lines, and assumes that the reader was drinking as well, what exactly does this mean for the interpretation of the book that is to follow this opening text, which constitutes both the subjectivity of the narrator who writes it down, and the readers who are called upon to interpret it? At this point, it should be clear what that means from the point of view that I have adopted here: the text was written in a Bacchic spirit, meaning that Alcofribas was inspired by wine to write using certain corporeal, visceral, and animal images as emblems for higher truths, and that the reader should interpret these images "joyfully," in a spirit of divine intoxication and ecstasy that ascends toward the highest forms of knowledge through the contemplation of the basest images. Rabelais's work is thus itself a kind of "banquet" in the Platonic sense, and must be read as an affirmation of the continuity and contiguity of the physical and the spiritual, the literal and the figurative.

The paradox of Rabelais's text is that characters of the type I have been describing should be called upon to interpret "en la perfectissime partie" (8), given their tendency to deform and denature any scrap of language (as in chapter five), and the identification of Alcofribas with their trickster's delight in linguistic transformation and even destruction. This Rabelaisian practice of generating narrative sequences through extended puns and syllepses, which appears perhaps in its purest state in the "propos des bienyvres," is in fact highlighted in the culmination of the Prologue in some of the most remarkable sentences to be found in the entire work. Alcofribas's performance as a subject type also reaches fruition in these final sentences, which are the logical conclusion of the sequence I have just been examining. The end of the Prologue reads as follows:

> Pourtant interpretez tous mes faictz et mes dictz en la perfectissime partie, ayez en reverence le cerveau caseiforme qui vous paist de ces belles billes vezées, et a vostre povoir tenez moy tousjours joyeux.
> Or esbaudissez vous mes amours, et guayement lisez le reste tout à l'aise du corps, et au profit des reins. Mais escoutez vietz d'azes, que le maulubec vous trousque: vous soubvienne de boyre à my pour la pareille: et je vous plegeray tout ares metys. (8)

As we have already noted, if we are to read these pages from a point of view that synthesizes theory and philology, we cannot ignore any of the linguistic and discursive details that they contain in order to privilege one interpretation over another. As Duval has noted, the final imperatives call upon the readers to "interpret in the most perfect of ways" this text which is highly "imperfect" in the sense that it develops so much of the time in a grotesque manner that would seem to be incompatible with spiritual messages. It could be, however, that the perfection to which Alcofribas refers here is much more concerned with the Bacchic idea that the most sublime of ideas is contained in the most base, visceral, and perhaps even disgusting of material forms. The superlative "perfectissime" clearly echoes the description of the most perfect of foods: "la mouelle est aliment elabouré à perfection de nature" (7). It could be, then, that the famous phrase, "interpretez en la perfectissime partie," means that the "perfection" that Alcofribas demands of his readers is precisely the same as the figurative digestion of the bone marrow, meaning that the "joyful" spiritual meaning of the text has to be "ingested" in the exact material form in which it is expressed on the page, while the spiritual lesson of the text can only be an "amplification" of these grotesque images. In other words, for Rabelais as for Plato, the "celestial" truth necessarily has to be expressed in material, visceral, physical, and corporeal "emblems" that must be kept in the mind as objects of meditation.

The rest of this remarkable sentence vacillates vertiginously between the serious and comic registers. The imperative "ayez en reverence" interacts ironically with its object "le cerveau caseiforme," which, as Huchon notes, signifies "en forme de fromage," and continues: "Le fromage est considéré au XVIe siècle comme une nourriture du fou" (1066). The ironic combination of the idea of reverence with a "cheese-shaped brain," which contains a marker not only of madness, but of jocularity and tricksterism (if we take "fou" to mean not only "madman" but "jester" as well), is indeed the quintessence of Rabelaisian style, which combines the alimentary register (the proper domain of the roguish character types mentioned above) with the most abstract of meanings. This type of irony continues in the rest of the sentence, in which the verb "paître," which Huchon translates as "repaître," combines both literary allusions with animalistic connotations. Both of these levels are at work in the famous characterization of the work itself as "belles billes vezées" that are literally and figuratively given to eat to the readers. Huchon reads these enigmatic lines as follows: "Mot de l'Ouest, formé sur *beille* (latin *botulus*, <<boyau>>) et *vezée* (onomatopée, <<soufflée>>); d'où <<chose vaine>>" (1066). The literal meaning of the end of this sentence is so absurd that it would almost be impossible to interpret it at face value: the readers cannot literally venerate the cheese-shaped brain that gives them inflated intestines to feast upon, nor are the various theses concerning the modes of reading Rabelais of any help when it comes to deciphering this crucial passage. The incompatibility of the two registers that are opposed in the two halves of the sentence cannot be resolved simply by claiming the priority of the first ("interpretez…en la perfectisimme partie") over the second ("ayez en reverence"). Furthermore, we cannot assume that the grotesque or burlesque images of the latter simply undercut the seriousness of the former.

The hypothesis that the literal, corporeal figures that complete the sentence constitute a kind of emblem or object of meditation that must be considered in its material aspects allows us to arrive at some kind of synthesis of this opposition. We have already noted the connotations of "cerveau caseiforme" that reinforce the jocular theme developed throughout the Prologue and the ensuing text. The alimentary theme is present as well in this implicit description of the author as fool and trickster, and it is precisely this semantic register that "takes over" the rest of the sentence, as well as the end of the Prologue, when the Bacchic elements of wine and drinking are substituted for food and eating in the final paragraph. We have already seen as well the way in which "perfectissime partie" echoes the "perfection" of the bone marrow as (intellectual) food; similarly, the figure of the empty intestines foreshadows chapter four of the work, in which a carnival feast of tripes precedes the "propos des bienyvres" and the birth of Gargantua. What are we to make of this second echo? In chapters four and five, the eating of tripes serves to "mieulx entrer en vin," (16) which in this context engenders the production of (perhaps meaningless and empty) discourse among the revelers inspired by abundant eating and drinking. To translate these sentences into comprehensible English, Alcofribas seems to be saying to his interpellated readers, "in my role as inspired, roguish jester, I offer you these vain discursive improvisations to 'feast' upon." If this is the case, then the echo of the "belles billes vezées" in chapters four and five reveals what has to be the most serious message of all in the Prologue and the work as a whole: Gargantua, the future Humanist Prince, and the founder of the Utopia of Thélème, is born precisely in the context of feasting, debauchery, superabundance, word games, and "joyful" indulgence in the fruits of the earth, wine and viscera most notable among them. In contrast to the Christian Evangelical message that has been read as the authentic "truth" of the work, Rabelais here seems to be saying that the new order of things that is the Renaissance has to grow out of a return to the "reverence" for the body and its functions, which manifests itself in the kinds of verbal improvisations that are the hallmark of Rabelaisian discourse. The emblem of the "belles billes vezées" as object of meditation thus may reveal this kind of truth as the ultimate meaning of the work. In other words, the ultimate lesson of Rabelais may be the immanence of truth in the realm of the physical, as opposed to its transcendence in an unattainable, metaphysical domain.

In this sense, the reading of Rabelais's text is literally the same thing as opening a bottle of wine for the type of Bacchic reader whom Alcofribas interpellates: "Crochetastes vous oncques bouteilles? Caisgne. Reduizez à memoire la contenence qu'aviez" (6). One of the most interesting features of the Prologue is the usage of imprecations and insults in the interpellation of its readers. Often these terms are couched in regional dialects or languages (as Huchon noted, "belles billes vezées" is a "mot de l'Ouest"). The reference to the bitch here prepares for the improvisation on the philosophical dog which immediately follows it. Furthermore, it is inscribed in an animal domain or register that is evoked consistently throughout the Prologue, as well as in the narrative literature devoted to tricksters and rogues. Essentially, this type of character is mainly concerned with satisfying his animal appetites in taverns and marketplaces. Within the upside-down discourse of these "bienyvres," the act of insulting another while drinking is a mark of affection and comradery, in which Alcofribas engages here. This kind of insult is repeated in a much more striking manner at the end of the Prologue: "Mais escoutez vietz d'azes, que le maulubec vous trousque : vous soubvienne de boyre à my pour la pareille: et je vous plegeray tout ares metys" (8). In this register, Alcofribas becomes utterly provincial, popular, local, and intimate, especially when it comes to male bonding with his drinking companions. This type of male homosocial behavior is a noteworthy characteristic of Rabelais, which often verges on the hyperbolic, as in the notorious chapters in the *Tiers Livre* (chapters 26 and 28) in which Frère Jean and Panurge "console" one another in long lists of epithets for the male genitals. In the Prologue, these kinds of imprecations are transferred to the basest of animal domains, and are conjoined at the end with an enigmatic curse in which Alcofribas wishes a crippling disease upon his imaginary interlocutors. In this way, the end of the text rejoins its opening, ironic dedication to the "verolez tresprecieux."

In the final analysis, the various echoes that may be heard in the final sentences of the Prologue interpellate the reader in a distinctive manner, and by means of this process, the figure of Alcofribas carries out the performance of his own identity as a subjective type. Whether we interpret these lines as ultimately serious or comic, several things are clear about the readers whom Alcofribas calls into being: they are the same kind of revelers who are present at the birth of Gargantua; they engage in the production of discourse as a language game which develops on the Bacchic theme of drinking wine; this discourse is figuratively like food and drink to them, while its consumption—the act of reading itself—is equivalent to eating; interpretation, for them, would have to be akin to digesting the most perfect of foods, which here is emblematized as bone marrow; finally, and as the end of the sentence makes clear, the "ingestion" and "absorption" of this kind of discourse constitutes "joyfulness" and "pleasure" ("à vostre povoir tenez moy tousjours joyeux." "Or esbaudissez vous mes amours, et guayement lisez le reste tout à l'aise du corps et au profit des reins."). In the Platonic context of the reference to the *Symposium* that opens the Prologue, this reference to the idea of happiness must be understood in the sense of the "possession of good and beautiful things" that is the heart of Socrates' citation of Diotima, but which must be accomplished through an initiation in bodily pleasures (Plato, *Symposium*, 204e-205a). Moreover, the imperative reference to bodily functions that closes the Prologue is inscribed in an ancient conception of the mind that was revived in Renaissance medicine. Humors rising from the stomach reached the brain and hence had an influence on thinking.[23] Alcofribas reverses this paradigm, and proclaims the "benefits" for the kidneys that can be had from a joyful reading of his text. The connection of the literal and the figurative in this explication of the body is clear: if eating and drinking wine while writing has a direct influence on the kind of thought of which one is capable, as Rabelais claims explicitly in the Prologue, then the consumption of that writing has a direct influence on the body, and benefits the kidneys—that is, the reading of this text has a salubrious diuretic effect, and causes the body to produce a fluid, whose importance for the medical interpretation of the body has been highlighted recently by Jeffery Persels. This kind of meditation on the "meaning" of Rabelais's text is Bacchic in the sense that it has to operate on all semantic levels at once, and cannot ignore the literal inscriptions on the page for the sake of giving priority to allegorical readings. Moreover, and from a contemporary theoretical point of view, Alcofribas performs a discursive subjectivity that is firmly grounded in this view of the body and its relation to thought. In other words, the voice that interpellates us as readers of a certain type in the Prologue is that of a Bacchic subject, who requires of us a certain kind of meditation upon and "digestion" of the "wine" of his narrative discourse. The knowledge that one might gain from this meditation is predicated precisely on one's ability to maintain a certain overabundant image of the body in one's mind, as the material in which and through which an inspired, intoxicated understanding of higher truths may finally be glimpsed.

Notes

[1] I wish to express my gratitude to the editors and outside readers of *EMF*, whose comments and suggestions were invaluable in the revision of this article for publication. This article was intended as a means of joining the conversation that so many sixteenth-century scholars have had concerning the Prologue to *Gargantua*. While it was going to press, we lost one of the greatest *seiziémistes*, Gérard Defaux, whose opinion of and reaction to this piece I will unfortunately never hear. With great sorrow, I dedicate this work to his memory.

[2] Michel Foucault provides the briefest possible definition of a theoretician's work: "J'appelle théoricien celui qui bâtit un système général soit de déduction, soit d'analyse, et l'applique de façon uniforme à des champs différents" (Foucault, *Dits et écrits*, 861). From this point of view, philology is a theory, since it is a general system of analysis that is applied uniformly to diverse works.

[3] It should be noted that my usage of the masculine article here is intentional, since it is clear that Platonic philosophy, especially in the *Symposium*, is blatantly male and androcentric. The same could be said of Rabelais.

[4] According to Mireille Huchon, the name "Alcofribas" was absent from the title page before this date: "La manipulation ironique est particulièrement sensible pour la figure du narrateur–qui est, jusqu'en 1542, non pas Alcofrybas Nasier comme dans *Pantagruel*, mais l'abstracteur de quinte essence. Contrairement à *Pantagruel*, où à l'instar du héros de l'*Histoire véritable* de Lucien, Alcofrybas Nasier était narrateur et acteur, le narrateur de *Gargantua* ne prend pas part à l'histoire" (Rabelais, 1039). Throughout this article, for the sake of convenience, I will use the name "Alcofribas" to refer to the narrator who "performs" in the Prologue.

[5] "I shall then suggest that ideology 'acts' or 'functions' in such a way that it 'recruits' subjects among the individuals (it recruits them all), or 'transforms' individuals into subjects

(it transforms them all) by that very precise operation which I have called *interpellation* or hailing, and which can be imagined along the lines of the most commonplace everyday police (or other) hailing: 'Hey, you there!'" (Althusser 301). On the role of interpellation in the performance of gender, see Judith Butler's introduction to *Gender Trouble*.

[6] In their response to Defaux, Terence Cave, François Rigolot, and Michel Jeanneret raise this point: "On peut se demander s'il est légitime de faire appel à la foi chrétienne de Rabelais ou d'Érasme pour assigner automatiquement à leur oeuvre un sens spirituel. G. Defaux semble ériger en *a priori* théorique la révélation de la parole divine (dont la valeur transcendante n'est d'ailleurs pas discutée), sans se rendre compte que cette valeur ne peut s'étendre au fonctionnement du langage humain, nécessairement imparfait, et *a forteriori* à l'écriture d'une oeuvre de fiction. Il pousse même si loin l'assimilation de la parole sacrée à la parole fictive qu'il se croit autorisé à invoquer Nicolas de Lyre et sons <<*sensus* (sic) *mysticum et spiritualem sub littera latentem*>>. Le même nivellement le conduit à assimiler deux ordres incompatibles—confusion entre le temporel et le spirituel qu'un Évangélique n'aurait pu admettre" (Cave et. al., 714-15).

Tristan Dagron makes a similar point: "En rapportant la discussion du Prologue aux catégories de l'exégèse médiévale, on oublie pourtant qu'elle porte moins sur le double sens lui-même que sur l'idée d'une <<sagesse poétique>> à l'origine de cette profondeur et que le modèle d'écriture est Homère et non l'Ecriture sainte" (79).

[7] Cave, Jeanneret, and Rigolot make a similar point: "Si Rabelais avait tout simplement voulu préparer son lecteur à recevoir un message univoque, on ne voit pas pourquoi il aurait choisi de parasiter un exposé sérieux par des interférences burlesques : thème de la mangeaille, comparaisons triviales, vocabulaire hyperbolique, etc. Par exemple, même si l'on reconnaît un sens positif à l'injonction : <<Interpretez tous mes faictz et mes dictz en la perfectissime partie>> (et Duval a raison de rappeler l'expression latine dont elle est issue), on n'a pas le droit d'oublier que le texte remet ce sérieux en question par un brusque changement de registre. L'objectivité impose de citer la phrase de Rabelais en entier et de ne pas raturer les termes burlesques qui suivent immédiatement : 'Pour tant, interpretez tous mes faictz et mes dictz en la perfectissime partie; ayez en reverence le cerveau caseiforme qui vous paist de ces belles billes vezées, et à vostre pouvoir, tenez moy tousjours joyeux.' C'est justement dans ce genre de télescopages, de paradoxes et de renversements (<<cerveau caseiforme>>, <<belles billes vezées>>) que réside l'immense différence entre Rabelais et les humanistes évangéliques de son temps—ce qui n'empêche pas Defaux et Duval de les assimiler" (712-13).

See also Duval, "Interpretation," 14: "For Rabelais, the question is rather one of putting the best light on the words and deeds of others, and of taking in good part (in the *best possible* part in fact: <<en la *perfectissime* partie>>) that which is well-intentioned, overlooking the faults and inadequacies that necessarily marr even the most successful of human undertakings." Here, as elsewhere, Duval relegates at least half of the actual words on the page to the realm of the irrelevant. Referring to the usage of the verb "calfreter," Duval writes: "While modern readers have naturally assumed that the word is used contemptuously, it is more likely that Rabelais's original readers, who took for granted the notion that Homer's poems contained real wisdom, saw in it nothing more than the burlesque diction that prevails throughout the prologue (cf. the image of the assiduous dog used comically to recommend serious allegorical reading)" (7, n. 12). From a rather different point of view, it could be argued that the "burlesque diction" is precisely where the "wisdom" of Rabelais resides, and for that matter it has to be examined seriously.

[8] "Toutefois, ces expositions présupposent que le sens littéral soit leur fondement; de même

en effet qu'un édifice qui glisse sur son fondement est voué à s'écrouler, de même toute exposition mystique qui s'écarte du sens littéral doit être tenue pour incorrecte et inappropriée, ou à tout le moins pour moins correcte et appropriée que toutes les autres de la même nature. Aussi, tous ceux qui veulent avancer dans l'étude de l'Écriture sacrée doivent commencer par l'intelligence du sens littéral, pour la raison principale que seul ce sens, et non le sens mystique, fournit l'argumentation pour prouver quelque chose ou pour éclairer un doute" (Delègue, 106).

[9] Lyra uses the example of the city of Jerusalem to describe these four levels of meaning: the word "Jerusalem" on the page signifies, in a literal sense, "une certaine cité qui fut autrefois la capitale du royaume de Judée"; in a moral sense, it signifies "l'âme fidèle"; in an allegorical sense, it signifies "l'Église militante"; finally, in an anagogical sense, it signifies "l'Église triomphante" (Delègue, 104).

[10] "Tout en admettant avec mes interlocuteurs [Cave, Jeanneret, Rigolot] que <<l'optimisme d'Érasme n'est jamais naïf ou banal>>—et encore moins <<simpliste>>—, je me garderais donc bien d'aller aussi loin qu'eux dans la présentation de ce qu'ils appellent <<la plénitude et ses pièges>>. Car s'agit-il vraiment pour eux de s'interroger sur <<l'écriture humaniste d'Érasme>>? Ne s'agit-il pas aussi, ne s'agit-il pas plutôt, de projeter sur cette écriture des concepts, des préoccupations et une problématique qui lui sont de toute évidence totalement étrangers? Suffit-il de constater que notre époque, comme celle d'Érasme ou de Rabelais, s'intéresse beaucoup au langage et à tout ce qui touche, de près ou de loin, à l'interprétation, pour en conclure aussitôt que nos spéculations et les leurs sont de nature identique? Qu'elles peuvent, sans courir le moindre danger, s'exprimer dans le même langage, à l'aide des mêmes concepts et des mêmes mots? Suffit-il de remarquer qu'après tout J. Derrida a lui aussi lu Platon, pour se sentir du même coup autorisé à appliquer aux textes d'Érasme et de Rabelais une problématique philosophique spécifiquement conçue par son auteur pour déconstruire les prétentions descriptives de la phénoménologie, et par delà la phénoménologie, celles de toute la métaphysique occidentale du sujet? Questions fondamentales, et qui reviennent toutes, au fond, à se demander si l'entreprise qui consiste à lire un texte *dans des termes qui ne sont pas les siens* est ou n'est pas une entreprise légitime" (Defaux, "Sur la prétendue pluralité," 718-19, my italics).

[11] "Partons, puisque nous y sommes déjà installés, de la problématique du signe et de l'écriture. Le signe, dit-on couramment, se met à la place de la chose même, de la chose présente, <<chose>> valant ici aussi bien pour le sens que pour le référent. Le signe représente le présent en son absence. Il en tient lieu. Quand nous ne pouvons prendre ou montrer la chose, disons le présent, l'étant-présent, quand le présent ne se présente pas, nous signifions, nous passons par le détour du signe. Nous prenons ou donnons un signe. Nous faisons signe. Le signe serait donc la présence différée" (Derrida, *Marges*, 9).

[12] The original reads as follows: "liber considerandus : liber habet similitudinem speculi: quod sicut in speculo apparent forme sensibiles: sic in libro relucent intelligibiles veritates. Unde et divina prescientia in qua relucent omnes veritates liber vocatur: in quo libro leguntur sancti apostoli et prophete qui hanc scientiam tradiderunt: et hoc est quod dicit glosa sup illud Esa. Xxxviii.a. Dispone domue tue etc. Glosa. Prophete in ipso libro prescientie dei in quo omnia scripta sunt legere possunt. Quod tamen non est sic intelligendus: prophete viderint ipsam dei essentiam que idem est cum eius prescientia: quia prophetica cognitio cum habeat enigma: evacuat in tali visione: cum dicit Apl's in Cor. Xiii.c. Pro tanto dicunt, prophete in libro prescientia dei legiste: quod per species divinitus impressas mentidum phetoru': et par lumen propheticum eis apportionatum: videbant suo modo veritates a dei scientia ad eos derivatan per revelationem...Habet tunc iste liber speciale una libra continet plures sensus : lui' ratio est: quo principalis huius libri auctor est ipse deux in cuius poteste est non solum uti vocibus ad aliquid significandum: quod etiam homines faccere possiunt

et faciunt: sed etiam rebus significant per voces utitur ad significandum alias res: et ideo commune, est omnibus libris voces aliquod significent" (Lyra, 3).

[13] "Βλέπομεν γὰρ ἄρτι δί ἐσόπτρου ἐν αἰνιγματι, τότε.δὲ πρόσοπον πρὸς πρόσοπον. For we see now through a glass obscurely, but then face to face" (Berry, 459). Berry translates ἐν αἰνιγματι as "obscurely," when it is clear that it could also be rendered as "in enigmas," which is more faithful to the meaning of the passage, especially from the point of view of a medieval exegete such as Nicholas de Lyra.

[14] "In his most ambitious analysis of such [binary] oppositions, Hegel went so far as to claim that, not only could alternatives be shown to be ultimately compatible when thought together within some higher-order notion (*Begriff*) that resolved or 'sublated' the opposition, but that one term in such opposition could actually be said to imply or require its contrary, that a 'positing' of such a notion would, to maintain consistency, require its own 'negating,' and that it was this sort of dialectical opposition that could be shown to require a sublation, or *Aufhebung* (a term of art in Hegel that simultaneously means in German 'to cancel,' 'to preserve,' and 'to raise up')" (Audi, 368).

[15] To use Derrida's famous formulation of this attitude, which had enormous implications for criticism on this side of the Atlantic: "On a donc toujours pensé que le centre, qui par définition est unique, constituait, dans une structure, cela même qui, commandant la structure, échappe à la structuralité. C'est pourquoi, pour une pensée classique de la structure, le centre peut être dit, paradoxalement, *dans* la structure et *hors de* la structure. Il est au centre de la totalité et pourtant, puisque le centre ne lui appartient pas, la totalité *a son centre ailleurs*. Le centre n'est pas le centre. Le concept de structure centrée—bien qu'il représente la cohérence elle-même, la condition de l'*epistémè* comme philosophie ou comme science—est contradictoirement cohérent.... A partir de ce que nous appelons donc le centre et qui, à pouvoir être aussi bien dehors que dedans, reçoit indifféremment les noms d'origine ou de fin, d'*archè* ou de *telos*, les répétitions, les substitutions, les transformations, les permutations sont toujours *prises* dans une histoire du sens—c'est-à-dire une histoire tout court—dont on peut toujours réveiller l'origine ou anticiper la fin dans la forme de la présence" (Derrida, *L'Écriture*, 410).

[16] Derrida expressed this point in much more abstract terms: "Dès lors [the moment of rupture between structuralism and poststructuralism] on a dû sans doute commencer à penser qu'il n'y avait pas de centre, que le centre ne pouvait être pensé dans la forme d'un étant-présent, que le centre n'avait pas de lieu naturel, qu'il n'était pas un lieu fixe mais une fonction, une sorte de non-lieu dans lequel se jouaient à l'infini des substitutions de signes. C'est alors le moment où le langage envahit le champ problématique universel; c'est alors le moment où, en l'absence de centre ou d'origine, tout devient discours—à condition de s'entendre sur ce mot—c'est-à-dire système dans lequel le signifié central, originaire ou transcendantal, n'est jamais absolument présent hors d'un système de différences. L'absence de signifié transcendantal étend à l'infini le champ et le jeu de la signification"(Derrida, *L'Écriture*, 411).

[17] See Duval's proclamation against the deconstructive view of the Prologue, which he maintained more than a decade after Regosin's reading of it: "The *Tiers Livre* has often been understood as a book about hermeneutics in which conflicting interpretations of ambiguous signs, words, and written messages illustrate the radical indeterminacy of all 'texts' and therefore the impossibility of any truly definitive interpretation of anything. Polyvalence and hermeneutic indeterminacy, according to this reading, are not only essential characteristics of the *Tiers Livre* but its principal subjects as well. This view is faithful neither to the letter nor to the spirit of the book" (Duval, *The Design*, 187).

[18] "The usefulness of Jeanneret's approach is limited by the fact that it tends to treat instances of polyvalence in Rabelais only as isolated facts about a 'text'. It does not go on to consider the function (much less the meaning) of these textual facts within the larger context of what

is, after all, not a 'text' but a *work* of literature" (Duval, *The Design*, 187 n. 1).

[19] See Duval, *The Design*, 188-89: "Erasmus's paraphrases [of the New Testament]...will tell us everything we need to know about interpretation in the *Tiers Livre*, and in Rabelais's books generally.... In these paraphrases we find the precise diction used by Rabelais throughout his works to define the way he would have his readers 'interpret' his books."

[20] "Comparé ici au subtil goût du vin et à la richesse de la moelle, le charme des images poétiques vient de ce qu'elles portent en elles ce 'plus haut sens,' et ce charme est vrai, réel, mais aussi vérace. Qu'il y ait un étagement de sens, là n'est pas la question. L'important, c'est que l'esprit soit logé dans la lettre, non comme une substance étrangère, ou une âme exilée, mais comme son 'bouquet' ou encore son 'entéléchie.' A la dialectique entre la lettre charnelle et la leçon spirituelle, qu'Erasme déduit du thème des Silènes, un autre modèle a bien été restitué, celui du charme de la séduction et de l'ivresse qui articule, dans un même continu, la qualité sensible (la figure) à une forme substantielle ou qualité occulte (la "doctrine plus absconce") qu'il faut laisser agir en nous, en gardant, si j'ose dire, le vin en bouche" (Dagron, 85-86).

[21] This characterization of identity as "fictive" has to be understood in the context of Butler's work on gender: "To claim that there is no performer prior to the performed, that the performance is performative, that the performance constitutes the appearance of a 'subject' as its effect is difficult to accept. This difficulty is the result of a predisposition to think of sexuality and gender as 'expressing' in some indirect or direct way a psychic reality that precedes it" (Butler, "Imitation," 725). The performance of identity is thus "fictive" since it is not based upon a "real" identity that precedes it. In the same way, Alcofribas's identity in Rabelais can be thought of as a fictive, discursive effect that does not necessarily represent an essence that exists prior to its appearance in the text.

[22] On these types of characters in Rabelais, see my article, "'*Un bon esmoucheteur par mouches jamais esmouché ne sera.*'"

[23] On Rabelais and Renaissance medicine, see my article, "Dr. Rabelais and the Medicine of Scatology."

Works Cited

Althusser, Louis. "Ideology and Ideological State Apparatuses." Tr B. Brewster In *Literary Theory: An Anthology*, ed. Julie Rivkin and Michael Ryan, 294-304. Malden, MA: Blackwell Publishing, 1998.

Audi, Robert, ed. *The Cambridge Dictionary of Philosophy*. Cambridge: Cambridge University Press, 1999.

Austin, J. L. *How to Do Things With Words*. Oxford: Oxford University Press, 1962.

Bakhtin, Mikhail. "The Chronotope of the Rogue, Clown, and Fool." *The Dialogic Imagination*. Ed. Michael Holquist. Trans. Caryl Emerson and Michael Holquist. Austin: University of Texas Press, 1981.

———. *Rabelais and His World*. Trans. Hélène Iswolsky. Bloomington: Indiana University Press, 1984.

Berry, George Ricker, ed. and tr. *The Interlinear Literal Translation of the Greek New Testament*. Chicago: Wilcox and Follett, 1952.

Butler, Judith. *Gender Trouble: Feminism and the Subversion of Identity*. New York: Routledge, 1990.

―――. "Imitation and Gender Insubordination." In *Literary Theory: An Anthology*, ed. Julie Rivkin and Michael Ryan, 722-30. Malden, MA: Blackwell Publishing, 1998.

Cave, Terence, Michel Jeanneret, and François Rigolot. "Sur la prétendue transparence de Rabelais," *Revue d'histoire littéraire de la France* June-July 1986: 709-16.

Dagron, Tristan. "Silènes et statues platoniciennes, à propos du Prologue du *Gargantua*." *Études Rabelaisiennes* 33(1998): 79-90.

Defaux, Gérard. "D'un problème l'autre : herméneutique de l'*'altior sensus'* et '*captatio lectoris*' dans le Prologue de 'Gargantua'." *Revue d'histoire littéraire de la France* March-April 1985: 195-216.

―――. "Sur la prétendue pluralité du Prologue de 'Gargantua'." *Revue d'histoire littéraire de la France* June-July 1986: 716-22.

Delègue, Yves, ed. *Les machines du sens: fragments d'une sémiologie médiévale (textes de Hugues de Saint-Victor, Thomas d'Aquin et Nicolas de Lyre)*. Paris: Éditions des Cendres, 1987.

Derrida, Jacques. *L'Écriture et la différence*. Paris: Éditions du Seuil, 1967.

―――. *Marges de la philosophie*. Paris: Éditions de Minuit, 1972.

Duval, Edwin. "Interpretation and the 'Doctrine absconce' of Rabelais's Prologue to *Gargantua*." *Études Rabelaisiennes* 18 (1985): 1-17.

―――. *The Design of Rabelais's* Tiers Livre de Pantagruel. *Études Rabelaisiennes* 34 (1997).

Erasmi, Desiderii. *Opera omnia*. Vol. 2, num. 5, *Adagiorum chilias tertia*, ed. Felix Heinimann and Emanuel Kienzle. Amsterdam: North-Holland Publishing Co., 1981.

Erasmus, Desiderius. *Collected Works of Erasmus*. Vol. 34, ed. and tr. R. A. B. Mynors. Toronto: University of Toronto Press, 1992.

Foucault, Michel. *Dits et écrits II, 1976-1988*. Paris: Gallimard, 2001.

―――. *L'Histoire de la sexualité I: la volonté de savoir*. Paris: Gallimard, 1976.

LaGuardia, David. "Dr. Rabelais and the Medicine of Scatology." In *Fecal Matters*, ed. Jeffery Persels and Russell Ganim. Aldershot, UK: Ashgate, 2004.

―――. "'*Un bon esmoucheteur par mouches jamais esmouché ne sera*': Panurge as Trickster." *Romanic Review* 8, no. 4 November 1997: 519-28.

Lyra, Nicholas de. *Postillae*. Thoringen: Hummelburg, 1501.

Persels, Jeffery. "Taking the Piss out of Pantagruel: Urine and Micturition in Early Modern French Literature." Paper read at the Guthrie Colloquium, Dartmouth College, September, 2000.

Plato. *Symposium of Plato*, tr. Tom Griffith. Berkeley: University of California Press, 1989.

―――. *The Dialogues of Plato*, tr. Benjamin Jowett. Chicago: Encyclopedia Britannica, 1952.

Rabelais, François. *Oeuvres complètes*, ed. Mireille Huchon. Paris: Gallimard, 1995.

Regosin, Richard. "The Ins(ides) and Outs(ides) of Reading: Plural discourse and the Question of Interpretation in Rabelais." In *Rabelais's Incomparable Book: Essays on His Art*, ed. Raymond C. La Charité, 59-71. Lexington: French Forum, 1986.

Spitzer, Leo. "Rabelais et les 'rabelaisants,'" *Studi Francesi* 12 (September-December 1960): 401-23.

Wimsatt, W. K., and Monroe C. Beardsley. "The Intentional Fallacy." in *Critical Theory Since Plato*, ed. Hazard Adams and Leroy Searle, 1015-22. New York: Harcourt, Brace, Jovanovich, 1971. (Originally published in *The Verbal Icon*. Lexington: University of Kentucky Press, 1954).

THE BIBLIOPHILE AND THE ARCHIVIST ON MONTAIGNE

Katherine Almquist

Twentieth-century Montaigne scholarship thought that an elite group led by the private collector Dr. Jean-François Payen drove nineteenth-century Montaigne scholarship (Simonin, Richou, Keffer). "L'immense mérite du Dr Payen," writes Trinquet, "c'est d'avoir orienté, attisé, passionné la curiosité des milieux littéraires, non plus seulement sur la pensée et le style de Montaigne, mais aussi—et surtout—sur la personne et sur la vie de l'homme. C'est lui qui suscita l'équipe peu nombreuse, mais ardente, des *Montaignologues*, comme l'un d'entre eux le nommera" (Trinquet, 178).

There is no doubt that Payen promoted his self-image as the leader of a Montaigne elite. "On ne se hasardait guère…à écrire sur Montaigne, sans avoir, au préalable, consulté le docteur," reflected Gabriel Richou in the 1870s (cited in Trinquet, 179). But, whatever Payen may have projected about himself, and, however convinced were twentieth-century scholars of this self-image, the historical record shows his superior role in the production of Montaigne biography to be so much myth. It is true that the production of Montaigne biography in the nineteenth century was constrained by the ambitions of certain intellectual elites. But it is wrong to assume that Montaigne was what brought these intellectuals together.

The most frequently mentioned members of the 'Montaigne elite' were Gustave Brunet, a Bordelais businessman, and Jules Delpit, a Gascon landowner. Even though Payen, Brunet and Delpit's association with Montaigne came from their efforts to publish Montaigne documents from the 1830s through the 1850s (Trinquet, 178-79), these men, with the exception of Payen, were not searching for and publishing Montaigne documents in order to promote the essayist and his biography. Montaigne was instead a marginal subject of their involvement in a large-scale preservation movement that included the edition and publication of historical documents.

In order to view Montaigne's marginality, he must be removed from the center of our field of vision. McGann rightly observes that historical scholarship prior to the advent of 'New Criticism' did not establish a means for critically evaluating its founding presumptions. When we return to historical scholarship or ask questions about prior historical method, we risk reproducing these presumptions. By allowing an author or a text the privileged role of categorizing principle, individuals and groups are brought into a limelight that may not be historically accurate in the most traditional philological sense. Bourdieu's method for defining cultural fields of production can help us to create categories upon which the author or text is merely contingent. It also brings to light the motivations that contributed to the creation not only of the literary works which we so admire, but also to the traditional literary historical method that we criticize (Bourdieu). Payen, Delpit, and Brunet's association with Montaigne makes them important in our eyes because Montaigne is our categorizing principle. Understanding their sometimes diffident regard for the essayist is possible when we let their professional concerns for document preservation and for government sponsorship define our field of vision.

In this article I have proceeded by following the intersection of the career trajectories of the so-called Montaigne elite: Payen, Brunet, and Delpit. Instead of focusing on Montaigne, however, I have opened up a wider lens to examine the positioning of each scholar with respect to the journals in which they published Montaigne documents. Most Montaigne scholars met through the *Bulletin du Bibliophile*, started by Techener in 1834 for private collectors, *belles-lettres* critics and *amateurs de livres*. This is a place where Payen felt most comfortable, and where Montaigne, as the witty, antisocial philosopher of the remote sixteenth century, found himself placed on a pedestal. The Montaigne elite then followed Brunet in the 1840s to the Academy of Bordeaux. The Academy's primary interests were the commerce, technology, and tourism of Guyenne, and in this commercial arena the arcane essayist and intellectual is marginalized. In the late 1850s, Brunet and Delpit form the *Archives Historiques de la Gironde* and bring Payen with them. In this journal, one that exists to publish extant French archives, significant documents relating to Montaigne's biography are published from the late 1860s onwards. Even in this journal, however, Montaigne is far from central to the professional interests of the archivists involved with it. By the early 1860s, neither Montaigne nor his *Essays* had achieved the stature of a national treasure deserving preservation.

Perhaps Montaigne's place in the national patrimony was challenged because of the reigning romantic image of the sixteenth-century thinker as a purely private individual. Even though he was one of the few sixteenth-century writers to attract the attention of the academies, he was portrayed by them as a speculative philosopher, safely locked in his library tower, whose book served as bedside meditation (Frame, *Montaigne in France*). French intellectuals strongly resisted breaking him out of the private sphere. When Alphonse Grün published his biography of Montaigne's public life in 1855, its success was largely due to the polemical argument that Montaigne had one. Villemain, who launched his academic career by winning an 1812 competition of the French academy to eulogize Montaigne, approached Grün's thesis with considerable reserve. Most damning to it was an extant letter in which Montaigne, as mayor, informed the city officials that he would not return to plague-infested Bordeaux for the election of the new mayor. "Sans doute, il était plus fait pour étudier les hommes que pour les gouverner," concluded Villemain (cited in Trinquet, 186).

Montaigne's biography was not only hampered by the image of Montaigne as a private man, but also the image of his *Essays* dominated it. The fragmentary, contradictory work reinforced the presumption of Montaigne's biographical fragmentation. "Chez Montaigne, montrer le maire actif aux prises avec l'épicurien nonchalant, le philosophe avec l'homme de cour, l'élève de Rome et d'Athènes avec le gentilhomme du XVIe siècle, le chrétien avec le sceptique, là est le véritable intérêt," observed Payen (*Documents inédits*, 5). The *Essays*' ability to inform the biographer's point of view was something that nineteenth-century Montaigne scholars recognized. Payen believed that Grün failed as a biographer for having presented Montaigne's personhood in facets, "Montaigne maire, magistrat, gentilhomme de la chambre, chevalier de l'ordre, etc.," when in fact "pour Montaigne, on peut dire qu'il est assez décousu pour qu'il ne soit pas bon de le découdre encore" (Payen, 5).

Frame demonstrates convincingly that Montaigne's popularity greatly diminished in the mid-nineteenth century as realism replaced the romantic ideal of the individual. Grün's exposé of Montaigne's conduct during the plague was sufficient reason for why "*les Bordelais n'ont pas encore élevé de statue à ce philosophe*," as Payen complains (*Documents inédits*, 21). The 'fragmentary Montaigne,' projected from his book, may have also impeded the writing of a coherent biography. Finally, the production of Montaigne's biography was severely hampered when the preservation movement could not decide on the criteria for conserving extant documents. Montaigne's biography could not become a central figure of French national history until the nation found a reason in the late 1860s to preserve his book.

The *Bulletin du Bibliophile*

The discourse on the place of documents in the national preservation movement is already evident in the early issues of the *Bulletin du bibliophile*. In 1834, the *Bulletin* was born as a circular advertisement for the rare book offering list of Techener, a Parisian bookseller.[1] Techener's cronies soon began to contribute small essays, letters, or commentaries. Charles Nodier and Gustave Brunet were intimately involved in this salon from its inception. By 1836 it had reorganized with a set of statutes and goals and increased its subscription price to 10 francs, proving its success. Techener decided that it would consist of his offering list, supplemented by "notices bibliographiques, philologiques et littéraires, par divers auteurs," edited by Nodier ("Avis," np). Brunet also contributed anonymous comments on bibliophilia on a monthly basis.[2]

Techener wanted his journal to cater to private book collectors untainted by professional aims or political intrigue. "Aucune entreprise ne fut jamais plus indépendante que celle-ci des mouvemens de la politique et des actes extérieurs des gouvernemens," he affirmed with autarchic elitism ("Préliminaires," 2). His readers and contributors were committed to *belles-lettres* criticism and followed the rare book and manuscript market in its "actualité … si piquant et si vif dans tous les goûts qui tiennent de la mode et de la fantasie" (5). They were dedicated to the production of text editions, "surtout des auteurs classiques anciens et modernes," editions "qui se distinguent par l'amélioration des textes, par la clarté des commentaires, et par le bon goût des illustrations, de façon à l'emporter, en quelque point, sur les éditions antérieures, et à faire baisser leur prix" (6). The editions of Firmin Didot set Techener's standard.[3]

Techener's book lovers were rebelling against the mammoth, commentaried *Œuvres complètes* of the eighteenth century. "Rabelais, Marot, le *Cymbalum mundi* de Desperriers, le *Longus* et le *Plutarque* d'Amyot, les *Essais* de Montaigne, ont été, à la vérité, réimprimés fort souvent dans le XVIIIe siècle, mais avec une insouciance ou plutôt avec un mépris de l'orthographie et du texte qui fait de la plupart de ces somptueuses éditions des monuments de mauvais goût," denounced Nodier in the first issues of the journal ("Auteurs," 6). Instead of these monoliths, so over-encrusted with "des clefs et des commentaires, clefs absurdes, commentaires insignifiants, dont le moindre défaut est de ne rien apprendre aux gens qui savent quelque chose," Nodier and Techener desired naked texts, stripped of decorative artifice, masterfully typeset and luxuriously bound, Rosetta stones in a world of triumphant arches. They set themselves this aesthetic standard because they were experts in what gave rare books their worth: "la seule recommandation d'une ligne de marge, du fer d'un relieur célèbre, ou de la signature mal déchiffrée d'un personnage célèbre" (Techener, "Préliminaires," 7). On the quality of their typesetting and paper alone, new editions of classic texts would become collectibles and "l'emporter, en quelque point, sur les éditions antérieures, et à faire baisser leur prix" (6).

The edition of Montaigne's *Essays*, as well as the discovery and publication of Montaigne documents, were well-placed within the interests of the *Bulletin*'s bibliophiles. It was the appropriate elite for Payen to cultivate. He was introduced to the *Bulletin* through Nodier's laudatory praise of his *Notice bibliographique sur Montaigne*, which was reviewed by Nodier in early 1838. Nodier championed the work as an example of the kind of bibliography that should be done by the public ministries that Nodier pretended to disdain. "Un tel ouvrage seroit un véritable monument national, et ce monument s'éleveroit sans effort si la France, qui a le bonheur de posséder des sociétés littéraires de toutes les espèces, possédoit, par hasard, une Société bibliographique" (3). Payen is preceded by the example of Brunet, whose bibliographical research on Rabelais, Marot, and La Fontaine "sont infiniment ... précieuses" (4). In Nodier's imagined "*Bibliographie classique de France*" (4), Payen's work would fill the chapter on Montaigne.

One would think that such praise would prompt a contribution by Payen to the next supplement of the *Bulletin*. But he waited until Brunet published an unedited 1582 letter of Montaigne in the August 1839 supplement. The letter was one of two retained in the private collection of a notable Bordeaux historian, Bernadau. Brunet observed that Montaigne had mistakenly dropped the "n" in his name, "avec une sorte de trait sur l'o" (721) and that, according to Fontaine's *Manuel de l'Amateur d'autographes,* "l'écriture de l'auteur des *Essais* est du nombre de celles dont la gravure ou la lithographie n'ont point reproduit la facsimilé" (722). Montaigne's letter is published by him hesitantly, reluctantly, and dutifully, since "elle n'est pas d'un intérêt bien vif, mais elle est courte, et il faut recueillir avec zèle tout ce qu'a tracé la plume à laquelle on doit les *Essais*" (721). His presentation of the letter demonstrates that he was a bibliophile under obligation, not a lover of Montaigne promoting a Montaigne elite.

By taking the initiative to publish and promote the edition of Montaigne documents, Brunet incited Payen to action. Payen immediately wrote a masterfully self-promoting letter to Techener which was later printed in the *Bulletin* (Payen, "Au Même"). "Personne autre que moi n'applaudit à la publication qu'a faite M. G. B., dans le Bulletin, d'une lettre inédite de Montaigne" (893), he gushed, because "tout ce qu'a tracé la plume qui a écrit les essais doit être recueilli avec zèle" (893). This zeal moved him to spend the rest of his letter pointing out Brunet's errors. Montaigne's signature tic is not a "*lapsus calami,* car je crois avoir positivement établi, dans ma *notice bibliographique sur Montaigne* (page 42), que l'auteur des Essais signoit toujours ainsi" (893). His opinion, based on the many extant signatures that he had examined, is only confirmed by Brunet's single exemplar (894). Finally, Brunet gravely erred in presuming that Montaigne's handwriting had never been reproduced. Not only had Montaigne's handwriting been reproduced by others, but Payen himself had published a facsimile of Montaigne's signature. If Brunet had any doubts as to who was the leader of Montaigne studies, then he need only consult "la Notice bibliographique précitée" (894).

Given that Brunet was third in command of the *Bulletin* that he had helped to found, Payen resembled a terrier attacking a doberman. Payen's actions suggest that he was not the leader in Montaigne publication or in document edition and that he knew it. Perhaps Brunet cultivated Payen's posturing for his personal amusement. Perhaps he had an eye on Payen's wealth and rich private collection.[4] In any case, at some point during this exchange, Payen and Brunet became friends.

The friendship between two private book collectors of easy means, disinterested in monetary or political gain, fit the professed aim of the *Bulletin*. In 1835, Nodier scoffed loudly, "[J]e n'ai pas l'ambition de la faire valoir comme un titre de candidature par devant l'Académie des inscriptions et belles-lettres, ou comme un droit à être porté dans la liste expectative des préfets" ("Échantillon," 8). Those that followed him, "cet essaim studieux tout entier qui compose son miel dans la poussière des chartes," should not expect to impress government agencies since "la moitié vient d'être sacrificiée par la chance capricieux du concours à l'*ultimatum* parcimonieux du budget" ("Auteurs," 4). Bibliophiles impassioned by "l'exploration de ces chartes vénérables de notre histoire, de ces *incunables* précieux de notre langage, trésor jusqu'ici méconnu qui étoit échu aux vers comme un patrimoine" (4), should support their habit by engaging in a remunerative profession and by conforming "aux devoirs de la morale" (5). This description precisely fits the profile of Payen and Brunet in the 1830s.

This professed disinterest in political or professional gain was belied by the speed with which the *Bulletin* aligned itself with the Ministry of Public Instruction, becoming a broadsheet for the ministry's activities and agenda. It also testified to a growing need for professional, paid archivists: Nodier protested too much. The *Bulletin* became a forum for the nascent preservation movement inasmuch as the movement concerned extant documents. In early 1837, it reprinted a significant report of Augustin Thierry to François Guizot, one of the directors of the Ministry of Public Instruction. Thierry had been funded by the ministry to research and write a history of the third estate, reclaiming their story through an exhaustive publication of documents in public archives: charters, privileges, statutes of the guilds.[5] The mission of this ministry to publish the "monumens de l'histoire du tiers-état" had come down from the National Assembly (Thierry, 384). In 1838, it published another report on the cataloging of all French public library holdings by the Ministry of Public Instruction (Grégoire, 63). These works, particularly those suitable for contemporary study, would be redistributed through the nation because "les monumens des arts étant un héritage commun, tous les départemens y ont droit" (70).

These ministerial reports show that the French government was driven in the 1830s to create a national patrimony of texts whose aesthetic, monetary, and patriotic value was that of monuments. The *Bulletin du Bibliophile* was supportive and aligned with this agenda. But the criteria for value set by the Ministry of Public Instruction did not always coincide with those of the *Bulletin*. The bibliophiles collected rare and expensive documents. Yet even though the archivist Grégoire admitted that "les exemplaires d'environ douze mille ouvrages imprimés au XVe siècle," were increasing in price "dans une progression exorbitante" (68), and that "une foule d'autres ouvrages imprimés posterieurement" were "actuellement très recherchés" (68), he affirmed that the real concern of the ministry and of the government in general was to find "matériaux abondans...[p]our travailler à neuf l'histoire de France, car cet ouvrage est à refaire" (68). Works that contributed to "une histoire bien faite de la féodalité, qui fut une des grandes erreurs de l'esprit humain" were welcome in the public collections, but those which might be placed "à l'*Index* de la raison" (70) were not. Grégoire even suggested selling these atrocities to other countries whose ideals were not those of new France.

Given Montaigne's dubious image as a speculative philosopher and private individual, it was not out of the question that his documents would be placed on the *Index* of reason. But the real problem was that, with the exception of a small group of scholars of like mind with Thierry and Guizot, the focus for the creation of a French national patrimony was mortar and stone. Thierry and Guizot's efforts were in the minority. The conservation movement made its way from the capital to the provincial Academy of Bordeaux in the late 1830s, at the same time that Brunet moved to Bordeaux. In the Academy of Bordeaux, the conservation movement was concerned with mortar and stone.

THE ACADEMY OF BORDEAUX

In reports to the Academy in 1840 and 1841, Ferdinand Leroy, adjunct assistant to the prefecture of the Gironde responsible for the conservation of monuments and soon to become the president of the Academy, told how the local Bordeaux government and erudite groups became involved in the national movement for monument conservation.[6] He retells the story laid out in the *Bulletin* and fills in its gaps. In the 1830s, the French academies and the government began to express concern about the conservation of French monuments. The initiatives started in the Ministry of Public Instruction. In 1833, this ministry organized a "[c]ommission chargée de diriger le grand travail d'une publication de tous les matériaux importants sur l'histoire intellectuelle et morale du pays, la philosophie, les sciences, les lettres et les arts" (Leroy,"Notice," 723). This is the commission which funded Thierry to write a history of the third estate. Two years later, the commission formed a committee "spécialement chargé de la publication des monuments inédits des sciences et des arts" (723). The *Comité de monuments inédits*, managed by Guizot, was more narrowly focused, however, on the preservation of three-dimensional monuments—buildings and ruins—and on writing their history. A second subcommittee, the *Comité des arts et monuments* was next founded in 1837 by an art historian named Salvandy in order to write art history and to find and publish ancient and modern supporting documentation for it (724). The aims of the subcommittees illustrate that works of art and architecture were understood to be the monuments worthy of preservation. The preservation of texts, such as those studied by Thierry, and of literary works, such as Montaigne's *Essays*, is trapped outside the clearly defined domains of the subcommittees. The preservation of extant documents mattered largely inasmuch as they contributed to the writing of the history of three-dimensional monuments.

The ambiguous place of document preservation in the national movement was only further confused by the different aims of the two government ministries interested in preservation. The writing of cultural and political history and the discovery of its source texts was the purview of the Ministry of Public Instruction. But the actual conservation of extant monuments fell to the Ministry of the Interior. In 1837 the Ministry of the Interior formed its own committee, a *Commission des monuments historiques* (725). This agency reviewed funding requests for preservation and repair (726). In each French department, an inspector-general of buildings was appointed to examine funding requests.

The considerable funds at the disposal of the Ministry of the Interior attracted the politicians in the region of Bordeaux. The Council General of the Gironde soon created a local commission seated in Bordeaux that mirrored the agenda of the Ministry of the Interior. The Council General went to the Academy in search of well-connected experts in preservation. The local committee's task was "la recherche et [...] la conservation des monuments et documents historiques" (727), but it, too, only preserved buildings. In its first years, it established a *statistique monumentale* of the Gironde, "inventaire exact de tous les monuments, ruines, ou souvenirs de monuments épars sur le sol du département, quel que soit leur âge, Gaulois, Romain ou Français, quelle que soit leur destination, religieuse, militaire, civile, domestique, quelle que soit leur nature, meuble ou immeuble" (727-28). The establishment of a local commission was a stroke of genius: it was quite successful in winning funding amounting to thousands upon thousands of francs.

By 1840 two government ministries and one local commission had taken up the banner of preservation. The confusion between their objectives must have been subject to public dispute, for Leroy took almost too much care to emphasize their distinction. "[Le ministre de l'intérieur] comprend tout ce qui touche à la réparation des édifices, à la partie matérielle, tandis que ce qui a trait à l'histoire, à la description de ces édifices, rentre plus particulièrement dans les attributions du Comité de l'instruction publique" (726). Yet the real ambiguity must have been particularly obvious to Brunet and to the "essaim studieux" of the *Bulletin du bibliophile*. Both ministries were interested in skilled conservationists. Both ministries hired archivists to inventory and to catalog. Neither ministry, finally, could articulate clearly how documents were situated in the national patrimony. The local commission in the Gironde only increased that confusion by taking jurisdiction over both architectural and textual artifacts. A young archivist and bibliophile seeking to establish himself with government monies would have good reason, therefore, to cultivate all three funding streams.

These funding streams probably explain why the Academy of Bordeaux so strongly supported the Council General of the Gironde's commission on monuments and documents. The aims of the national conservation movement fit generally into the Academy's interest in promoting the Gironde's regional riches.[7] Lemonnier, the president of the Academy in 1840, deplored the fact that Bordeaux had not matched the economic advances seen in other regions since the revolution: "[I]l est superflu de rappeler par quel enchaînement de circonstances funestes Bordeaux est demeuré si longtemps étranger à la grande révolution qui s'est faite depuis cinquante années dans les habitudes du monde commercial [...], pourquoi, le Nord et l'Est se sont couverts de manufactures, [...] tandis que Bordeaux, isolé sur sa plage sablonneuse, n'a pu remplacer par de nouveaux liens ses anciennes relations brisées" (Lemonnier, 546). The treatment of historical objects by the Academy reflects its forward-looking stance. Before the arrival of Brunet, never more than sixteen percent of works submitted to the Academy from outside its membership concerned historical study of any kind. Those that did were topographical, archeological, or antiquarian in nature. Only once was a text edition mentioned, that of Thomas More's *Utopia* (1839). If the Academy of Bordeaux became involved in conservation, it was because such conservation promoted the region of Guyenne.

Even Brunet retreated from his love of textual artifacts when he was accepted into the Academy in 1841. In his acceptance speech, he delivered a comparative essay of world newspaper readership. Beginning his story with the hypothetical existence of newspapers in the classical age, a satirical approach that subtly mocked his new colleagues, he sketched a comparative study on the growth of newspapers in European countries up to the present day.[8] His point was to decry the effect of the print industry and of its readership, both unstable and fleeting, on the timelessness of literary works: "[l]a critique sera forcée de s'occuper de plus en plus de la presse périodique; cet être toujours affamé, toujours insatiable, n'est point exempt de reproches; on l'a déjà remarqué, il est mortel au génie; il épuise, à son profit, la satyre, la gaîté, l'esprit, la chanson, le roman, l'histoire, le poëme, le petit vers, le grand vers; au lieu du volume durable, fait avec conscience, médité à loisir, écrit lentement, il donne une feuille en l'air, qui va, qui vient, qui disparaît, qu'on ne retrouve plus [...]" (596). With masterful skill, Brunet presented a commercial topic that nevertheless gave an apology for literary works: Montaigne's slowly written *Essays* were among the only texts worthy of monumentality.

Payen joined the Academy of Bordeaux as a correspondant member in the early 1840s, trailing Brunet from the *Bulletin du Bibliophile*. Jules Delpit, who studied under a colleague of Brunet's, soon joined them. Payen had begun publishing his *Documents inédits* with Jannet and Techener in Paris.[9] In 1844, Brunet published a brochure on the annotations of the 1588 edition of the *Essays*, also with Techener in Paris.[10] With these three members in the same Bordeaux society, there was a nucleus of individuals concerned with French literary history, with document collection and preservation, and with Montaigne. Yet Montaigne simply was not their primary concern. Delpit, though a bibliophile and rare document collector, epitomized the ambition of young archivists who sought funding from the government ministries.

Jules Delpit received his bachelors in law in Paris in 1830 at the age of twenty-two (Ducaunnès-Duval, et. al., 10). After his graduation, however, he immediately began lessons at the newly refounded *École des Chartes*, eventually becoming a student of Guérard. His cousin Martial, five years his junior, was also a student there. Four years later, his father's death left him an independent landowner, and he began working in archives in Paris and in the provinces on a "nouvelle histoire de Bordeaux" (14).[11] By 1837 he fell under the protection of Thierry: his cousin Martial had become Thierry's secretary and right-hand man (Thierry, 407). Through this connection, in 1842, the Ministry of Public Instruction appointed Delpit as a correspondant charged with cataloging French documents in the Guild Hall and elsewhere in London. Villemain, who was then director of the ministry, commissioned him.[12] In the year prior to his voyage to England, Delpit had published an article in the *L'Indicateur* on "Materiaux pour servir à l'histoire de la Guyenne" (12). Just days prior to receiving an official letter from Villemain, he published another article on Bordeaux documents in English archives in the *Mémorial bor-*

delais (Delpit, "Introduction," iv). It is clear that the thirty-two-year-old Delpit harbored the ambition not only to become the official historian of Bordeaux but also to become publicly recognized as such.

One would think that Villemain's professional association with Montaigne would transmit to the Gascon a responsibility to look for Montaigne documents in London. His instructions nevertheless clearly restricted Delpit's work to the Guild Hall and "toutes les pièces pouvant servir au Recueil des monuments inédits de l'Histoire du Tiers-Etat, publié par M. A. Thierry" (Ducaunnès-Duval, 15, letter dated March 11, 1842). Delpit was to seek out only charters and other documentation of the establishment of the French state. These constraints did not keep him from proposing his own project for funding by a ministry grant, one that did not concern Montaigne. Delpit wanted to publish an exhaustive inventory of all documents in London archives: "l'histoire générale, l'histoire de nos diverses provinces, et les monuments littéraires" (16). The ministry initially accepted his proposal. This success meant a great deal: he had finally achieved the kind of recognition and financial support that Thierry enjoyed. With such recognition, he could rise in the ranks of French intellectuals towards the Academy and the Institute, or, in the very least, he could receive a permanent appointment as an archivist. As an independently wealthy landowner, Delpit was clearly in competition for the prestige and political connections of a government position.

Delpit chose a topic that he felt would be funded. Neither literary, nor Montaigne-oriented, it was nevertheless too arcane to fit within the government's aims for rewriting the national history. By November 1842, Delpit had returned to France. At the end of the month, he received a flattering request from Villemain to research "l'origine, aux principaux caractères et aux différentes vicissitudes du régime municipal [...] au moyen des documents locaux qui sont à votre disposition, et que vous voudriez bien prêter de nouveau le concours de votre zèle et de vos lumières" (19, letter dated November 24, 1842). He completed his work in early January 1843, and he did not hear from the academician again until April. By this time, for some reason, he had become discredited within the ministry. It is only under Thierry's ultimatum that Villemain sent Delpit once again to London, this time in the company of his cousin Martial—and perhaps under his cousin's tutelage. Nevertheless, Villemain rejected Delpit's conditionally-accepted proposal (22, letter dated June 2, 1843). It was "trop vague et trop étendu pour pouvoir être adopté sans d'importantes modifications." It was more of an uncritically assembled, exhaustive catalog. Delpit had not succeeded in finding a subject worthy of conservation in the French national patrimony. What is worse, since he could not find a good criterion for assimilating a "recueuil de pièces," he was not even a good historian. He simply was not in the same league with the great Thierry.

During Delpit's second trip to London in the summer of 1843, he seemed even more distracted from his appointed task. He corresponded with François Mignet, of the Ministry of Foreign Affairs, on whose behalf he did a great deal of research, comprising among other things an annotated catalog of correspondence of the "State papers office" with France from November 1558 to the end of 1562. Villemain himself distracted Delpit from his task by requesting that he change projects and transcribe a number of letters of Catherine de Medicis for another edition of documents funded by the Ministry of Public Instruction. In the last days of his stay, he even served as tour guide for two secretaries of Mignet. He had turned into a distracted secretary, trusted on archival errands, incapable of directing a historical project on his own.

This lack of support did not stop the indefatigable Delpit from submitting a new proposal to Villemain for a work based on the French documents in London. Once again, the committee was guardedly interested in his proposal for a volume on "documents inédits extraits des archives d'Angleterre" (28), but they demanded transcriptions of all pieces to be included before granting their approval. It is entirely likely that Delpit did not even know which papers he would include. Within weeks, the proposal was formally rejected, unworthy of the collection. He published them with his own funds in 1847.[13]

Twice in one year, Delpit was blocked by ministerial forces from ascending to the rank of publicly funded historian. The independent proprietor responded by cutting ties with Paris and by retreating to his home in Izon in early 1844. He left Paris, but he did not give up his ambition, following it to the Academy of Bordeaux and to Brunet.

By 1844, Delpit had met Brunet as well as Arnaud Detcheverry, the archivist for the city of Bordeaux, through shared interests in historical questions and documentary research (Delpit, "Introduction," xxv-xxvi). The three men set their sights on the funding streams available to the local *Commission des monuments et documents*. They came up with a plan to publish nothing less than the complete archives of the *Ancien Régime* municipal government of Bordeaux: the *Jurade*. They made their proposal to Rabanis, head of the local commission, former president of the Academy, chairholder in history and *doyen* of the University of Bordeaux.

Rabanis had come to Bordeaux around 1835 to occupy the seat of history at the *collège royal*. "[J]eune encore, sentant sa force, et plein d'enthousiasme pour les nouvelles théories historiques, [il] crut qu'il lui serait facile de raconter les faits que d'autres, sans doute, avaient dû suffisamment fouiller, et qu'il n'aurait qu'à les plier aux théories nouvelles" (Delpit, xx). After writing an "introduction brillante et facile," Rabanis soon discovered that the primary research of the documentary sources of Bordeaux history had not been done, "et qu'il lui serait impossible de les étudier sérieusement pendant que l'imprimeur composerait le récit des premières siècles" (xxi). For the next fifteen years Rabanis assimilated "les documents que sa position, et les sympathies qu'il avait su gagner, lui avaient fait découvrir" (xxi). Delpit had little respect for Rabanis's ability to network in the intellectual societies of Bordeaux and to capitalize on the private collections of their notable members, even though Delpit and Brunet, who had edited a letter of Montaigne's kept in a private collection, did precisely the same thing.[14] Delpit's antimony to Rabanis was also methodological: Rabanis was not an archival researcher, a student of Thierry, dedicated to documentary research and to preservation. He followed instead Michelet's "théories nouvelles."

Delpit and Brunet's proposal was doomed to failure from the beginning. It was inspired by a bibliophilic zeal for documents and text editions. The audience of their proposal, the Academy, was overwhelmingly invested in the preservation of three-dimensional monuments. Their proposal was furthermore directed to the wrong ministry. It made sense that Delpit change venues after having alienated the entire Ministry of Public Instruction, but the Ministry of the Interior simply did not fund projects for the conservation of documents. While the *local* committee of the Gironde pretended an interest in documents, even this committee had never sought to conserve one.

Rabanis was instrumental in the rejection of Delpit's proposal. While it was circulating among members of the Municipal Council, he presented a negative evaluation of it. Even though Delpit envisioned "six à huit volumes, publiés dans trois ou quatre années" (xxvi), and for funds in the amount of 750 francs per year, he asserted that, in fact, the amount could rise as high as 7-8000 francs. He strongly encouraged the commission to support the endeavor in principle without making financial commitments of any kind.

The reasons for the rejection of the proposal could be many, from personal enmity to a conflict between the agenda of the municipality and the generality of the Gironde. It does appear very likely that Delpit's proposal *could* eventually have cost the municipality on the order of 8,000 francs. Gras, the departmental archivist, received a stipend of 2,000 francs a year for his work of setting order to the chaotic, post-revolutionary departmental archives. For that sum, in the course of two years, he had accomplished no more than the triage and the preliminary labeling of the stores.[15] Given the size of the archives of the *Jurade*—over two hundred and fifty years of decisions and deliberations—it was unlikely that transcription and publication of even a fraction would cost less. Rabanis was an economic realist.

Delpit interpreted the rejection as a personal betrayal. Not only did he feel that Rabanis had materially misrepresented his proposal, but also Rabanis might have done so out of jealous competition. Delpit's scathing depiction of the historian's incompetence with primary documents bears witness to a grudge held for over twenty years and to the elitist prejudice of the bibliophile and trained archivist. But it also hints at Delpit's ambition: if Delpit advanced—with the support of the municipality—Rabanis's own position as the recognized historian of Bordeaux might have been jeopardized.

Delpit and Brunet did not succeed in receiving public funding for the next fifteen years. In the meantime, both men committed themselves to assiduous committee work within the Academy of Bordeaux. In the late 1840s and early 1850s, Montaigne was occasionally—if rarely—introduced by them as a subject of discussion.[16] In the early 1860s, they finally succeeded in receiving municipal funding for one of their projects, the *Archives historiques de la Gironde*. Delpit and Brunet's inability to launch their projects was as much a question of political positioning as it was of methodological approach. As we have seen in the case of Delpit, the private collectors who felt comfortable in the *Bulletin des bibliophiles* made no effort to commercialize their proposals to the whims and interests of potential funding sources. It is entirely likely, therefore, that this elitism played a role in the establishment of the journal that became identified with Delpit.

THE *ARCHIVES HISTORIQUES DE LA GIRONDE*

Brunet was the first president, and Delpit was the general secretary of the *Archives historiques de la Gironde*, founded in 1859. Delpit remained at the helm as general secretary until his death in 1892.[17] It was first sold to an extensive and impressive subscriber list for fifteen francs a volume. Despite much enthusiasm, after the first year's print run, the subscription list fell short of costs, and a moderate grant from the Municipal Council of Bordeaux was requested.

The reports of the Municipal Council on their approval of the funding request communicate a significant change in the positioning of historic documents. Textual artifacts had been metaphorically subsumed into the architectural conservation movement. Both Denjoy and Bonnet, who examined the proposal for public funding, used similar metaphors. Denjoy compared the work of Delpit, Brunet, and his compatriots to the stonemasons who supplied the materials for the great medieval cathedrals: "quand une grande construction se prépare, il faut d'abord amasser sur place les pierres de diverses natures et de dimensions différentes: il faut les tailler et les bien choisir; il faut sonder et creuser le sol pour y asseoir des fondements solides et inébranlables. Ainsi l'histoire, avant de l'écrire" (*AHG* (1860), vii). The monuments to the French national patrimony were no longer merely its ancient buildings of mortar and stone but also the modern constructions of historical writing. Documents found in archives were the raw materials in the production of history, not the substance of history itself. They were rare jewels in need of a textual setting. "Un jour viendra où cette publication incessante portera ses fruits; la mine historique sera fouillée et ouverte à tous; les hommes doués de facultés supérieures qui font l'histoire y pourra puiser les éléments alors certains et complets de leurs compositions achevées ou brillantes" (viii). Once elitist collectors of rare works, Brunet and Delpit had been reduced to the status of technicians, skilled workers digging in the ground for "les pierres gallo-romaines [...]; les inscriptions gravées [...] sur le bronze des cloches, sur le marbre des tombes ou sur les piliers des églises; les ceaux des actes [...]; les meubles et les monuments" (viii). At best they share the work of museum curators, labeling and ordering their findings, so that a historian may come later to use these found objects to create history's textual monuments.

Delpit and Brunet had nevertheless created for themselves a provincial journal that met the needs of the bibliophile and archivist. As neo-Benedictines, they were marginalized, out of time, just as the *Bulletin* bibliophiles had preferred. Their work still required the critical faculties of *belles-lettres* criticism. Denjoy called it a "noble entreprise, oeuvre de dévouement et de science, d'érudition sobre, de choix judicieux et de saine critique" (vii). Most importantly, Delpit had finally won for himself a grant that—this time—applauded him for doing what he did best: the frenetic publication of everything. "*Publier les documents*, voilà ce que veut faire la Société," declared Bonnet grandly, "et pas autre chose; et comme elle ne fera pas autre chose, elle pourra en publier beaucoup; l'énergie, l'activité, le savoir des hommes qui la dirigeront, les ressources qui seront réunies, ne seront pas éparpillés sur mille objets divers, sur des travaux de toute nature; tout sera concentré sur la publication de documents, et dès lors cette publication sera sérieuse, abondante : elle pourra devenir immense" (viii). Delpit has succeeded in finding a group that was not appalled by his greatness of scale but impressed by it. It is no surprise that these men were the commercial leaders of the city of Bordeaux.

With the success in receiving funding, Delpit and Brunet had changed professions. They were no longer private collectors but publically-funded technicians, and this placed them in a different category than men such as Payen.[18] This distinction can be read between the lines of Delpit and Brunet's correspondance with Payen as early as the 1850s. While Delpit and Brunet were quite cordial, encouraging his donations to the nascent *Archives historiques,* Delpit did not restrain himself from chiding Payen, on whose behalf he had conducted numerous searches in the archives for documents related to Montaigne:

> quand je vous donne indication ce que vous jugez utile de m'en reporter ayez le bonté de me rappeler les dates et autres indications que je vous avais donné, sans quoi j'ai beaucoup de peine à les retrouver. Ainsi, je ne sais vraiment où est cette lettre autographe d'une dame de Belcier [...] dont vous m'avez parlé. Je ne la trouve ni parmi mes autographes *classés*, ni parmi les papiers qui sont à la biblioth. de Bordeaux, il faut qu'elle soit à Izon. Si vous m'aviez donné exactement l'indication de la signature du Sr de Mattecoulon j'aurai peut-être pu vous envoyer un calque, mais n'ayant pas trouvé M. Gras, je ne vous envoie que ce que j'ai trouvé. (Z Payen 711, letter dated 13 January)

When Payen asked questions about the departmental archives, in particular about those of the Parliament of Bordeaux, he was repeatedly told by Brunet that they were too hard for him to master: "c'est une rude besogne [...]. Maintenant, pour savoir s'il y a moyen d'extraire des archives quelque détail montaignesque d'un peu de valeur, le mieux que vous pouvez faire, c'est d'écrire à l'archiviste, M. Gras. Vous lui avez déjà écrit, ce me semble. [Faites]-le si vous voulez: spécifiez bien vos demandes. Je lui porterai votre lettre si vous me l'adressiez et m'entendrai avec lui. Il est obligeant et peut-être [arriverons y] à quelque petite découverte" (Z Payen 711, 14 March 1853, unsigned letter from Brunet to Payen. Spelling modernized). As late as 1859, even though Delpit's tone was quite informal, and even though they continue to participate in the same bibliophilic endeavors—sharing auction-lists and information—still, Delpit scolded Payen. "Pour avoir des renseignements sur quoique ce soit, n'oubliez jamais de rappeler les dates. Comment voulez-vous que je demande à Mr Gras, le discours de Montaigne mentionné dans les Ephemerides, il faut que j'aille à Izon que je fouille vos publications et que je revienne pour fixer cette date que vous pouvez donner sans vous deranger" (Z Payen 711, letter dated 10 April 1859). He did not hesitate to kid Payen over Payen's enmity with the rival Montaigne biographer Alphonse Grün.[19] "Le président et Montaigne se pourvurent reellement du conseil d'Etat? Vous n'avez qu'à le demander au directeur des archives judiciaires, votre ami Mr Grün" (10 April 1859). Delpit, Brunet, and Payen were still compatriots, working with a similar love of documents and obscure historical points. Yet Delpit and Brunet had not only become Payen's intellectual and technical superior; they censured his access to the archives. If bibliophiles and archivists could be envisioned to be in a competition in the nineteenth century, the archivists had won.

Throughout the nineteenth century, archivists could not situate Montaigne's place in the preservation of the French national patrimony. As early as the 1830s, those who sought funding from the Ministry of Public Instruction proposed volumes on the letters of Henry IV, of Catherine de Médicis, of the *Princesse palatine*. By the 1860s, these interests had not changed. Even though a significant number of Montaigne documents are published in the *Archives historiques de la Gironde* in the 1860s, including his last will and testament, an interest in the biographical Montaigne was not the motivation for preserving them in print. When archivists penetrated the archives in search for documents on greater figures of the French national patrimony, when local archivists methodically cataloged the notary records, they chanced upon documents relating to Montaigne.

Since 1860 or 1861, one of Delpit's pet projects had been to fund a printed catalog of Series E in the departmental archives of the Gironde through the *Archives historiques*. Even though the municipality had turned down his funding proposals, departmental archivists Gaullieur and Ducaunnès-Duval continued to read through and annotate Series E as part of their daily work, transcribing interesting documents as they went. It is in this way that, in 1866, Gaullieur published twelve documents of which only two are directly related to Montaigne and his family.[20] The other documents are equally noteworthy records left by past figures from Guyenne. In 1868, the proportions reverse: Gaullieur and Ducaunnès-Duval together published twelve documents of which nine are directly related to Montaigne and his family, and Delpit published one coming from the Montaigne archive of the municipal library. Yet, once again, each Montaigne document was included in a long list of documents published by the archivists. It was by chance that Montaigne's happened to be in the notary record being cataloged, along with those of other notable figures from Bordeaux.[21] It was sheer happenstance that Paul Raymond, an archivist working on the history of the *Basses Pyrénées* and that Roborel de Climens, a chartist funded by the Committee on Public Instruction, found and published documents on Montaigne while searching for letters of famous and important Renaissance figures. This pattern continued until Théophile Malvezin published his "Michel de Montaigne, son origine et sa famille" in the *Actes* of the Academy of Bordeaux in 1874. Even Malvezin followed up his research on Montaigne's genealogy with a monograph on the "Histoire des Juifs à Bordeaux,"[22] one that situated Montaigne within a radically different field of reference.

Montaigne's biography was marginalized until almost the end of the century (Bonnefon 1892).[23] By 1868, however, his *Essays* had achieved monumentality at the price of tragedy.

In June 1862, the municipal archives burned, and vast stores of documents were lost. Delpit blamed Rabanis and the municipal leaders directly for the loss: "[L]incendie du 13 juin 1862 n'a-t-il pas donné quelques regrets aux conseillers municipaux qui pouvaient empêcher de périr près de deux cents registres de la Jurade?"(Delpit, "Introduction," xxvi). The disaster attracted the attention of the Ministry of Public Instruction and its funding for the preservation of textual artifacts. In 1864, it suggested that Bordeaux publish its municipal archives as a contribution to the patrimony of the city.

It is important to consider the promotional value of the municipality's conservationist goal. Less inspired by the archivist's desire to preserve any shred of the past, no matter how insignificant, the municipality wanted to tout the historical riches of the large commercial city throughout the world. More than an "édifice publique les habitants de Bordeaux pourraient seuls admirer," it would be a "monument impérissable, qu'elle éléverait au passé de la cité, [qui] irait dans toutes les bibliothèques témoigner toujours du goût éclairé de la municipalité, de son intelligente application aux sciences, de son respect pour ceux qui l'ont précédée dans la voie qu'elle suit, et surtout de son amour pour son pays" (xxix, citing a municipal proclamation). In 1865, it approved a sum of 5,000 francs towards the publication of the municipal archives.

With the assurance of a funding stream from the Ministry of Public Instruction for textual artifacts, with the desire to promote the 'great riches' of Bordeaux, interest turned to the annotated copy of the *Essays* in the possession of the municipality. In 1868, a mayoral proclamation declared that its edition would "rendre absolument sien un de ses monuments, qui ne doivent jamais périr, laisser ce soin à nos successeurs c'est risquer de tout perdre" (cited in Keffer, 27-29). The language of the description suggests that the *Essays* had attained the same monumentality as Bordeaux's famed historical architecture: its city gates, its great bell, its churches and cathedrals. The *Essays* would be conserved as a work of art or architecture, but Montaigne's biographical documents would not receive equal consideration until the middle of the twentieth-century (Frame, *Biography*).

In the early nineteenth century, there existed an outlet for private collectors and for a marginal movement for the conservation of texts. These elite collectors and self-taught archivists fed into a national movement to conserve a patrimony of monuments. By the end of the century, archival research was no longer a prestigious activity reserved for the bibliophiles. It was the domain of professional archivists working for publically-funded entities. As independently wealthy bibliophiles were replaced by professional archivists, of whom Jules Delpit embodied the transition, the demands of an archetypal national story imposed its contingencies on the ambitions of the archivists. They would prefer to discover the letters of Catherine de Medicis to a secondary political figure and dubious skeptical philosopher from Bordeaux. The Committee on Public Instruction wanted great names. All Montaigne had done was to write a great book. In the end, Montaigne's book achieved monumentality sooner than did his biography.

Twentieth-century Montaigne scholars have tended to presume that people worked on Montaigne in the nineteenth-century because Montaigne mattered generally. To properly view the nineteenth-century Montaigne, he needs to be accurately situated at the margins of historical greatness. Closer to the center of our field of vision, we would find Techener and Brunet. Closer still would be Nodier, Villemain and Thierry. In the center of our field of vision we find competing historical methodologies and the ministries that supported them. It is well worth considering, however, if Brunet predicted the accurate context for viewing the nineteenth-century reception of Montaigne: the journalistic medium, of academies and historical societies, is where we see the nineteenth and twentieth-century Montaigne transform into a national monument.

Notes

[1] The *Bulletin du bibliophile* is published under this title by Techener in Paris until 1857, at which time it becomes the *Bulletin du bibliophile et du bibliothécaire*. Later it becomes the *Bulletin du bibliophile et du bibliothécaire et de la Société des Amis de la Bibliothèque Nationale et des grandes bibliothèques de France*.

[2] Brunet's monthly column is full of dry wit, remarkable erudition, and a taste for scatology that merit further study by scholars interested in the reception of early modern literature.

[3] Techener is referring to the publishing house that produced *Essais de Monsieur Michel de Montaigne*, ed. J.-A. Naigeon, Paris: Didot, 1802. See Desan.

[4] I am indebted to George Hoffmann for the suggestion that Brunet and Delpit cultivated Payen in the hopes of eventually securing Payen's collection for their own purposes.

[5] Augustin Thierry (1795-1856), *Recueil des monuments inédits de l'histoire du tiers-état. Ier série: chartes, coutumes, actes municipaux, statuts des corporations d'arts et métiers des villes et communes de France: région du Nord*. Paris: Firmin-Didot frères, 1850. 4 vols.

[6] Founded in the early eighteenth-century, the Academy of Bordeaux "se releva pour ainsi dire des ruines révolutionnaires" in 1797 as the *Société d'histoire naturelle*. (Leroy, "Discours," 478). In the first decades of the nineteenth century, it saw many modifications to its

statutes, the most significant being a move in 1838 to open its proceedings up to the public. This change in statutes led to the creation of its quarterly *Actes*. The *Actes de l'Académie royale des sciences, belles-lettres et arts de Bordeaux* is jointly published in Bordeaux and Paris by various printers from 1839-47, at which time it changed title to *Recueil des actes de l'Académie des sciences, belles lettres et arts de Bordeaux*. In 1860 it again changed title to *Actes de l'Académie impériale des sciences, belles-lettres et arts de Bordeaux*. In 1871 it changed title again to *Actes de l'Académie nationale des sciences, belles-lettres et arts de Bordeaux*. The journal continues publishing throughout the twentieth century.

[7] The standing committees of the sciences were called "1: Sciences mathématiques, physiques et chimiques; 2: Sciences naturelles et agricoles; 3: Sciences physiologiques et médicales" "Réglement de l'académie royale des sciences, belles-lettres et arts," *Actes* 1, no. 1: 12.

[8] Brunet dryly comments, "Avant le déluge, il existait déjà, au dire de quelques érudits [citation of four eighteenth-century works in Latin], des livres, des bibliothèques, des académies; je serais donc en droit, remontant jusqu'à ce grand cataclysme, de rechercher si les aïeux de Noé lisaient aussi un journal" (Brunet, "Essai," 568).

[9] The *Documents inédits ou peu connus sur Montaigne* are originally published as brochures with Jannet and then the last with Techener in 1847, 1850, 1855, and 1856.

[10] *Les Essais de Michel de Montaigne, leçons inédites, recueillies par un membre de l'Académie de Bordeaux, sur les manuscrits autographes conservés à la bibliothèque publique de cette ville*, Paris: Techener, 1844.

[11] In 1837, Pierre Bernadau publishes a *Histoire de Bordeaux depuis l'année 1675 jusqu'à l'année 1836*. Delpit will later scoff at the merits of this publication, one which is in direct competition with his own aims at producing the definitive history of the region (Delpit, "Introduction," xxiii-xxiv).

[12] See Frame, *Montaigne in France,* on Villemain.

[13] *Collection générale des documents français qui se trouvent en Angleterre*, Paris: Veuve Dondey-Dupré, 1847.

[14] *Revue Historique de droit français et étranger*, 7 (1861): 461-524.

[15] See Ferdinand Leroy, "Notes sur les archives de la préfecture de la Gironde et de quelques villes du département," *Actes* 2, No. 3 (1841): 491-533.

[16] Brunet publishes his facsimile of Montaigne's annotations to the *Edition de Bordeaux* in an early appeal for the edition of this text. In 1855, some letters of Montaigne's are re-printed in the *Actes* and become the subject of polemic between Payen and Grün (Trinquet).

[17] This journal will publish continually until 1903. Without Delpit's nurturing, it could not last.

[18] About half of the participants in the *Archives historiques* are appointed archivists for a city or a department; the other half private collectors, of which the majority are titled nobility or members of the clergy. It is something of a fusion between bibliophilic and archival zeal.

[19] Alphonse Grün publishes a *Vie Publique de Michel Montaigne*, Paris: Librairie D'Amyot, 1855, using materials cribbed from meetings with Payen and others, which Payen takes to be a personal betrayal. Delpit helps Payen's cause in the polemic that ensues. See Trinquet.

[20] Gaullieur publishes the "Vente et revente de la terre de Montagne (1477)" and the "Testament de Thomas Ayquem, chanoine (5 August 1541)."

[21] Gaullieur and Ducaunnès-Duval publish "Contrat de Mariage de Michel Eyquem de Montaigne et de Françoise de Lachassaigne (22 September 1565)"; "Contrat de Michel Eyquem de Montaigne et de Françoise de Lachassaigne (deuxième rédaction) (22 September 1565)"; "Caution fournie par Joseph de Lachassaigne pour la dot de sa fille (22 September 1565)"; "Connaissement des marchandises chargées par Raymond Eyquem sur le Nicolas de Saint-Paul (22 November 1477)"; "Hommage à l'archevêque de Bordeaux de la terre et château de Montagne (9 November 1530)"; "Procuration donnée par Michel de Montaigne

(22 Mai 1566)." With the exception of the 15th century *hommage*, all are found in Series E of the Archives départementales de la Gironde (ADG), in the minutes of the notary Léonard Destivals (*AHG* 10 (1868): 163-76). Later in the year, they publish the "Partage de la succession de Pierre Eyquem de Montaigne entre ses quatre fils (22 August 1568)." It is in ADG series E, in the minutes of the notary J. Castaigne (*AHG* 10 (1868):252-56). Emile Lalanne transcribes a copy of Guillaume de Lachassaigne's last will and testament (13 May 1587) from ADG. He doesn't specify which records, but it is likely to be from the notary records in Series E (*AHG* 10 (1868): 274-87). At the same time, Delpit publishes "Quittance donnée pour la livraison de deux accusés (17 July 1536)" from the municipal library, "Cartulaire du château de Montaigne" (*AHG* 10 (1868): 250-52). Early in the year, however, Gaullieur publishes "Mandement d'Odet de L'Omagne au seigneur de Rignac (11 May 1462)" from the ADG notary minutes (*AHG* 10 (1868): 90-92), and Ducaunnès-Duval transcribes a "Bulle d'Urbain VIII accordant une dispense pour un mariage au 4ᵉ degré de parenté (5 December 1640)" from the private collection of M. de Sentou, for Gustave Labat. Neither of these documents are related to Montaigne. At the very end of the year, Gaullieur publishes "Lettres de renvoi au parlement de Paris d'un procès entre les archevêques de Bordeaux et de Bourges (24 September 1460)" from ADG Series G (records of the archdiocese), and "Ratification de la vente de la seigneurie de Montagne" (17 April 1509), found in ADG Series E notary minutes (AHG 10 (1868): 501-10). Only one of the two documents is directly related to Montaigne.

[22] Malvezin's work on Montaigne first came out in the first trimester of *Actes* (1874). It was later republished under the same title as a monograph in Bordeaux by Lefebvre, 1875. His *Histoire des juïfs à Bordeaux* is published in Bordeaux by Lefebvre in 1875.

[23] Even Paul Bonnefon, who writes a two-volume biography of Montaigne, was a scholar of La Boétie.

Works Cited

Actes de l'Académie nationale des sciences, belles-lettres et arts de Bordeaux. 31 vols. Bordeaux: 1839-50.

Archives historiques du département de la Gironde. 27 vols. Bordeaux: Gounouilhou, 1859-92.

Bonnefon, Paul. *Montaigne: l'homme et l'œuvre.* Paris (Bordeaux): Rouam (Gounouilhou), 1893.

Bourdieu, Pierre. *The Field of Cultural Production: Essays on art and literature*, ed. and intro. Randall Johnson. New York: Columbia UP, 1993.

Brunet, Gustave. "À M. l'Editeur du Bulletin du Bibliophile." *Bulletin* 4(1839): 720-21.

———. "Essai sur la statistique de la presse périodique dans les cinq parties du monde, lu le 25 novembre 1841, en séance publique." *Actes* 3, no. 4 (1841): 565-97.

Bulletin du bibliophile. Paris : Techener, 1. sér. (1834)-9e sér., no. 22/23/24 (1850).

Delpit, Jules. "Introduction." *Archives municipales de Bordeaux* 1 (1867).

———. "Lettres inédites de Françoise de Lachassaigne veuve de Michel de Montaigne." In Inventaire...., Gabriel Richou and François de Lachassaigne, 274-76.

Paris : Techener, 1878.

Desan, Philippe. "Naigeon et l' "avertissement" censuré de l'édition des *Essais* de 1802." *Montaigne Studies* 10(1998): 7-78.

Ducaunnès-Duval, A. F. Habasque, and Charles Marionneau. "Jules Delpit." *Archives historiques du département de la Gironde* 27 (1892): 9-70.

Frame, Donald. *Montaigne in France (1812-1852)*. New York: Columbia University Press, 1940.

———. *Montaigne: A Biography*. New York: Harcourt Brace & World, 1965.

Grégoire. "Rapport sur la bibliographie." *Bulletin du Bibliophile* 3 (1838): 63-72.

Grün, Alphonse. *La Vie publique de Montaigne*. Paris: Librairie D'Amyot, 1855.

Keffer, Ken. *A Publication History of the Rival Transcriptions of Montaigne's 'Essays'*. Lewiston, New York: Edwin Mellen Press, 2001.

Lemonnier, Charles. "Discours de M. Lemonnier, Président de l'Académie, prononcé en séance publique, le 28 novembre 1840." *Actes* 2, no. 4 (1841): 563-71.

Leroy, Ferdinand. "Discours prononcé par M. Ferdinand Leroy, président de l'Académie." *Actes* 4, no. 4(1842): 471-96.

———. "Notice historique et archéologique sur l'ancien prieuré de Cayac, près de Gradignan (Gironde), suivie de l'examen de cette question: la loi de 1833 sur l'expropriation forcée pour cause d'utilité publique est-elle applicable à la conservation des monuments?" *Actes* 2 No. 4 (1841): 717-58.

McGann, Jerome J. "A Point of Reference." In *Historical Studies and Literary Criticism,* ed. Jerome H. McGann, 3-24. Madison: University of Wisconsin Press, 1985.

Nodier, Charles. "Des Auteurs du seizième siècle qu'il convient de réimprimer." *Bulletin du bibliophile* 1 (février 1835): 1-11.

———. "Échantillon curieux de statistique." *Bulletin du bibliophile* 1 (août 1835): 1-12.

———. "Notice bibliographique sur Montaigne, par M. Payen." *Bulletin du bibliophile* 3 (janvier 1838): 3-4.

Payen, Jean-François. "Au Même." *Bulletin du bibliophile* 4 (1839): 893-94.

———. *Registres secrets du Parlement de Bordeaux. Extraits faits principalement (par M. Payen) au point de vue de Montaigne et de la Boétie*, in-quarto manuscript notebook with interfiled letters and cuttings, 1853, BN Z Payen ms. 711.

———. *Documents inédits de Montaigne*, Fasc. 1-4, Paris: Techener; Jannet [bound as one], 1847-1856.

Richou, Gabriel and François de Lachassaigne. *Inventaire de la collection des ouvrages et documents réunis par J.-F. Payen et J.-B. Bastide sur Michel de Montaigne [...] Suivi de lettres inédites de Françoise de Lachassaigne*. Ed.

Jules Delpit. Paris: Techener, 1878.

Simonin, Michel. "Le zèle et la compétence: le docteur Payen, Reinhold Dezeimeris et les études montanistes au XIXe siècle." *Montaigne Studies* 10 (1998): 79-120.

Techener, Jacques. "Avis sur le bibliophile." *Bulletin du bibliophile* 1 (décembre 1835): np.

——. "Préliminaires." *Bulletin du bibliophile* 2 (janvier 1836): 3-10.

Thierry, Augustin. "Rapport à M. le Ministre de l'Instruction publique, sur la Collection des documents historiques relatifs à l'histoire du tiers état." *Bulletin du bibliophile* 2 (1837): 384-89; 404-409.

Trinquet, Roger. "Centenaire d'un livre et d'une polémique, «La Vie publique de Montaigne» par Alphonse Grün." *Revue d'Histoire Littéraire de la France* 56 (April-June 1956): 177-203.

La Barque de Dante:
Delacroix, Michelangelo
and the Anxiety of Influence

William Cloonan

In 1822 the twenty-four year old Eugène Delacroix was completely unknown. Yet a mere five years later he was "a famous artist, one of those at the center of the French School, an artist who mattered, even if his works were harshly or even severely judged" (Jobert, 66). He would maintain this position of importance until his death in 1863. This sudden burst into the limelight and the creation of a reputation that endured throughout his career were due in large measure to three canvases Delacroix completed before the end of the decade: *The Barque of Dante* (1822), *Scenes from the Massacre of Chios* (1824), and in 1827-1828, *The Death of Sardanapalus*. It was, however, *The Barque of Dante* which "immediately established his reputation as a major talent" (Johnson, *Catalogue*, 74). In his *Dante et Virgile d'Eugène Delacroix* Sébastien Allard suggests that "[c]ette première réussite au Salon constitua le moment peut-être le plus décisif de toute la carrière d'un peintre avide de reconnaissance et pour qui 'la gloire n'était pas un vain mot'" (10). The canvas made such a powerful impression that eventually it would be copied by "Courbet, Manet, Degas, Cézanne, Gauguin and a multitude of lesser painters" (Johnson, *Delacroix* 1979, 18).

In addition to *The Barque of Dante* offering an impressive display of Delacroix's artistic talent, elements in the picture provide intriguing indications of the young painter's grasp of the art world politics of the day. The fastest path to commercial success in early nineteenth-century France was to show successfully at a salon, and *Barque* was consciously prepared for the Salon of 1822. As James Rubin remarks in *Eugène Delacroix, Die Dantebarke: Idealismus und Modernität*, 1987: "Mit...*Dante und Vergil fahren über den Styx* hoffe der junge Delacroix im Salon der offiziellen französischen Kunstausstellung 1822, die Augen der Öffentlichkeit auf sich zu lenken"(5).

Since the jury was largely academic, Delacroix created statuesque figures whose forms and poses clearly referenced earlier Masters, a ploy intended at least in part to appease traditional tastes, thus perhaps lessening the jurors' apprehensions before the boldness of the coloring. In 1822, the hierarchy of pictorial genres

Michelangelo (1475–1564). Last Judgement, detail of Christ and Virgin Mary, Sistine Chapel, Vatican Palace, Vatican State. Credit: Art Resource, NY.

Delacroix, Eugene (1798–1863), Dante and Virgil in Hell; also called Dante's Boat. 1822. Oil on canvas, 189 x 246 cm. Louvre, Paris, France. Credit: Réunion des Musées Nationaux/Art Resource, NY.

was still very much in place, with large historical paintings at the top, followed by portraits, landscapes and still lifes (Jobert, 56). The *Barque* is a relatively big canvas (75 by 97 inches), yet given the ongoing political turmoil in the France of the 1820s, it would have been unwise for an ambitious young painter to show a picture that purported to comment on contemporary historical events. Fortunately for Delacroix, in terms of the aesthetic theory that reigned from the seventeenth century to the early portion of the nineteenth, the definition of a "history painting" was remarkably broad. Subsumed under that heading were "mythology, sacred history, history properly speaking, or subjects drawn from literature" (Jobert, 56). In addition to showing respect for tradition by incorporating blatant allusions to the Old Masters, Delacroix was shrewd enough to draw attention to his own modernity and intellectual cultivation by placing Dante directly in the picture.[1]

At the Salon of 1822 *The Barque of Dante* made a largely positive impression. No less an artist than the Baron Gros famously referred to it as "du Rubens châtié," and then offered to take Delacroix under his wing to prepare him for the Prix de Rome (Johnson, *Catalogue*, 75). Even those less well-disposed, such as the reactionary critic, Delécluze, who described *Barque* as "une vraie tartouillade," nonetheless conceded that it contained figures whose "contours et la couleur sont pleins d'énergie" (Johnson, *Catalogue*, 75). Probably the most remarkable commentary was supplied by Adolphe Thiers, at the time a newly-arrived lawyer in Paris and a sometime journalist, who, in relation to Delacroix's achievement with this canvas, wrote:

> Il jette ses figures, les groupe, les plie à volonté avec la hardiesse de Michel-Ange, et la fécondité de Rubens. Je ne sais quel souvenir des grands artistes me saisit à l'aspect de ce tableau; j'y trouve cette puissance sauvage, ardente mais naturelle, qui cède sans effort à son propre entraînement. [...] Je ne crois pas m'y tromper, M. de Lacroix (sic) a reçu le génie. (Johnson, *Catalogue* 1981, 75)

Delacroix began constructing his image as a genius with *The Barque of Dante* by consciously building on the accomplishments of his illustrious predecessors. In his *Catalogue*, Lee Johnson provides a succinct résumé of many of the possible sources from which Delacroix borrowed: the woman on the right clinging to the boat from Michelangelo's *Night*, the boatman, Charon, from the Apollo Belvedere, a combination of the pose of God the Father from the Sistine Chapel and a head from Géricault's *Raft of the Médusa* for the horizontal figure on the left. He further suggests that the arrangement of the drapery folds in Michelangelo's statue, *Rachel*, is copied for the depiction of Dante's clothing, and a figure in Ruben's *Hero and Leander* for the person in the water (75). While this list is not exhaustive, it certainly demonstrates Delacroix's indebtedness to earlier artists. Nevertheless, as obvious as all these allusions are, and as typical as it was in Delacroix's day to cite illustrious predecessors, there remains one reference that has not been noted, and whose ostensible brazenness raises questions about the extent of the young painter's ambitions in *Barque*. I am referring to the figure of Virgil in the Delacroix canvas and its striking resemblance to the image of Christ in Michelangelo's *Last Judgment* (1536-1541).

Despite all the grimaces and frenzied gesturing of the damned in *Barque*, the most imposing personage is Virgil. Such a Virgil has no precedents in pictorial art, and, to my knowledge, has not been copied since. His thick, muscular body is of Michelangelesque inspiration, but his most riveting feature is the handsome, clean-shaven, youthful face, whose beauty is accentuated by the serenity of his countenance during the chaotic crossing of the waters in Phlegyas's skiff toward the City of Dis. Since *The Divine Comedy* was only completed shortly before the poet's death in 1321, it is not entirely surprising that the Dante figure in the painting appears somewhat wizened, but the portrait of Virgil is clearly at odds with accepted historical facts. It was common knowledge that Virgil died in 19 CE at the age of 48. Delacroix's rendering of Virgil is not that of a middle-aged man. Thus at the center of Delacroix's ambitious canvas is an imposing albeit somewhat incongruous figure, almost as imposing and incongruous as the image of Christ in *The Last Judgment*.[2]

Michelangelo's Christ initially appears extremely unorthodox. On first viewing, the figure can seem more Apollonian and pagan than Christian and traditional. This apparent departure from the norm has prompted even art historians to seek after hidden meanings or radical breaks with orthodoxy in Michelangelo's beardless deity. As late as 1968, Leo Steinberg could suggest that this Christ was "a Christ unknown to the faithful" (49). More recent scholarship, however, has shown this not to be the case. The figure of the beardless Christ turns out to have had a long history in the iconography of Western Christianity.[3] Valerie Shrimplin makes clear that, whatever Michelangelo's personal reasons for electing to paint the Christ-figure in this fashion, he was in no sense breaking with tradition: "It is...erroneous to suggest that in the Italian Renaissance the beardless Apollo-type Christ was completely out of the ordinary and unknown, or that it implied heresy at the time, although the type was admittedly less common" (2000, 155).

The reason for this little aside concerning the putatively radical nature of Michelangelo's Christ has to do with Delacroix's actual knowledge of *The Last Judgment*. He had never been in Italy before painting *The Barque of Dante*, and, in fact, he would never go there, although he frequently talked of such a voyage (Jobert, 44). His knowledge of Renaissance art stemmed from what was available in the Louvre and other French provincial museums, as well as from an extensive consultation of prints and copies. His acquaintance with *The Last Judgment* was through secondary sources, and he had never been to Italy where he might have seen other examples of the beardless Christ, so it is perfectly plausible to suspect that Delacroix, like many other people then and now, found in the Christ figure a challenging and unorthodox image.

The similarities between Michelangelo's Christ and Delacroix's Virgil are striking. Both figures have the signature Michelangelesque bodies, those massive forms; both have clean-shaven faces that resemble each other; both have rather deep-set, heavily lidded eyes; and, to a greater or lesser degree, both are departures from more canonical or expected depictions. Perhaps the most disquieting quality in both figures is the composure of the two countenances. While, given the dramatic moment depicted, Virgil's calm could seem out of place to a person unfamiliar with *The Divine Comedy*, Delacroix's rendering is amply justified. In Canto VIII, Virgil's impassivity contrasts sharply with Dante's terror. Delacroix was very familiar with Dante,[4] and was quite true to the poem in depicting Virgil as he did. Still, in terms of the picture itself and without reference to its literary source, Virgil's detachment produces an almost jarring effect. Michelangelo's Christ is even more impressive in this respect. At the very moment when he is condemning the damned to eternal punishment, his face, in the words of John Dixon, "is calm, impassive…[displaying]…a firm, unsentimental compassion" (68). Equally noteworthy is the way the frightened Dante's raised right arm and left arm which links with Virgil's forearm and hand, echo the positioning of Christ's arms in the fresco.[5]

While there is nothing unusual about an ambitious, talented young painter quoting liberally (and obviously) from Old Masters in order to curry favor with an academically-minded jury, or simply to acknowledge a genuine debt, I do not think that Delacroix's referencing of Michelangelo's Christ in *The Last Judgment* can be entirely explained in these terms. The other allusions to Michelangelo are perfectly straightforward and have no function beyond their role as visual citations, marks of homage on the part of a fledgling artist toward his admired predecessor. The evocation of the Christ figure in Delacroix's Virgil is, on the other hand, at once startling and somewhat idiosyncratic. Also, because of the centrality of Virgil in the painting (except for Dante, the function of the other figures is essentially decorative), the puzzling Christ-Virgil association invites study. James Rubin has remarked that "*Die Dantebarke* ist ein Kunsterliches Programmbild," (*Die Dantebarke*,30), and albeit from a very different perspective from Rubin's, I agree totally with this statement. I believe the program in question involves an unconscious challenge on Delacroix's part to Michelangelo's greatness, and that the challenge most overtly manifests itself in the Christ-Virgil parallel. To explain the full extent of this challenge will first require an examination of Delacroix's complex relation to Michelangelo, the man and the myth, as well as an analysis of the French painter's self-positioning amid the aesthetic and social controversies of post-Napoleonic France. In formulating my conclusion I will draw heavily on Harold Bloom's *The Anxiety of Influence* (1973). Before I address these two issues however, it seems appropriate to say something about the historical time line involved in these discussions.

The Barque of Dante (1822) is Delacroix's first major piece and marks the beginning of his public career. Although Delacroix is justly famous for his *Journal 1822-1863*, as the dates indicate, he did not begin them until the year of *Barque*, and so they have little to say about this particular painting. Finally, even though Delacroix would eventually launch what would become a second career as a literature and art critic, in 1822 this was still very much in the future. As Michele Hannoosh remarked about the thinking and writing of the young Delacroix: "the early years…have none of the radically innovative features and none of the philosophical reflection on writing and painting of the later ones" (*Painting*, 5-6). Obviously then, the materials I will draw upon in examining Delacroix's attitude toward Michelangelo, as well his own involvement with the aesthetic politics of nineteenth-century France, will all postdate this breakthrough painting. I consider myself to be justified in employing this approach since I intend to demonstrate how the reflections and decisions of a more mature artist retrospectively clarify a series of choices that were undoubtedly to a great extent instinctive or unconscious for the young painter.

Although Michelangelo was not the only predecessor cited in *Barque*, or the sole painter from the past who interested Delacroix,[6] he was by far the artist with whom the French painter most closely associated himself. Nothing illustrates this bond more dramatically than a canvas Delacroix did in 1849-50, *Michelangelo in His Studio*, currently hanging in the Musée Fabre at Montpellier. According to Barthélémy Jobert, in this work, "Delacroix, reaching his fifties, saw himself as a meditative Michelangelo, whom he portrayed seated between the *Moses* and the meditative *Madonna*, the sculptor's shears at his feet, the writer's book lying on the floor beside a box of drawings. He did the painting for himself " (45).[7]

This powerful homage to Michelangelo, not to mention to himself, was no sudden gesture on Delacroix's part. It was rather the culmination of a longstanding and developing association; "from 1830 on Delacroix more or less consciously projected himself onto Michelangelo" (Jobert, 45). This projection took different forms, from the relatively trivial to the deeply significant. In *Michelangelo in His Studio*, the Michelangelo/Delacroix figure is draped with a red cape, an image that would recall for Delacroix's contemporaries the French artist's omnipresent red scarf (Jobert, 45). Evidence of Delacroix's more substantial encounter with Michelangelo emerges from five sources: passages in his *Journal*, in the *Supplement* to his journal, two essays he published in 1830 in *La Revue de Paris* that focused on Michelangelo, along with an 1837 essay on *The Last Judgment* which appeared in the *Revue des deux mondes*. The essays from the *Revue de Paris* and the one from the *Revue de deux mondes* have been reprinted in *Eugène Delacroix: Ecrits sur l'art*, edited by François-Marie Deyrolle and Christophe Denissel in 1988, and I will cite them from this source.[8]

It is in the writing of Delacrois that the full measure of his complex and conflicted relation/association with Michelangelo appears. Delacroix's earliest extended commentaries on Michelangelo are found in volumes 15 and 16 of the 1830 *La Revue de Paris*, reprinted as "Michel-Ange" in *Ecrits*. Toward the end of the essay the French painter directly addresses *The Last Judgment*. The most surprising part of Delacroix's discussion concerns his description of the face of Christ: "Le Christ a l'air dans cette peinture d'un être animé seulement à la vengeance.... C'est un juge impitoyable, sourd aux cris de l'horrible désespoir de ces millions de damnés qui le supplient en vain" (118).[9] Passing from the Christ figure to that of his creator, Delacroix claims that "La peinture des sentiments tendres n'avait jamais été dans le génie de Michel-Ange" (118). The description of the angry, impatient Christ conforms to the common perception of Michelangelo's character, a judgment which the comment on his putative inability to depict tenderness only reinforces. For Delacroix, there appears to be an implicit association between the personality of the Christ figure and that of Michelangelo.[10]

Despite the somewhat atypical description of Christ's face, to which I shall return, the tone here is generally laudatory, a fact which makes all the more shocking a *Journal* entry of October 4, 1854: "*Le Jugement dernier*...ne me dit rien du tout. Je n'y vois que des détails frappants comme un coup de poing qu'on reçoit; mais l'intérêt, l'unité, l'enchaînement de tout cela est absent. Son *Christ en croix*[11] ne me donne aucune des idées qu'un pareil sujet doit exciter" (480). While it is true that this entry also reflects Delacroix's impatience with a fellow painter and friend named Chenavard, whose unconditional admiration for Michelangelo seemed to have gotten on Delacroix's nerves, the language here is undoubtedly strong, and certainly negative.[12]

To complicate matters further, in the *Supplément au Journal*,[13] a passage from August 16, 1844 provides yet another opinion about Michelangelo and his *Last Judgment*: "Je regarde Michel-Ange comme le plus grand peintre sans en excepter Raphaël....*Le Jugement dernier* est le seul tableau qui m'a donné des frissons" (863).

The simplest way to make some sense out of these seemingly conflicted if not contradictory statements would be to suggest that while Delacroix always admired Michelangelo, over time his enthusiasm for *The Last Judgment*, perhaps never really strong, waned. Whatever virtue simplicity might possess, in this case it certainly leaves some important questions unanswered. Why is Delacroix so adamant in his description of Christ's face as filled with anger? How can he refer to the creator of the *Pietà* as incapable of tenderness? To what extent did extraneous, even psychological factors contribute to Delacroix's denigration of *The Last Judgment* in his October 4, 1854 journal entry?

As is the case for students of art history today, in Delacroix's time knowledge of original works frequently came filtered through reproductions and guided by the appraisal of a powerful critical voice. In 1817 Stendhal published *Histoire de la peinture en Italie*, a book that had a great influence on Delacroix and his generation.[14]

In Stendhal's rather selective history, Michelangelo has pride of place. For Stendhal, Michelangelo is before all else the artist of terror: "the emotion Michelangelo seemed born to imprint into souls by means of marble and color" (in *Stendhal and the Arts* 1973, 80). Given Stendhal's stature in artistic and intellectual circles, his strong judgment might well have affected Delacroix's view of both the Christ figure and Michelangelo's own artistic strength, since it is obvious that in his discussion of Christ and the Italian painter/sculptor, the French painter is conflating the two. In a previously cited passage from "Michel-Ange," I noted that Delacroix offered the rather surprising judgment that "La peinture des sentiments tendres n'avait jamais été dans le génie de Michel-Ange." He then continued, "Dans cet ouvrage [*Le Jugement dernier*], plus que dans tous les autres, il donna carrière à son goût pour le terrible" (118). In his *Dictionnaire des beaux-arts*[15] Delacroix has the following entry: "Terrible. La sensation du *terrible* et encore moins celle de l'*horrible* ne peuvent se supporter longtemps.... Le *terrible* est dans les arts un don naturel comme celui de la grâce" (194-95, emphasis in text). The emotion referred to here is overwhelming terror mingled with an insidious, yet deeply satisfying pleasure. The artist he cites as an example is, of course, Michelangelo.

Certainly, Delacroix's assertion that Michelangelo did not have a genius for the depiction of the "tender" flies in the face of common knowledge, not to mention common sense. The French painter had access to numerous reproductions of Michelangelo's art, as well as to some originals. *The Dying Slave* was in the Louvre and must have provided a more nuanced sense of the Italian's talents. Delacroix must have known that the creator of the *Pietà* and *The Dying Slave* had little problem rendering tender sentiments, and even in his own, *Michelangelo in His Studio* (cited above), Delacroix depicts a tenderly rendered Madonna to the right of the Michelangelo-Delacroix figure.

Whether Delacroix was doing it consciously or not, he appears to have been creating a very idiosyncratic image of his Italian predecessor, and Stendhal's *Histoire* just may supply the key to unlocking Delacroix's intentions. Stendhal concludes his text with a proclamation that the nineteenth century is in search of strong emotions and that this "thirst for energy will bring us back to Michelangelo's masterpieces" (87).[16] Michelangelo, Stendhal insists, will be the reigning influence "until art has given us emotional power free from physical power" (87). A new artist must be able to rival Michelangelo in the depiction of strong emotions. The rather enigmatic "free from physical power," would seem to suggest that the new artist would be working in a medium other than sculpture whose very massiveness contributes to the overall emotional effect. This new artist then, will equal his predecessor's achievement, but also move beyond him, in part by working in a subtler element. For Stendhal, the reference to such a new artist was not merely a rhetorical ploy, but a real possibility: "If Michelangelo were born in our enlightened days, imagine what heights he might achieve!" (81). It is my contention that Delacroix imagined himself to be the artist capable of assuming Michelangelo's mantle.[17]

A glance at Delacroix's self-positioning in the artistic and social milieu of his era reveals a man skillful at keeping his deepest intentions to himself while providing a degree of encouragement to the various factions desiring to situate him in a particular camp. In this respect, Delacroix's *Liberty Leading the People* (1830) is one of the most misleading pictures of the nineteenth century. While the canvas celebrates the overthrow of the Bourbons in the revolution of 1830, it was painted five months after the fact by an artist with vaguely liberal leanings, but who had also enjoyed Bourbon patronage. What appealed to Delacroix was much more the drama of the moment than the larger political implications. According to Jobert, and despite *Liberty*, Delacroix "is among the least political [artists] of the century, or in any case one of the least committed to the service of any cause, except for Greek independence" (27). More revealing still is the fact that "he never declared or publicized his political opinions during this period when France was changing regimes just about every twenty years. He...received commissions from all the governments from the Restoration onward" (27). Far from espousing any political views that might please or annoy perspective patrons, Delacroix was more interested in connecting with the right people. He led a very successful forty year career in Paris where he knew everyone of importance and did not hesitate to use his connections to further his career (27). The nature of Delacroix's ambitions was certainly not political, and if one or several of his works appeared to be addressing a social issue it was primarily a case of circumstances rather than commitment. As Sébastien Allard observes: "Il tenait essentiellement à attirer l'attention sur lui par ses qualités de peintre et son inspiration, non au moyen d'un scandale politique" (32). To the extent that the painter had a radical, revolutionary side, it expressed itself in his artistic technique much more so than in the content of his pictures, but even here, on the canvases themselves, one can observe a relatively rapid disassociation from the political: "Between the years of 1822 and 1831...Delacroix's protagonist changed from a personality split between social concern, weak as it was, and egocentric detachment, to one that was completely asocial, detached, and self-possessed. This is the 'heroism' of disengagement" (Brown, 253).

In artistic matters Delacroix's convictions were elusive. James Rubin, in an essay entitled "Delacroix's *Dante and Virgil* as a Romantic Manifesto," quite correctly situates him in the Romantic camp and even finds that *The Barque of Dante* is "a manifesto, announcing a group of themes and formal concerns that will inform the Romanticism of the 1820s" (48). While there is doubtless merit in this claim, it also points to an ambiguity in much of Delacroix's work. Of course he was a Romantic; his spectacular subjects, rough finish and scumbling attest to that in every instance, but he was a Romantic of a somewhat peculiar sort: a Romantic with an inordinate respect for tradition. Hugh Honour points out that while many Romantics "were inspired by opposition to the aesthetic doctrines of classicism, to the rationalism of the Enlightenment, or to the political ideals of the French Revolution, many others were not, and they included Delacroix"

(14). In addition, if *Barque* were indeed a Romantic manifesto, it managed to be one without making any "decisive break from the long line of European history paintings" (Honour, 47).

The core of Delacroix's Romanticism is found less in themes or techniques,[18] than in his obsession with himself, his talents, his potential, in a word, in his very Romantic certainty of his own genius. Jobert speaks of his "iron will at the service of a formidable creative power" (15), and Delacroix codified his own Romanticism as "the free manifestations of my personal impressions, my aversion for the stereotypes of the schools, and my repugnance for academic formulae" (Honour, 22). The artist's description of himself is something of a Romantic stereotype, but elements, besides natural talent, that do separate him from many other Romantics are his great knowledge of, and lifetime involvement with painterly tradition, as well as the pronounced tendency to measure his achievements against the great artists who had come before him. Commenting on Delacroix's journal and letters, Stephanie Mora remarks that they "portray a man who sought…to follow in the footsteps of his great and famous predecessors"(72). Principal among them, I have been suggesting, is Michelangelo, and while Mora proposes that the French painter sought to equal his predecessors, I would now like to argue that the similarities between Virgil and the Christ of *The Last Judgment* coupled with the literary context provided by *The Divine Comedy* strongly imply that Delacroix's deep-seated and doubtlessly unconscious intention in *The Barque of Dante* was to begin the process of surpassing Michelangelo.

When Harold Bloom's *The Anxiety of Influence: A Theory of Poetry* first appeared in 1973, it created quite a stir due to its audacious proposal that living poets blessed with great talent often display a complex love-hate relationship to their equally gifted forerunners. He called this "the anxiety of influence." It seems to me that with very little tweaking (the substitution of "painter" for "poet," "painting" for "poetry," "artistic" for "poetic"), the general lines of Bloom's theory can also prove useful in the study of art history. According to Bloom:

> Poetic influence—when it involves two strong, authentic poets—always proceeds by a misreading of the prior poet, an act of creative correction that is actually and necessarily a misinterpretation. The history of fruitful poetic influence, which is to say the main tradition of Western poetry since the Renaissance, is a history of anxiety and self-saving caricature, of distortion, of perverse, wilful revisionism without which modern poetry as such could not exist.(30)

Bloom argues that "strong poets make…history from misreading one another, so as to clear the imaginative space for themselves" (5). That is to say, the artist must find a fault that is not necessarily there, and then show how he has triumphed over the very difficulty that had handicapped his predecessor. In elaborating his theory Bloom lists six ways in which this "misreading" can take place. At least three of them (*clinamen, tessera,* and *kenosis*[19]) seem germane to the discussion of the relationship between Michelangelo and Delacroix. I will first of all explain these concepts and then apply them to the discussion of Delacroix and Michelangelo.

Bloom never claims that all six elements have to be present in any example of the "anxiety of influence," and they are not all of equal importance. *Clinamen* is "the central working concept of Poetic Influence" (42). Bloom takes the idea from Lucretius where it means a "swerve of atoms," and applies it to art in the following manner: "A poet swerves from his predecessor...which implies that the precursor poem went accurately up to a certain point, but then should have swerved, precisely in the direction that the new poem moves" (14). A *clinamen* occurs when the latter-day admirer/emulator of a strong artist suddenly breaks with him, and moves beyond into areas the great predecessor was unable to enter.

For Bloom, "*Tessera*...is completion and antithesis.... A poet antithetically 'completes' his precursor, by so reading the parent-poem as to retain its terms but to mean them in another sense, as though the precursor had failed to go far enough" (14). Once again the emphasis is on the young artist finishing a task that proved beyond the ability of the Old Master.

Kenosis occurs when "the later poet, apparently emptying himself of his own afflatus, his imaginative godhead, seems to humble himself as though he were ceasing to be a poet, but this ebbing is so performed in relation to a precursor's poem-of-ebbing that the precursor is emptied out also, and so the later poem of deflation is not as absolute as it appears" (14-15). In less-Bloomian language, *kenosis* points to a form of false modesty. The young artist, really quite confident in his own abilities, insists upon his awe in the face of his esteemed precursor, but in the very admission of personal unworthiness, elements emerge which suggest the new artist's eventual triumph over his admired model.

Bloom insists that "the stronger the man, the larger his resentments, and the more brazen his *clinamen*" (43). What I am suggesting about Delacroix would make him brazen indeed. When the unheralded Eugène Delacroix appeared upon the scene in 1822, his *Barque of Dante* already possessed "strength and originality...not anticipated in the earlier paintings" (Jobert, 62). The young artist was also extremely well-versed in the literary and visual art of Western culture. His aim was to make a dazzling impression in the public sphere and on the academic-minded jury. Yet given his ego, his ambition, and his deep-immersion in the art of the past, along with his choice of subject and theme, he might also have been, in the best Romantic tradition, couching his admiration for a past master in a way that recalls kenosis. His very homage to the Renaissance artist amounted to a challenge directed at none other than his frère-ennemi, Michelangelo.

In viewing *Barque* with *The Last Judgment* in mind, a pattern rapidly emerges. Delacroix's Virgil resembles Michelangelo's Christ. I have earlier suggested that the

French painter conflated Michelangelo with his Christ figure, and Delacroix, in his turn, would be associating himself with the Italian painter/sculptor throughout his life. So imagine for a moment that the Christ of *The Last Judgment* is, in Delacroix's eyes, an image for Michelangelo, while the Dante in *The Barque* represents the debuting Delacroix.[20] The French artist then reprises the Christ figure, and models his Virgil after him. This is an homage to Michelangelo to be sure, but also the start of a more complicated process. The scene depicted by Delacroix is drawn from Canto VIII of *The Inferno*, at the very beginning of *The Divine Comedy*. At this juncture, Virgil dominates the cringing and fearful Dante, who has achieved some success in his career, but who, like Delacroix at the time of *The Barque*, has yet to fulfill his potential. However, in the course of the journey from Hell to Paradise, this power relationship between Dante and Virgil will change; it will in fact reverse itself. In Canto XXVII of *The Purgatorio* Virgil is forced to stop, and here one finds the clearest example of a *clinamen*. Virgil has carried Dante, and to a degree the poem, up to a certain point, a very exalted point, but now he has reached the limits of his forces and can go no further. Dante, however, will continue onward, move beyond him, surpass him and eventually achieve the ultimate experience of visual splendor, the Beautiful Vision. Despite starting from a position of considerable inferiority to the older artist, Dante was eventually able to continue forward, to make the "swerve" in Bloom's terms, and go where Virgil could not. The audacious suggestion of *The Barque* is that this pattern will repeat itself with Delacroix and Michelangelo.[21]

In this, his first significant painting, the bold young artist provides one of the greatest, indeed most outrageous examples of the hubris of the Romantic ego by implicitly predicting that he, Eugène Delacroix, aged twenty-four, would in time outdo the great Michelangelo. While, aside from the obvious desire to make a name for himself, it is impossible to determine Delacroix's deeper, unconscious aims in painting *The Barque*, Bloom makes an intriguing comment about the *clinamen* in relation to the artist's consciousness of the extent of his own ambition: "the *clinamen* always must be considered as though it were simultaneously intentional and involuntary" (44-45). Combining the "intentional" and the "involuntary" in one concept is surely contradictory in purely rational terms, but Bloom is talking about the complex mechanism of the human psyche, which does not shy away from the contradictory. Given Delacroix's ambition, his respect for tradition in general and Michelangelo in particular, it seems fair to *speculate* that Delacroix believed one of the factors that would help determine his future greatness would be his achievements in comparison to those of Michelangelo, and that perhaps without ever consciously formulating his intentions, he was driven to establish his claim, as quickly as possible, to be the artist capable of equaling and in time surpassing his great predecessor. Delacroix, an admirer of the Italian poet, imagined himself playing Dante to Michelangelo's Virgil in a context that foretold the eventual triumph of the former over the latter: Dante over Virgil, Delacroix over Michelangelo.

What characterizes this relationship is the great love of the younger man for his elder's accomplishment coupled with a strong sense of indebtedness, but also an envy and a desire to outdo him. All of which leads to a pictorial enactment of the anxiety of influence.

Delacroix was always aware how much he, along with generations of artists, owed Michelangelo. In a passage from his *Journal* of August 9, 1850, he wrote: "La fréquentation de Michel-Ange a exhalté et élevé successivement au-dessus d'eux-mêmes toutes les génerations de peintres" (263),[22] and in his essay "Michel-Ange" he was even more effusive:

> Il faut…oublier toutes les idées que nous faisons le plus habituellement sur la grâce et sur la beauté. Les ouvrages de Michel-Ange donnent incontestablement la sensation la plus épurée et la plus élévée qu'il soit possible d'éprouver par un art. (102)

This is high praise indeed, but one must be cautious about accepting it at face value. According to Bloom, *kenosis* is a complicated procedure where the modern artist breaks away from his precursor in the very act of praising his putative master while demeaning himself. The combination of Delacroix's genuine admiration for Michelangelo, along with the rhetorical excess of his praise for him, conform in part to what Bloom means by *kenosis*. Yet what finally completes the *kenosis* is the French painter's seemingly contrived reservations about aspects of his otherwise-revered predecessor's talent.

Delacroix was loathe to criticize the great Italian artist, yet in two areas he did qualify his praise. One involved Michelangelo's writing, notably his sonnets: "S'il n'eût fait que ses sonnets, il est probable que la posterité ne se fût pas occupée de lui" (January 25, 1860, 757). This is from a nineteenth-century artist who had already achieved an additional degree of celebrity from his essays and from portions of his *Journal* which he permitted Théophile Silvestre to quote in 1853 for an article about Delacroix's painting.

I have already referred to the other alleged weakness Delacroix had discerned in his predecessor, namely that "La peinture des sentiments tendres n'avait jamais été dans le génie de Michel-Ange" (*Ecrits sur l'art*, "Michel-Ange," 118). While *The Barque* provides plenty of evidence of the terrible and terrifying (Michelangelo's great strength according to Delacroix), one would be hard-pressed to uncover examples of tenderness in this work. However, at the outset of this essay, I noted that Delacroix's great reputation was forged in the 1820s on the basis of three paintings of which *The Barque of Dante* was the first. If we turn our attention briefly to the second painting, *Scenes from the Massacre of Chios* (1824), we find a near perfect blending of the tender and the terrifying with the wounded and dying Greeks, complete with nursing mother, portrayed as conquered yet dignified in defeat. These figures contrast sharply with the ferocious Turks, one of whom is dragging away a half-naked Greek woman. In terms of the anxiety of influence theory, this second canvas provides an example of *tessera*: " in *tessera* the later poet provides what his imagination tells him would complete the otherwise "truncated" precursor poem and poet" (Bloom, 66). Just as Dante (Delacroix) will eventually surpass the Virgil (Michelangelo) who appears in *The Barque*, *Scenes from the Massacre of Chios* captures in paint an emotional state that was beyond the capacity of an otherwise supremely gifted artist. In this painting, Delacroix, by successfully combining the terrible and the tender, achieves a level of perfection which, according to him, not even the great Michelangelo could manage.

Notes

[1] "La représentation...d'un épisode mettant en scène Dante lui-même, bien qu'absolument inédit à cette date, correspondait donc au goût d'une élite cultivée, cosmopolite et moderne, qui entendait rompre la 'grande muraille de Chine' que le classicisme avait érigée autour de la France" (Allard, 38).

[2] Even before turning to the Christ figure, it is worth noting that in the lower right section of *The Last Judgment*, there is a depiction of Charon and his boat, the very motif that Delacroix reprises.

[3] In her *Sun Symbolism and Cosmology in Michelangelo's The Last Judgment* (2000), Valerie Shrimplin provides an extensive discussion of the beardless Christ in Christian iconography. She notes that examples abounded in Northern Italy, where the most prominent was the Christ figure in St. Mark's in Venice. For her, "Michelangelo's Sun-Christ perhaps forms the culmination of a visual tradition that was formulated in the very beginning of the Early Christian period" (138). See also John Dixon, *The Christ of Michelangelo*, especially pages 68-77.

[4] Delacroix had a friend read him portions of Dante during the composition of *Barque*. (Johnson *Delacroix*, 76).

[5] Sébastien Allard notes this similarity as well: "Peut-être le geste de Virgile se couvrant la téte...est-il inspiré de la position du bras du Christ infligeant le châtiment sur la fresque du Vatican" (80).

[6] "Delacroix was engaged during his whole life in a continuing dialogue with the artists of the past" (Jobert, 44).

[7] In an essay devoted to Michelangelo that Delacroix published in *la Revue de Paris* in 1830, and reissued in *Ecrits* as "Michel-Ange," he proposes an image of the painter/sculptor that contains elements which would later figure in the 1849-50 painting:

> Je me figure le grand Michel-Ange durant ces instants où, l'imagination obsédée par les créations de Dante ou par la lecture des livres saints, sa main dessinait, à la clarté de sa lampe, quelques-unes de ces figures gigantesques dont l'impression ne s'efface jamais quand on les a une fois senties. Durant ses grands travaux, il dormait peu, toujours vêtu pour être prêt à chaque instant à obéir à l'inspiration. Je me le figure à une heure avancée de la nuit, pris de peur lui-même au spectacle de ses créations, jouissant le premier de la terreur secrète qu'il voulait éveiller dans les âmes (96).

[8] I will be citing from the Deyrolle and Denissel edition. In this text the two essays from the *Revue de Paris* are published together under the single title of "Michel-Ange," while the essay from the *Revue de deux mondes* is entitled "Sur *Le Jugement dernier*."

[9] In a passage from "Sur *Le Jugement dernier*," Delacroix reinforces this opinion about the Christ figure: "Le Christ de Michel-Ange n'est ni un philosophe, ni un héros de roman; c'est Dieu lui-même, dont le bras va réduire en poudre l'univers" (281).

[10] Earlier in this essay Delacroix draws a strongly Romantic portrait of Michelangelo that

might also be an association with himself in his less confident moments. The imagined speaker here is the Italian artist: "Je suis un homme fini, je n'ai plus d'idées, tous mes rivaux valent mieux que moi: la preuve, c'est que le public les favorise. On me dédaigne, peut-être je le mérite. Qu'importe la gloire! Qu'importe l'avenir" (96).

[11] This is doubtless a slip of the pen on Delacroix's part. According to André Joubin, who established the notes for the *Journal*: "C'est certainement une erreur de lecture. Il s'agit du Christ en *Juge* qui domine toute la scène du *Jugement dernier*"(480).

[12] In an article entitled "Delacroix as Essayist: Writings on Art," Michele Hannoosh discusses, with particular reference to Poussin, how Delacroix's attitudes toward artists could undergo radical changes over the course of time. Unlike the Poussin model, and with specific regard to this citation where Michelangelo expresses disinterest if not dislike for *The Last Judgment*, the change here seems to me a sudden and abrupt reversal, an opinion for which nothing had prepared the reader, and one that is never reiterated.

[13] There is a break in the *Journal* between 1824 and 1847. In his edition, Joubin publishes what writings of Delacroix survive from this hiatal period in a supplement.

[14] See Rubin, "Delacroix's *Dante and Virgil* as a Romantic Manifesto," especially pages 51-2.

[15] When Delacroix was around sixty years old, he undertook to bring together diverse thoughts and construct a dictionary of the fine arts. Drafts of this project were incorporated into his journal.

[16] In "Sur *Le Jugement dernier*" Delacroix makes a similar, somewhat grandiose claim for Michelangelo's enduring importance: "L'art ne sortira pas du cercle que Michel-Ange a tracé autour de lui" (286).

[17] In his *Die Dantebarke* James Rubin argues that the choice of theme and the form of artistic expression on Delacroix's part constitute "der erste in einer lebenslangen Reihe von Versuchen, Gegensätze in Kunst des 19 Jahrhunderts zu überwinden und eine Malerei zu schaffen, die eines Tages Klassizismus und Moderne vereinen würde" (5). While obviously Rubin's "Gegensätze" refer to a variety of artistic conflicts in which Delacroix was involved, I would suggest that the French painter was also involved on a psychological level to overcome (überwinden) the powerful influence of Michelangelo, and with regard to Rubin's quite plausible claim that Delacroix was seeking to eventually unite in his art the Classical and the Modern, it is worth noting that in "Sur *Le Jugement dernier*," he referred to Michelangelo as "le père de l'art moderne" (285).

[18] Stephanie Mora points out that Delacroix's technical prowess and innovation have somewhat obscured his adherence to tradition: "the artist's loose brushwork, his free use of color, his expressive rendering of subject matter, and the freedom of movement he gave to his figures...caused him to be regarded as an opponent of tradition" (59).

[19] Bloom italicizes these terms throughout his book, and I am following his practice.

[20] Throughout his *Die Dantebarke* James Rubin stresses Delacroix's great admiration of Dante, and that "[am] meisten identifizierte sich Delacroix mit Dante" (34).

[21] In *The Anxiety of Influence* Bloom cites a letter he received from the Italian scholar, John Freccero, where Canto XXVII is discussed. Freccero is commenting on the moment that follows Virgil's departure and Beatrice's appearance: "So the dark eros of Dido is transformed by the retrospective redemption of Beatrice's return...poetry becomes stronger than Death and for the first time in the poem, the Pilgrim is named as Beatrice calls him: '*Dante*' (123, emphasis in text). The suggestion that in *The Divine Comedy* Dante can only achieve his full stature as a poet, signaled by the first mention of his name, when Virgil departs is comparable to my argument that Delacroix could only achieve greatness by challenging and surpassing Michelangelo.

[22] In an entry for January 25, 1857, he reiterates this judgment, practically verbatim.

Works Cited

Allard, Sébastien. *Dante et Virgile aux Enfers d'Eugène Delacroix*. Paris: Editions de la Réunion des musées nationaux, 2004.

Bloom, Harold. *The Anxiety of Influence: A Theory of Poetry*. Oxford: Oxford University Press, 1973.

Brown, Roy. "The Formation of Delacroix's Hero Between 1822 and 1831." *Art Bulletin* 66, no.2 (June 1984): 237-54.

Delacroix, Eugène. *Dictionnaire des Beaux Arts d'Eugène Delacroix*. Reconstituted and edited by Anne Larue. Paris: Hermann, 1996.

———. *Ecrits sur l'art*. ed. François-Marie Deyrolle and Christine Denissel. Paris: Séguier, 1988.

———. *Journal 1822-1863*. Introduction and notes by André Joubin. Paris: Plon, 1980.

Dixon, John. *The Christ of Michelangelo*. Atlanta: Scholars Press, 1994.

Hannoosh, Michele. *Painting and the Journal of Eugène Delacroix*. Princeton: Princeton University Press, 1995.

———. "Delacroix as Essayist: Writings on Art." In *The Cambridge Companion to Delacroix*. ed. Beth S. Wright. New York: Cambridge University Press, 2001.

Honour, Hugh. *Romanticism*. New York: Harper & Row, 1979.

Jobert, Barthélémy. *Delacroix*. Princeton: Princeton University Press, 1998.

Johnson, Lee. *Delacroix*. New York: Norton, 1963.

———. *The Paintings of Eugène Delacroix: a Critical Catalogue 1816-1831*. Oxford: Clarendon Press, 1981.

Mora, Stephanie. "Delacroix's Art Theory and His Definition of Classicism." *Journal of Aesthetic Education*. 34, no. 1 (Spring 2000): 57-75.

Rubin, James. "Delacroix's *Dante and Virgil* as a Romantic Manifesto." *Art Journal* 52 (Summer 1993): 48-58.

———. *Eugène Delacroix' Die Dantebarke: Idealismus und Modernität*. Frankfurt am Main: Fischer, 1987.

Shrimplin, Valerie. *Sun Symbolism and Cosmology in Michelangelo's The Last Judgment*. Kirksville: Truman State University Press, 2000.

Steinberg, Leo. "Michelangelo's *Last Judgment* as Merciful Heresy." *Art in America* 63 (1968): 49-63.

Stendhal. *Stendhal and the Arts*. Selected and edited by David Wakefield. London: Phaidon, 1975.

Roland Joffé's *Vatel*:
Refashioning the History of the Ancien Régime

Stephen Shapiro

The premiere of Roland Joffé's film *Vatel* at the 2000 Cannes Film Festival struck hope in the hearts of dix-septièmistes who delighted in the release of yet another prominent film that promised to expose what is often perceived as the rarified, elitist culture of the classical period to a wider, popular international audience.[1] The story of the *maître d'hôtel* who commits suicide rather than suffer personal and professional humiliation when a shipment of fish fails to arrive for a banquet in honor of Louis XIV is a *fait divers* with the gothic appeal of the *histoire tragique* that seems ideally suited to a cinematographic adaptation. Yet while the film serves up elaborate costumes, extravagant feasts, and a tragic love story, *Vatel* also presents a number of puzzling historical distortions. After all, Madame de Sévigné, the principal source for the details of Vatel's suicide, makes no mention of the film's central plot dynamic: a love affair between the *maître d'hôtel* and Anne de Montausier, a fictive lady-in-waiting to the queen. The film also claims that Vatel committed suicide to maintain his freedom after the Prince de Condé wagered and lost his devoted steward in a card game with Louis XIV. Other details have been doctored: Vatel makes up for the lack of meat at one meal by creating an ersatz meat pie passed off as unicorn, and the expensive fireworks display that Sévigné claims was ruined by clouds instead claims the life of a stable boy in an accident.

Yet before cataloging all the *entorses* and bemoaning a lack of historical sophistication we would do well to question the fidelity or correspondence model of criticism that measures films against an authentic historical referent (such as a text or a document) in order to judge whether they maintain historical integrity. Even the contemporary seventeenth-century accounts of the festivities at Chantilly are shifting and unstable. In spite of its hallowed status as historical evidence, Madame de Sévigné's report is itself a literary creation that gathers disparate facts into story forms. In fact, the differences between her preliminary account of April 24, 1671 and her retelling of the story in a second letter of April 26, 1671 offer a rare glimpse of historical re-interpretation as temporal distance and additional information allow for a story to be re-emplotted in a different way. The first letter breaks the news abruptly and eulogizes Vatel with a string of epithets: "Vatel, le grand Vatel, maitre d'hôtel de M. Fouquet, qui l'était présentement de Monsieur le Prince, cet homme d'une capacité distinguée de toutes les autres, dont la bonne tête était capable de soutenir tout le soin d'un Etat" (234). The second letter, which Sévigné explains "n'est pas une lettre, c'est une relation..." contextualizes the events, portraying Vatel as a perfectionist who takes every detail to heart (235). We see fatigue and mental disorder overcome Vatel ("La tête me tourne, il y a douze nuits que je n'ai pas dormi"), Condé's attempts to reassure his steward ("rien n'était si beau que le souper du Roi [...] ne vous fâchez point: tout va bien"), and a detailed account of the suicide itself (235). Sévigné records the king's reactions to the suicide ("Le Roi [...] comprenait l'excès de cet embarrass") and comments on the festivities' success ("Tout était parfumé de jonquilles, tout était enchanté") (236). In spite of their abundant details and refashioning, Sévigné's accounts are deliciously ambiguous: when she concludes her second letter, she throws her hands up in exasperation, declaring "je jette mon bonnet par dessus les moulins," leaving generations of readers grasping for meaning (236). Does she indict the fête's excess and agree with Louis XIV's reactions? Does she paint a still life *vanitas vanitatum* where she highlights the specter of death that lies behind the sumptuous celebration?[2] Does she offer a stinging critique of royal hegemony by alluding to Fouquet (for whom Vatel worked at Vaux-le-Vicomte) and the Fronde (the festivities at Chantilly were perhaps intended to reconcile the ex-Frondeur Condé with a triumphant Louis XIV)?

The ambiguity of Madame de Sévigné's narration of Vatel's dramatic suicide has allowed for a torrent of cookbooks, plays, novels, and even an opera that adapt Vatel's story. These abundant and diverse adaptations point to historical subject matter's infinite recycling as subsequent generations refashion the past according to their own cultural circumstances and mentalities. This study takes as its point of departure Raymond Aron's declaration that, "nous retenons du passé ce qui nous intéresse. La séléction historique est dirigée par les questions que le présent pose au passé" and proposes not only to survey the variety of different ideological uses of Vatel's story but also to focus on what Joffé's *Vatel* reveals about the contemporary Western historical imagination's perception of seventeenth-century France (17-18).

Two main currents emerge from the various re-emplotments of Vatel's story in nineteenth-century France. First, Vatel came to represent the French culinary tradition, thereby becoming a *de facto* symbol of the superiority of French culture. Secondly, his story became a vehicle for the exploration and criticism of social structures, particularly the rigid hierarchies of the ancien régime. Vatel is by far best known as a culinary artist, although his association with gastronomy is historically suspect because the archival records of both Fouquet's and Condé's households clearly show that he was never a cook but rather a *maître d'hôtel* with duties ranging from bookkeeping to supervision of the grounds. Antonin Carême writes in *L'art de la cuisine française au XIXe siècle* (1833) that "le cuisinier français est mû dans son travail par un point d'honneur inséparable de l'art culinaire: témoin la mort du grand Vatel" (367). Vatel's reputation has sold cookbooks such as the nineteenth-century *L'art d'accomoder le poisson suivant les principes de Vatel et des grands officiers de Bouche* (nd), and his name has truly become synonymous with French culinary talent ever since Proust used it as a substantive for a gourmet or grand chef. In the twentieth century, circles of gastronomes celebrate French culinary excellence under the auspices of the Vatel Club.[3] The myth lives on today: the *Larousse Gastronomique* continues to include an article on the ill-fated *maître d'hôtel,* and his spirit still looms large at the chateau at Chantilly where groups can reserve a special banquet hosted by a bilingual *sommelier* in period costume. When Bernard Loiseau committed suicide in the spring of 2003 amidst (false) rumors of the impending loss of one of his three stars in the *Guide Michelin*, the *exemplum* of Vatel's perfectionism and desperation was evoked as an historical parallel.[4]

As a symbol of French culinary excellence, Vatel has become, by extension, a representative figure of French cultural and political hegemony. In the seventeenth century, foreigners began to praise French culinary achievement as a by-product of the absolute monarchy's prosperity, placing it on par with the Sun King's other accomplishments in the realm of culture, such as literature, music, or architecture.[5] Nineteenth-century France took this notion one step further, making French culinary excellence an illustration of the superiority of French civilization. As Pascal Ory explains, in the multitude of French aphorisms that equate a people with their cuisine (e.g. Brillat-Savarin's "dis-moi ce que tu manges, je te dirai ce que tu es") "il s'agit de conclure métonymiquement, *via* la suprématie, jugée évidente, de la cuisine française, à la superiorité de la 'civilisation' française" (3743). This metonymical operation depends on the creation of a history of culinary excellence to root French achievement in a trans-historical, indigenous tradition lest it appear as a merely temporary moment of glory linked to a particular and fleeting set of historical circumstances. As an historical *exemplum,* Vatel has been pressed into the service of the genealogy of French gastronomy which trades on the authority of the past to enhance the status of the present and perpetuate the sense of a seamless heritage of superiority.

Nineteenth-century authors were also drawn to the possibilities offered by Vatel's story for treating questions of class. Eugene Scribe's comedy *Vatel, ou le petit fils d'un grand homme* (1825), focuses on Vatel's son, a haughty, aristocratic pretender who seeks to advance his family's position by arranging an appropriate marriage for his own son (the *petit fils* of the great Vatel) who unfortunately loves Manette, "une cuisinière bourgeoise, domestique du caissier de Son Excellence" (218). Vatel *fils* is a pretentious snob who treats Manette with a condescending attitude of *noblesse oblige*: "A quoi servirait l'instruction," he berates his son's lowly lover, "si nous ne la répandions pas dans les basses classes de la société" (319). The short play concludes with Manette saving the day for the overworked Vatel by preparing a comically simple and ridiculous dish of macaroni and chestnut puree for the king's table. Her efforts earn her an heroic elevation evocative of

Rodrigue's ascent in Corneille's *Le Cid*: "laisse agir ton père," the young Vatel's mother tells her son at the play's conclusion, "le talent ennoblit tout à ses yeux, et où il y a du mérite il n'y a plus de préjugés" (346).

The anonymous *Vatel, tragédie (si l'on veut) ou drame burlesque en trois actes et en vers par un gastronome en défaut* (1845) also focuses on the class structures of kitchen workers. The author's *avertissement* underlines a painstaking effort at portraying class differences through language. Vatel, he writes, "que je fais sortir d'une classe obscure, doit avoir les manières d'un nouveau parvenu," while Brochard (who turns the *broche* or spit in Vatel's kitchen), "dont l'origine est à peu près celle de Vatel [...] s'exprime en termes vulgaires, et par son ensemble annonce un homme du commun" ("Avertissement"). In the play, Vatel is exceedingly ambitious: he describes his efforts for Louis XIV in terms reminiscent of Corneille's heroic register: "Le souper de Louis doit completer ma gloire; Il me faut figurer à jamais dans l'histoire" (46). Likewise, he is protective of his social status and forbids a marriage between his daughter Augustine and Brochard. When the *marée* fails to arrive, Vatel's dashed social ambitions dictate the suicide that follows: "dans l'espoir d'enchainer à jamais ma fortune, dans l'espoir d'ennoblir et l'office et mon nom, Et de fonder enfin une illustre maison [...] La marée ou la mort! Il y va de ma gloire! Il faut savoir mourir pour vivre dans l'histoire" (51).

The humor in both of these short comedies emerges from the dissonance between Vatel's position and his elevated conception of himself, making him a manic figure not far from Molière's *Bourgeois Gentilhomme*. In both plays, members of the lower classes upstage Vatel, bridge the gap between *maître de cuisine* and *cuisinier,* and restore the pretentious cook's distorted vision of class distinctions to clarity. These plays transpose noble aristocratic discourse into the decidedly un-noble, working class setting of the kitchen, thereby offering a safe space for the criticism of aristocratic values where the bourgeois and working class can mock the aristocratic pretensions of Vatel and identify with the simple, common-sense, egalitarian heroes. These comedies enact the very social confrontations between a nobility of blood and a nobility of talent that rocked French society as the succession of Empire, Restoration, July Monarchy, and Second Empire imposed a series of new, competing social values. Both plays also reflect the role culinary arts played in a collective examination of class and social order: the Empire's creation of a new aristocratic order turned to gastronomy to give it the legitimacy of the order it replaced. Jean-Paul Aron, in *Le mangeur du XIXe siècle*, explains that, "L'Empire qui réinvente les institutions seigneuriales [...] entreprend de relever l'usage des tables princières." Under the restoration, gastronomy becomes linked with aristocratic achievement and symbolizes a new social order: "la restauration la [la table] récupère dans le système des mentalités patrimoniales: ainsi, paradoxalement, elle l'insère dans l'équipement culturel de la nation, elle l'emploie à sceller l'union de l'ancienne éthique et de l'idéal égalitaire" (55). These early-nineteenth-century comedies capitalize on the thematic resonance between Vatel's story and the new institution of the restaurant which democratized gastronomy in order to examine the mixing of social classes and new patterns of social mobility.

The interest in class distinctions that often dominates the adaptations of Vatel's story goes beyond the bounds of nineteenth-century social criticism and often focuses on indicting the very foundation of the aristocracy of the ancien régime. An invented love story between the celebrated steward and an aristocratic courtier surreptitiously enters the historical record through Bouillet's 1845 biographical dictionary which vaguely attributes it to an indefinite and unnamed "*on*" : "On a expliqué autrement cette mort," he writes, "en disant qu'épris d'une des dames de la cour, il [Vatel] lui fit l'aveu de sa passion le jour de cette fête, et que se voyant repoussé il s'était tué de douleur" (1835). Louis Lurine develops this hypothesis in a romance *nouvelle à l'eau de rose* entitled "La véritable mort de Vatel" (1854) in which assumed identities, the crossing of class lines, and melodrama come together as Vatel falls under the spell of "Denise" who is later revealed to be the Duchesse de Ventadour. Vatel's suffering and suicide are the result of his impossible love for a duchess who has cruelly and capriciously deceived him: "j'ai provoqué..." he laments, "la curieuse coquetterie d'une femme de qualité; elle s'est amusee à me séduire, à m'enchanter, à me perdre...et moi, crédule, je vous ai aimée, madame la duchesse!" (169). Moura and Louvet's biography of Vatel also evokes lovesickness as the true reason for Vatel's suicide: "Ils [certains auteurs] veulent, en effet, qu'une dame de qualité se soit déguisée en fille de chambre pour s'attacher à plaire au grave Maître d'hôtel, et se faire ensuite un jeu de sa déconvenue" (214). In their story, Vatel the domestic is humiliated for the pleasure of his aristocratic masters: "Et ce devait être un jeu singulièrement plaisant que de regarder, dissimulé derrière une tenture, les agaceries de la Marquise accoutrée en chambrière et d'entendre ensuite ses rieuses confidences" (215). The addition of the love plot casts Vatel in a subordinate position, oppressed by his masters and an elaborate hierarchy, and makes him the victim rather than the deluded enforcer of social hierarchy.

Vatel concentrates on developing the exploitation, corruption, and decadence of the ancien régime in sexual, social, and economic terms by adapting this myth of a love affair between the *maître d'hôtel* and an aristocratic courtier. The film's main focus on the romance with a fictive Anne de Montausier, one of Queen Maria Theresa's ladies-in-waiting, denounces the courtly ethic of sexuality that privileges dynastic concerns and commodifies women in order to portray ancien régime court society as a realm of immoral decadence. At the film's beginning, the parameters of an aristocratic code of sexuality are laid out: Vatel learns that because "the king accomplished his duty with the queen just the other day," Louis XIV will not need rooms close to his wife, but instead requires access to his mistress (Madame de Montespan). Once the requirements of dynasty (the transmission of power, wealth, and heritage) are accomplished, sexual play is dangerously unfettered and inextricably linked to abusive power relations as the king orchestrates a network where sex, favor, and social advancement are traded amongst the Queen, the Duchesse de La

Vallière, Madame de Montespan, and Anne de Montausier, Vatel's love interest.

Joffé inveighs against this sexual economy by showing its ravages. When Montespan's fortunes rise, the duchess drives the former royal mistress La Vallière to tears as the two women cross paths on a staircase, remarking cruelly, "I am going up and you are going down, madam." Madame de Montespan receives her comeuppance when she loses her place at the king's side to Montausier and retreats in tears. Montausier, too, has a precarious grip on Louis XIV's attentions and is aware that she might be a pawn in the King's quest to keep Montespan in line. Louis XIV's brother, Philippe d'Orléans, driven to decadence by the indolent, meaningless life he leads at court, channels his energies into his homosexual circle and preys on a young boy from Vatel's kitchen. Philippe's predatory nature is a family trait he shares with the king: "We Bourbons," he declares, "are unpredictable when deprived of our pleasure." The Duc de Lauzun shamelessly trades on his favor with the king to extort sexual services from the women of court. For him, women are interchangeable sexual commodities. When Montausier rebuffs his advances by refusing to accept a delicate flower arrangement, he immediately offers it to the first woman from the court to cross his line of sight, along with the same passionate *billet doux* supposedly inspired by Montausier's singular charms.

Joffé contrasts this exploitive sexual manipulation with the relationship between Vatel and Montausier. Unlike the other members of the royal party who look down on Vatel as a servant, Montausier, he recounts, "treats me like a human. She's the only one who has a heart." Their relationship develops along a trajectory that echoes *La Carte du Tendre*: Vatel is the perfect lover whose attentions advance from *petits soins* (he helps Montausier clean up a broken bird cage) to *grands services* (he sacrifices his own parrot to save her canaries from being butchered to ease Condé's gout) and culminate in a mutual esteem. The couple's ultimate destruction illustrates how the moral decadence of the court society wins out over the bourgeois notion of the intertwining of sex, love, and marriage.

Sexual mores and social hierarchy are, however, only elements of Joffé's grander scheme to establish the monstrosity of the court of Louis XIV. To this end, Joffé highlights the court's squalor and filth and its erasure of humanizing responses to suffering. Images of the courtly world of luxury and refinement are juxtaposed with images of dirty kitchen workers slaving over hot fires while rats lurk just behind the gilded splendor of salons where the court gathers for entertainment. Bourgeois codes of modesty have not secreted bodily functions away: we see (and hear) Louis XIV "passing hot stones" on his *chaise percée* in view of a roomful of servants, courtiers, and his political advisors (Colbert and Condé). A servant ceremoniously wipes the King's behind, provoking a *frisson* of decadent disgust that disorients the modern viewer, who could not imagine not taking care of this need personally. Chambermaids and the queen herself urinate in chamber pots in plain view and servants have sex in the open with no regard for privacy or bystanders' sensibilities. By refusing to acknowledge that "les courtisans du XVIIe et XVIIIe siècles se lavaient et éliminaient leurs excréments comme lui," these images create what Hélène Himmelfarb terms an air of "exotisme baroque" that erects a reassuring barrier between us and the past: "la certitude de l'immondice et de la touffeur Versaillaise [sont] nécessaires à la démonstration de la monstruosité radicale de la monarchie absolue, et à l'affirmation du progrès bourgeois" ("Versailles," 243). Joffé's highlighting of dirt, grime, and bodily fluids points to a primitive world where a lack of bourgeois cleanliness and modesty signifies a base society.[6]

The monstrosity of absolute monarchy also emerges from the film's depiction of how it eradicates the labor (and misery) that produces royal splendor. Throughout the film, Louis proudly describes the elaborate plans for Versailles, but the royal visit is almost ruined when a worker from the kitchens accosts the king and blames him for her son's death on the *chantiers* at Versailles. The woman's anger is discounted as the rantings of a madwoman, preserving the fiction of royal infallibility. When Condé apologizes later for the incident and informs the king that the woman was flogged, the king pretends to have long erased the unpleasant reminder of Versailles's true cost from his memory: "What madwoman, Prince?" he asks, "We saw no madwoman, Prince." As Montausier and Vatel stroll through an alleyway adorned with flowers, Vatel recounts the travails of the poor villagers who picked the flowers for "a few sous." When Montausier counters that it is an honor for the poor to be creditors of the king, Vatel tersely replies that his parents died from this honor, shattering the aristocratic logic that effaces the true condition of the poor. The elaborate feast and fireworks presented on the second night of the festivities draw accolades from the court and particularly impress Louis XIV, but behind the stage a stable boy dies when the cords that raised a singer into the air strangle him to death in an accident. Vatel relates the boy's story to Montausier, lest the dead worker's name fade into anonymity. By exposing a system of silence that effectively erases the very human costs of pleasure and consumption, *Vatel* indicts the absolute monarchy as an immoral world.

By pitting the upstairs (the king, court, and nobility) against the downstairs (the workers), the exploiters against the exploited, and sexual predators against prey, *Vatel*'s villanization of court society overshadows the theme of culinary excellence that is the story's prevalent myth. Vatel's skills and artistry are subsumed into the context of the opposition between freedom and slavery that Joffé emphasizes in his portrayal of the court of Louis XIV. At the beginning of the film, Vatel believes that his artistic talents afford him the power to defy nature, surmount the vicissitudes of the kitchen, and even shape the political and historical landscape of France. While he describes the elaborate banquet of fish that will be served from ice sculptures representing Neptune's tribute to Helios, god of the sun, the Prince de Condé asks whether the ice will melt under the heat of the torches. Vatel responds confidently, "I forbid it to melt, my Prince." At every turn, Vatel projects control over the festivities, remaining coldly unflappable in the face of the many crises that erupt: when eggs for a custard dessert refuse to set, he calmly beats eggs and sugar together into the whipped cream (*crème Chantilly*) that he is still credited (falsely) with inventing. To serve unexpected extra guests for whom there is no roast he creates a mushroom pie that looks and tastes like meat. Nothing falls outside his realm of expertise: "I have it in my power," he explains to Montausier, "to create, to astonish." He believes that no less than the future of France lies in his hands: "The visit of His Majesty is the supreme test. If I please him, his benevolence will restore my master to his position and the destiny of France." Yet, when he learns that he was a prize won by Louis XIV in a card game and will serve a new master at Versailles, the illusion of his liberty is shattered. His final note to Montausier reveals that his suicide is a desperate effort to preserve his mastery. "Madame," he writes, "I thought I was the master of these festivities, but indeed I was their slave. In the last three days I have come to understand that I treasure freedom above all. Between Condé and Versailles, the path is narrow and I have taken it." As the film closes, a voice-over informs us that even in death Vatel's grand gesture has been eclipsed by the absolutist machine of Louis XIV: "Of course no one dared tell the king the truth, but soon the word went around that Vatel killed himself because of the fish—which flattered His Majesty and pleased his courtiers." The ultimate monstrosity of ancien régime France, the film implies, is its enslavement of the creative culinary genius who must die to escape its clutches.

Even the representation of the food and banquets is juxtaposed with this condemnation of the seventeenth-century political order. Joffé emphasizes the feasting at Chantilly as a political performance: "There is always a reason behind a royal visit," explains Gourville, Condé's secretary, as he informs us that the Duc de Condé has invited Louis XIV in an effort to obtain a military commission that will solve his dire financial problems. The war Condé yearns to command is presented as a vanity campaign against the threat of the Protestant Dutch republic that prints seditious pamphlets: "No king," declares Louis XIV, "is free from free thinkers. Especially if they're as rich as the Dutch." As a medium of symbolic exchange, food is pressed into service to further personal economic interests, to flatter and maintain the absolute monarch, and to suppress political dissidence, thereby painting the ancien régime as a profligate society where conspicuous consumption and dubious morals go hand in hand.

Why then does *Vatel* shy away from celebrating the glory of French gastronomy in favor of an indictment of the ancien régime? In an era when French culture has come under attack by the United States, European integration, and global economic forces, Vatel's story would seem to offer the opportunity to fight back on the cultural front with one of France's great weapons: its internationally recognized culture of gastronomy. Joffé's film, however, is not destined for a French audience. The $36 million film was produced in English and conceived as an international product for both American and European audiences. Just as patronage dictated artistic standards, messages, and tastes in the early-modern period, so too does it continue to influence the representation of history in our own time where the royal patron has been replaced by an international mass-market audience that votes with its wallet. To assure an appealing cosmopolitan melange, *Vatel* is a multi-national cultural production: the English director Roland Joffé[7] collaborated with Australian (Tom Stoppard) and French (Jeanne Labrune) screenwriters and Italian composer Ennio Morricone under the auspices of media conglomerates from Europe and America ("une co-production Franco-brittanique: Légende Entreprises-Gaumont; Nomad; Timothy Burrill productions; TF1 Films Productions; avec la participation de Canal +") who financed the film. The principal cast assembles French actor Gérard Depardieu (Vatel), American Uma Thurman (Anne de Montausier), and the British stars Tim Roth (Lauzun) and Julian Sands (Louis XIV). The combination of internationally recognized Hollywood commodities with multi-national funding and talent points to an effort to eliminate a particular national point of view in order to appeal to a diverse international audience.[8] The separation of Vatel's story from the realm of French gastronomy and culinary preeminence (with their subtext of French cultural superiority) shows how modern mass culture tends to efface cultural differences, seek the lowest common denominator, distance itself from national specificity, and develop simple archetypal plots. In this sense, Joffé's *Vatel* constitutes what I would call a post-nationalist history film in which questions of national or cultural difference yield to simple archetypes.

In its quest for an international mass audience, *Vatel* appeals to the common denominator of contemporary Western ideology: the triumph of liberal democratic capitalism. Almost all Western societies can easily identify with and understand the defeat of totalitarian regimes that exploited their people, negligently gambled human life, capriciously marched off to war, and dangerously abused power for personal ends. In the wake of democratic capitalism's defeat of fascism and communism, as well as the abolition of slavery, and the establishment of rights and representative government, the late twentieth century has, in the eyes of many, reached what Francis Fukuyama terms "the end of history" or "the end point of mankind's ideological evolution and the universalization of Western liberal democracy as the final form of government" (4). By villainizing the ancien régime, *Vatel* highlights the differences between contemporary bourgeois liberal democracy and the unjust regimes of the past, thereby inviting us to revel in our own progress.

At the same time, however, *Vatel* casts doubt on triumphant liberal democracy. In an age when war still can be understood as motivated by individual whims and where consumption and wealth still come at substantial human, social, and environmental cost, Joffé's film points to the emptiness and immorality of democratic capitalism. The film suggests an analogy between Louis XIV's court and present day scandals of government and corporate abuse where corruption, the commodification of labor, and even sexual intrigue still exist. While Tyco Corporation fired employees in a downsizing campaign, Chief Executive Dennis Kozlowski embezzled some $600 million to finance a $2 million birthday party featuring an ice sculpture of Michelangelo's *David* that sprayed champagne from its penis. Kozlowski's excesses are but one of a legion of parallels to Vatel's elaborate banquet for Louis XIV at Chantilly.[9] The vagaries of ancien régime "decadent" sexuality resonate with our own obsessions with presidential sexual behavior. *Vatel* also incites us to continue to pose the question "What is to be done?" and suggests that progress (social, political, and economic) is at best slow paced and, at worst, a self-deluding myth.

Vatel's polyphony points in several directions: its ambiguity problematizes its assertions, points to history's malleability, and shows how historical material can serve a variety of ideological viewpoints. Though the film revels in the free play of signifiers and avoids commitment to a single ideological stance in an effort to be something for everyone, it does consistently represent seventeenth-century France as an unjust, exploitive political regime. In the wake of the tremendous influence of Saint-Simon's chronicle of the underside of Versailles's splendor and Michelet's portrait of the "Décadence morale du XVIIe siècle," it would appear that, for a late-twentieth-century Western audience, the court of Louis XIV represents not a pinnacle of civilization, but rather an apex of sexual, social, and political corruption against which to measure contemporary progress or decline. So popular is the notion of ancien régime sexual license, for example, that Roland Mousnier laments that "les noms de Henri IV et de Louis XIV n'évoquent absolument plus rien, sinon peut-être les maîtresses, car, à la radio, à la télévision, dans certains revues et livres, il y a encore des histoires de fesses, considérées comme l'histoire" (61). Himmelfarb remarks that American tourists to Versailles routinely equate the absolute monarchy with brutal abuse of power with their incessant question, "Where did they kill people?" (258). Yet Saint-Simon and Michelet hardly lend themselves to such Manichean conclusions: their work is valuable precisely because it is richly nuanced in its examination of the complexity and contradiction of the *grand siècle*.

When faced with the alterity of the past, however, the international film industry prefers a simplistic and anachronistic denunciation of monarchy's consumption, power, and hierarchy that is easily understood by a modern audience. This treatment parallels *Vatel*'s own representation of a Turkish-themed banquet created by the *maître d'hôtel* for Louis XIV at Chantilly.[10] *Vatel*'s *Turquerie* tames the otherness of the Turk by translating it into figures that are both familiar and disarmed: the spectacle presents children in black face and billowing Turkish garb, an exotic landscape (palm trees, flowers, and eastern birds), and oriental music, thereby divorcing the Turk from a context of cultural and political meaning and thus reducing him to a few non-threatening cultural stereotypes.

While some might argue that film as a genre is necessarily reductive, it is no more reductive than written history which also must pick and choose from the material at its disposition and organize it into a story form. Indeed certain films, such as the recent French *films d'auteur Louis, enfant roi* and *Le Roi danse*, free themselves from the economic constraints of the international marketplace and remind us of the complexity involved in representing the past. Both of these cinematic adaptations of seventeenth-century French history admirably skirt commonplaces about the *grand siècle* and Louis XIV's rise to power and offer a nuanced view of the Sun King's early years. Yet, by adopting the simplest of plot structures that touch universal or highly general archetypal themes rather than national particularities and the complexities of the past, *Vatel* fails as history, and ultimately has very little to teach us about early-modern France. While *Vatel* does show how the *grand siècle's* significance is being continually re-evaluated and refashioned over time, it also points to the necessity for literary critics and historians to open up and foster the dialogue between the present and the past to bring out the ambivalence and elusiveness of seventeenth-century France's absolutist regime.

NOTES

[1] *Vatel* followed *Tous les matins du monde* (1991), *Louis, enfant roi* (1993), *The Man in the Iron Mask* (1998, the first film of international mega-star Leonardo Dicaprio after the blockbuster *Titanic*), *La Lettre* (1999, a modern adaptation of *La Princesse de Clèves*), *Le Roi danse* (2000), and *Saint-Cyr* (2000).
[2] See Cagnat on the commonplace of "la mort dans la fête" 444-47.
[3] See Trubeck, on these professional associations and their contribution to the particularly French notion of *haute cuisine*.
[4] See Richburg for more on Loiseau and the *Guide Michelin* as well as the suicide of Chef Alain Zick in 1966 following the loss of a Michelin star.
[5] See Mennell for examples of British commentary on French gastronomy during the reign of Louis XIV.
[6] See Elias on how removing the body's distasteful functions from sight has been interpreted as a sign of civilization and societal progress.
[7] Joffé's previous directorial credits include *Goodbye Lover* (1999); *The Scarlet Letter* (1995); *City of Joy* (1992); *Fat Man and Little Boy* (1989); *The Mission* (1986); and *The Killing Fields* (1984).
[8] For an examination of the cosmopolitan functioning of the international film industry, see Morin.
[9] The parallel is particularly fortuitous since Joffé's *Vatel* features an elaborate set of ice sculptures representing mythological characters and themes.
[10] The exotic *Turquerie* is modeled on seventeenth-century France's fascination with Turkey in the wake of the Ottomans' defeat of the Venetians and a band of French volunteers in Cyprus. Tensions were only heightened when a Turkish envoy snubbed Louis XIV during his mission in France, raising doubts about Louis's claims to glory. Molière's *Bourgeois Gentilhomme*, Racine's *Bajazet*, and La Fontaine's "Songe d'un habitant du Mogol" responded to the irritation of the visit by the Turkish ambassador.

WORKS CITED

Anonymous. *Vatel, tragédie (si l'on veut) ou drame burlesque en trois actes et en vers par un gastronome en défaut*. Poitiers, 1845.

Aron, Jean-Paul. *Le Mangeur du XIXe siècle*. Paris: Payot, 1989.

Aron, Raymond. *Dimensions de la conscience historique*. Paris: Plon, 1961.

Barnwell, H. T. "The Vatel Letters and the Narrative Art of Mme De Sévigné." *Seventeenth-Century French Studies* 8 (1986): 185-96.

Bouillet, Marie-Nicolas. "Vatel." *Dictionnaire universel d'histoire et de géographie.* Paris, 1845.

Cagnat, Constance. *La mort classique: Ecrire la mort dans la littérature française en prose de la seconde moitié du XVIIe siècle.* Paris: Champion, 1995.

Carême, Antonin. *L'art de la cuisine française au XIXe siècle.* Paris, 1833.

Château de Chantilly. *Les Fastes de Vatel.* December 1, 2003. <http://www.chateaudechantilly.com/html/6lieu/texte_produits.htm>.

Cussy, Marquis de. *L'art culinaire.* Paris, 1848.

Elias, Norbert. *The History of Manners.* Trans. Edmund Jephcott. New York: Pantheon, 1982.

Farrell, Michèle Longino. "Writing Letters, Telling Tales, Making History: Vatel's Death Told and Retold." *French Review* 66, no. 2 (1992): 229-42.

Fukuyama, Francis. "The End of History." *The National Interest* 16 (1989): 3-18.

Himmelfard, Hélène. "Versailles en notre temps." In *Destins et enjeux du XVIIIe siècle,* ed. Yves-Marie Bercé, et al., 139-52. Paris: PUF, 1985.

———. "Versailles." In *Les Lieux de mémoire,* ed. Pierre Nora, 235-92. Paris: Gallimard, 1997.

Lazareff, Alexandre. *L'exception culinaire française.* Paris: Albin Michel, 1998.

Lurine, Louis. "La véritable mort de Vatel." In *Ici l'on aime,* 153-74. Paris, 1854.

Mennell, Stephen. *All Manners of Food: Eating and Taste in England and France from the Middle Ages to the Present.* Oxford and New York: Blackwell, 1985.

Michel, Dominique. *Vatel et la naissance de la gastronomie.* Paris: Fayard, 1999.

Morin, Edgar. *L'esprit du temps.* Vol. 1. Paris: Grasset, 1975.

Moura, Jean and Paul Louvet. *La vie de Vatel.* 9th ed. Paris: Gallimard, 1929.

Mousnier, Roland. "Que représente le XVIIe siècle pour un homme du XXIe siècle?" In *Destins et enjeux du XVIIe siècle,* ed. Yves-Marie Bercé, et al., 61-68. Paris: PUF, 1985.

Ory, Pascal. "La Gastronomie." In *Les Lieux de mémoire,* ed. Pierre Nora, 3743-69. Paris: Gallimard, 1997.

Richburg, Keith B. "Did Ratings Slide Kill a Great Chef of Europe?" *Washington Post,* February 26, 2003.

Scribe, Eugene. *Vatel, ou le petit fils d'un grand homme.* Paris, 1825.

Sévigné, Marie de Rabutin Chantal. *Correspondance.* Ed. Roger Duchêne. Vol. 1. Paris: Gallimard, 1972.

Trubeck, Amy. *Haute Cuisine: How the French Invented the Culinary Profession.* Philadelphia: University of Pennsylvania Press, 2000.

Vatel. Dir. Roland Joffé. Perf. Gerard Depardieu, Uma Thurman, Julian Sands, and Tim Roth. Miramax, 2000.

Sans peur, sans reproche et sans perruque : la figure du Philosophe dans le cinéma français contemporain (1988-2001)

Ugo Dionne

1. Introduction. *Où l'on fait connaissance avec nos héros*

Le chevalier Grégoire de Fronsac, personnage principal du *Pacte des loups* de Christophe Gans (2001), n'est d'abord qu'une silhouette, une figure minuscule que l'on devine à peine sur l'horizon. Flanqué de son fidèle Mani — « Iroquois de la tribu des Mohawks », ramené des guerres du Canada, dont les époustouflantes performances martiales constituent l'un des plaisirs coupables du film — , il apparaît au fond d'une vallée pluvieuse, et se taille lentement un chemin jusqu'au premier plan. La séquence peut rappeler, au cinéphile nostalgique, la très progressive arrivée de Sharif Ali, dans *Lawrence d'Arabie* de David Lean ; mais l'accoutrement des deux hommes (dont les redingotes trempées n'ont rien à envier aux caches-poussière d'*Il était une fois l'Ouest*), le trot mesuré de leurs montures, le hiératisme de leurs mouvements, tout cela évoque plus sûrement encore les riches heures du western à l'italienne. Le télescopage des genres se poursuit aussitôt, alors que Mani dépêche, à l'aide d'un énorme bâton, quelques soldats sadiques qui s'attaquaient à deux pauvres hères ; plus que ceux de Clint Eastwood et d'Omar Sharif, ce sont désormais les spectres de Batman ou de Jackie Chan qui sont convoqués. Ce n'est qu'une fois passé cet étonnant préambule qu'est révélé le visage de Fronsac, jusqu'alors caché sous le col replié de son manteau ; c'est alors seulement que le marquis d'Apcher, narrateur en instance de guillotine, pose en voix *off* le détail de la situation. Nous sommes en 1767. Fronsac, « naturaliste au Jardin du Roi », est précédé d'une « réputation bien établie de libertin et de bel esprit ». Tel un nouveau (ou un premier ?) James Bond, il a été envoyé par Sa Majesté Louis XV pour enquêter sur la déjà trop célèbre bête du Gévaudan. Il y laissera son acolyte, mais dévoilera en échange un vaste complot antiphilosophique, combattra un fauve rapporté d'Afrique, aimera une séduisante espionne du Saint-Office, sera emprisonné, empoisonné, ressuscité, et ramènera du Gévaudan une jeune et noble épouse, sauvée *in extremis* des griffes de son frère difforme et incestueux, lui-même versé dans les pratiques de combat extrême.

Grégoire de Fronsac, encyclopédiste, playboy, fine gâchette et adepte du *kung fu* (il prouvera à maintes reprises qu'il n'a rien à envier à Mani, en matière de prouesses physiques et acrobatiques), est le spectaculaire point d'aboutissement d'un processus d'héroïsation du personnage de Philosophe, amorcé à la fin des années 1980. Il nous semble en effet—c'est l'intuition qu'il s'agit de tester ici—que depuis une quinzaine d'années (donc depuis le Bicentenaire de la Révolution française, et ceci contribue sans doute à expliquer cela...), le Philosophe est devenu un archétype, un *mythe* cinématographique proprement français. Alors qu'il n'était auparavant qu'une figure ambiguë, souvent en retrait, condamnée par son âge, son inaptitude ou son indécision à une certaine retenue (quand ses projets démiurgiques ou son rationalisme cruel n'en faisaient pas tout bonnement le « méchant » de la fable), le Philosophe a été propulsé au rang de héros, de « jeune premier ». Dans cette figure jusqu'alors plutôt négligée, au profit du chevalier, du mousquetaire ou de l'aventurier picaresque (façon Cartouche ou Fanfan), la France et son cinéma ont trouvé un type à la fois national et universel, une réponse gauloise au *pistolero* américain, au samouraï japonais ou à l'agent secret britannique.

Fronsac constitue le *terminus ad quem* de cette évolution : on ne peut sans doute aller plus loin dans la virilisation du Philosophe, ou dans le phagocytage plaisamment postmoderne des grands mythes héroïques du septième art. La voie lui a cependant été tracée par d'autres personnages « philosophiques », apparus dans le cinéma français des deux dernières décennies. Le point de départ de notre inventaire est ainsi fourni—un peu arbitrairement peut-être—par le comte Savinien de Kerfadec, aristocrate partisan des Lumières, interprété par Philippe Noiret dans *Chouans !* (1988) Ce film de Philippe de Broca—dont on aura plus loin l'occasion de souligner l'extrême ambivalence—est suivi de près par *les Deux Fragonard* de Philippe Le Guay (1989), sorte de suspense gothique sur lequel planent les ombres stupéfaites d'Alfred Hitchcock et de Révéroni Saint-Cyr, et qui met en scène (ou aux prises) les deux frères Fragonard : Honoré le peintre et Cyprien l'anatomiste. Notre série devient plus fournie au milieu des années 1990, alors qu'apparaissent coup sur coup sur les écrans trois films à cadre et à propos dix-huitiémistes. Le marquis Grégoire Ponceludon de Malavoy, le héros de *Ridicule* (Patrice Leconte, 1996), n'a que très rarement recours à la violence physique ; avec son arme de prédilection, le mot d'esprit, il fait cependant aussi souvent et cruellement mouche que Fronsac avec son coup de savate ou de fusil. Dans *les Caprices d'un fleuve* de Bernard Giraudeau (1996), le chevalier Jean-François de la Plaine, incarné par Giraudeau lui-même, est puni d'un mauvais duel par Louis XVI, qui le nomme gouverneur de la colonie africaine de Cap Saint-Louis. C'est dans ce milieu étrange et étranger que le personnage, d'abord un peu frivole, un peu trop « parisien », va (s')assimiler le message de tolérance des Lumières—se liant amoureusement, d'abord avec une mulâtre, puis avec une jeune esclave qu'on lui a donnée en cadeau et dont il a fait sa fille. Quant au *Beaumarchais* d'Édouard Molinaro, d'après Sacha Guitry (1996), il se mérite, par sa fine lame, sa carrière d'espion, son « insolence » et son effronterie mêmes, une place à l'intérieur de ce petit panthéon cinématographique. Avec l'arrivée du XXIe siècle, le processus d'héroïsation du Philosophe a encore tendance à s'accélérer. *Le Pacte des loups* est précédé de peu par le *Libertin* d'Éric-Emmanuel Schmitt et Gabriel Aghion (2000), qui raconte une journée de la vie de Diderot, réfugié au château du baron d'Holbach après l'interdiction de l'*Encyclopédie* ; c'est d'ailleurs dans la crypte de la chapelle d'Holbach que sont installées les presses sur lesquelles sont imprimés les volumes de l'ouvrage condamné.

En nous appuyant sur ce corpus, nous tenterons de définir et de comprendre ce nouveau mythe, ce nouveau type cinématographique du Philosophe. Nous dresserons d'abord un inventaire des traits distinctifs, des éléments qui caractérisent ou qui « signifient » le Philosophe au cinéma—procédant ainsi à ce qu'on pourrait appeler, en forçant un peu la note, une *mythologie*, voire (en prenant le terme dans son sens à la fois le plus large et le moins technique) une *sémiologie* du personnage philosophique. On verra notamment que le Philosophe se distingue par son *débraillé*, par l'indiscipline hautement calculée de sa mise ou de sa coiffure; on envisagera aussi le rapport intime qu'il entretient avec les choses, l'univers concret, rapport qui prend au cinéma le double visage du *libertinage* et de l'*expérimentation*. Dans un second temps, nous nous intéresserons au processus d'héroïsation lui-même; nous en retracerons les étapes, de la représentation encore ambiguë de *Chouans!* ou des *Deux Fragonard* à la consécration définitive du *Libertin* et du *Pacte des loups*.

Les films qui servent de fondement à ce petit essai relèvent tous, à un degré ou à un autre, d'un certain cinéma « populaire » (en autant que cette catégorie puisse être transférée de la littérature au cinéma, où les frontières qualitatives nous semblent par définition plus perméables). En effet, c'est dans la mesure où elle réussit à s'imposer dans ce cinéma de divertissement, ce cinéma « grand public » de samedi soir ou de dimanche après-midi, que la figure du Philosophe atteint une véritable dimension mythique. Ce pan volontiers dévalué de la production cinématographique n'est peut-être qu'un épiphénomène, en regard des travaux académiques, artistiques ou littéraires qui transforment et configurent notre perception du XVIIIe siècle ; il n'en offre pas moins un aperçu saisissant sur l'imaginaire historique de la France, sur ce qui l'obsède, ce qui l'habite, ce qu'elle valorise ou privilégie. Nous avons nous-même privilégié les œuvres de pure fiction, mettant délibérément de côté les reconstitutions historiques « sérieuses » ou officielles, lesquelles nous paraissent relever d'une autre démarche, didactique et commémorative : les Philosophes qui nous intéressent ici sont bien des Philosophes *fictifs*, des *personnages* de Philosophes. Nous nous sommes cependant cru autorisé à inclure quelques figures « d'après modèle »—Honoré et Cyprien Fragonard, Beaumarchais, Diderot—que leur évidente fictionnalisation, et leur réinvestissement manifeste par le mythe philosophique qu'il s'agit justement d'analyser, font résolument passer du côté du fantasme, de la fantaisie la plus débridée[1].

2. Mythologie du Philosophe. *Où l'on apprend comment nos héros s'habillent, se portent et se comportent*

L'*incarnation* cinématographique du Philosophe se résume exactement à cela ; il s'agit moins d'une mise en scène que d'une mise en chair, d'une *incorporation*, dans laquelle tout concourt à une revendication farouche de la physicalité. Le Philosophe de cinéma est d'abord un corps ; et c'est ce corps qui est chargé de signifier la Philosophie, de la rendre visible, de la rendre spectacle. Il y a un négligé, un débraillé, qui désigne immédiatement l'homme des Lumières. Ce débraillé philosophique se caractérise notamment par une mise en bataille, une chemise complaisamment ouverte, un costume endossé à la diable. Le corps du personnage éclairé refuse d'être contenu, d'être contraint ; il refuse de se décorer, de se camoufler, de se cacher sous les gilets ou les jabots. Le vêtement lui répugne, comme la forme épidermique de l'Autorité. Tous les héros Philosophes participent de ce protocole, d'Honoré Fragonard à Grégoire de Fronsac ; celui qui va le plus loin, dans ce rejet de la gangue vestimentaire, est cependant le Diderot d'É.-E. Schmitt, qui dans une scène emblématique (dont le film, comme la pièce avant lui, a fait un large emploi publicitaire), se promène nu dans les jardins du château d'Holbach. Le débraillé fait ici place à l'indécence, la liberté à la licence, le refus de l'autorité à la Révolution déclarée—dont elle n'est jamais séparée que par quelques bouts de tissu[2].

Plus encore que de chairs révélées, cependant, la Philosophie est affaire de *poils*. La pilosité faciale agit déjà comme indice des Lumières : les « vrais » hommes éclairés, de Fragonard à Diderot ou à Fronsac, arborent une barbe de trois jours, savamment mal taillée, à mi-chemin du menton glabre de l'aristocrate et de la barbe garnie du bonhomme ou du vilain. Le véritable signe de « philosophéité » se trouve toutefois quelques centimètres plus haut. De même que la romanité hollywoodienne résidait toute entière, selon une célèbre mythologie de R. Barthes, dans la mèche rabattue sur le front d'un James Mason ou d'un Marlon Brando, de même l'appartenance au parti des Lumières se traduit par un cheveu long, un peu gras, ou tout au moins humide, comme liquéfié à l'issue d'un long corps à corps avec la Vérité. Toute la société encyclopédique réfugiée dans la crypte de la chapelle d'Holbach se confond en une grande masse échevelée, où il est difficile de distinguer Diderot de son bras droit Abraham ou des ouvriers qui travaillent sous leurs ordres : tous ont le même air exténué, la même peau couverte de sueur, et (surtout) la même tignasse foncée, rebelle et déferlante. Grégoire de Fronsac, lui, tient sa crinière en respect à l'aide d'une boucle ; mais c'est un respect fragile, et le chevalier saura libérer sa chevelure au moment de l'assaut final contre les forces de l'obscurantisme et de l'Antiphilosophie[3].

Le débraillé philosophique se définit, corrélativement, par une série de refus, d'absences assumées. Absence de poudre, notamment, et de mouches : dans le système visuel du film des Lumières, le héros Philosophe, toujours exposé, toujours presque nu, ou en bonne voie de l'être, se distingue de l'aristocrate grimé, fardé, paré, dont l'aspect fantomatique et farineux trahit la décadence et l'oisiveté. *Les Caprices d'un fleuve* pose ainsi, dès ses premières scènes, un contraste entre le cercle noble et européen que quitte Jean-François de la Plaine—cercle de spectres chuchotants, complotants, médisants, serrés dans d'étroites antichambres, et plongés dans un perpétuel clair-obscur—et le monde ensoleillé, relâché, « libéré » qu'il découvre en Afrique. Même opposition fondamentale dans *les Deux Fragonard* (alors que la vitalité débordante d'Honoré jure avec l'entourage momifié, mouché et poudré de l'odieux Salmon d'Anglas) ou dans *le Pacte des loups* (où les « bons » et les « mauvais » aristocrates se reconnaissent à l'épaisseur relative de leur maquillage). L'équation de la noblesse décadente et de la poudre n'est cependant jamais mieux établie que dans ce tableau initial de *Ridicule* où le talc, complaisamment soufflé par les femmes de chambre de madame de Blayac, enveloppe son corps d'une nuée blanchâtre, lui fournissant une sorte de carapace lactée contre le monde et ses cruautés. Chez P. Leconte, la poudre remplit d'ailleurs un rôle de baromètre moral : la propre corruption de Ponceludon de Malavoy est directement proportionnelle à sa blancheur, à la quantité plus ou moins abondante de grimage qui recouvre sa figure ; son ultime retour à la raison et à la vertu coïncidera avec la révélation de son visage, désormais lavé de tout fard comme de tout blâme.

Il reste par ailleurs à faire toute une sémiologie cinématographique de la *perruque*, qui jouxterait et compléterait celle du cheveu. Les personnages éclairés—nos commentaires sur la chevelure philosophique le laissaient déjà entendre—se promènent tous *tête nue*. Ils font écho au coup de force opéré, dès le XVIIIe siècle, par les grands ennemis du postiche (les Rousseau, les Franklin, les Diderot), dont le propre dénudement capitulaire n'était du reste pas toujours lié à une affirmation libertaire. Chez le Philosophe de cinéma, cependant, ce lien est insécable : le personnage refuse d'être couvert, d'être chapeauté ; il fuit ce qui imposerait un carcan à sa tête, donc à sa pensée même, ainsi alourdie, empêchée par un faste qu'il s'agit justement de récuser. Dans ces circonstances, le *retrait* de la perruque acquiert une importance particulière ; il accompagne une épiphanie, ou souligne, d'un geste lourdement symbolique, une prise de position éclairée. C'est lorsqu'il apprend qu'il a enfanté un petit Africain—que son sang et son sort sont désormais indissolublement liés à ceux du « continent Noir »—que Jean-François de la Plaine, dans un mouvement lent, ému, concerté, fait tomber sa prothèse, coupant ses derniers liens avec la métropole et renonçant au reste de son autorité politique. Le Diderot de Schmitt et Aghion n'accepte pour sa part de porter perruque que pour complaire à ses hôtes, au moment du déjeuner. Une discussion tendue avec le cardinal d'Holbach (frère intégriste du Baron) rend cependant le postiche de plus en plus incommode ; jeté négligemment sur la tête, il s'en échappe progressivement, remontant peu à peu sur le front du Philosophe, avant que celui-ci ne le jette énergiquement sur la table, ponctuant par ce mouvement un article de son *credo*[4]. Même geste théâtral pour Beaumarchais, se délestant de sa perruque de magistrat pour redevenir libre penseur, et croiser le fer avec un aristocrate en furie. Le dénouement de la chevelure peut agir comme une variante atténuée de ce topos : c'est aussi pour marquer son refus d'une civilité frileuse, de convenances réductrices, que Fronsac, au moment de venger son « frère » iroquois, abandonne une boucle dont le spectateur avait déjà pu remarquer l'incapacité à contenir la toison rebelle. La perruque est ainsi un artifice que l'on rejette, un déguisement que l'on renie, un masque que l'on retire, retrouvant par le fait même une naturelle (et bien théorique) simplicité. Dans la pénultième scène de *Ridicule*, c'est d'ailleurs un *véritable* masque que laisse tomber Ponceludon de Malavoy à la suite de son trébuchement, s'exposant ainsi à la moquerie générale, et s'excluant pour toujours de la comédie versaillaise.

La dégaine philosophique présente ainsi plusieurs significations conjointes. L'indiscipline du vêtement et de la mise du Philosophe renvoient d'abord, métonymiquement, à sa propre indiscipline, son propre « désordre » intellectuel et moral. La liberté de parole et de pensée ne saurait se plier au code vestimentaire en vigueur, lequel n'est jamais qu'un conformisme, un asservissement, une invitation à rentrer dans le rang. Le costume du Philosophe—ou son absence—devient ainsi une question de principe. Plus : c'est un mode de réflexion, s'inscrivant d'emblée dans le combat pour les Lumières ; c'est un pamphlet, un manifeste en action—un manifeste fait de toile, de tissu, de poils, et d'un épiderme méthodiquement révélé. Dans le système des personnages du film « dix-huitième », cette manière d'être, cette façon d'habiter son corps, distinguent par ailleurs le Philosophe des figures aristocratiques, c'est-à-dire de *l'ordre* dans ce qu'il a à la fois de plus arbitraire et de plus sclérosé. La santé du Philosophe—santé dont fait foi ce corps exhibé, affirmé—rend plus remarquable encore la dégénérescence, le pourrissement fardé du corps aristocratique. Cheveu rare, dentition pourrie, oeil vague, chair blafarde : les nobles roués du cercle de Salmon d'Anglas, dans *les Deux Fragonard*, préfigurent ceux des *Caprices d'un fleuve* ou du *Pacte des loups*. Ici encore, le sens, la portée, la *valeur* d'un personnage sont immédiatement divulgués par son aspect physique. La vétusté de l'Ancien Régime, la décrépitude de ses élites titrées, se matérialise, selon cette vision toute républicaine, dans une série de dents gâtées, et dans une surenchère d'étoffes et de rubans[5].

Le Philosophe de cinéma ne se définit pas uniquement par son allure—ce qu'on oserait presque, considérant le média dont il s'agit, appeler son *look*. Il se caractérise aussi par son rapport aux choses, son sens du concret. Le Philosophe entre directement en contact avec le monde, avec la matière ; il s'abaisse volontiers à des tâches qu'un esprit moins pratique dédaignerait. Honoré Fragonard et Ponceludon de Malavoy sont représentés la faux à la main, secondant leurs paysans aux champs; le comte de Kerfadec va jusqu'à faire sa propre lessive, et se gausse de sa belle-fille qui lui en fait le reproche. Le matérialisme du Philosophe ne se cantonne cependant pas dans ces activités domestiques ; il prend essentiellement deux visages, plus spectaculaires, donc plus efficaces dans ce type de représentation : celui du *libertinage*, et celui de l'*expérimentation*.

Ce corps qu'ils dédaignent de cacher, les Philosophes en jouissent sans ménagement. Leur quasi-nudité n'est pas qu'une affirmation intellectuelle : c'est aussi une manière d'être *toujours prêts*, de profiter de toute occasion érotique. Aussi Honoré Fragonard, dans les premières minutes du film de Ph. le Guay, sort-il des bras d'une soubrette pour aller se blottir entre deux jeunes femmes manifestement consentantes. Beaumarchais est un amateur de chambrières et d'actrices, que la vie conjugale et un cocuage enfin partagé ne parviennent pas à assagir. Ponceludon de Malavoy, personnage « vertueux », jouit pourtant avec allégresse des faveurs de la scélérate Madame de Blayac. Grégoire de Fronsac, qualifié d'emblée de « libertin », confirme sa sulfureuse réputation au bordel de Mende. Le vieux comte de Kerfadec lui-même n'hésite pas à lutiner une de ses servantes, sous une reproduction des *Hasards heureux de l'escarpolette*—le tableau qui forme le centre de l'intrigue des *Deux Fragonard*. Quant à Diderot, le titre de la pièce d'Éric-Emmanuel Schmitt le réduisait déjà, de toutes manières, à cet élément d'aventurisme sexuel ; comme l'affirme un des ahurissants intertitres initiaux : « *Qu'est-ce que l'on était libre* (et leste !), *quand on inventait la liberté !* »

S'il ne recule devant aucune aventure, le Philosophe est toutefois appelé à se *ranger*—c'est, semble-t-il, son inéluctable destin, en prise avec le conformisme satisfait de tout cinéma populaire. Ponceludon de Malavoy épousera Mathilde de Bellegarde, la jeune femme éclairée que les fastes de Versailles, et les appas de Fanny Ardant, lui ont fait un moment négliger. Grégoire de Fronsac sauvera Marianne de Morangias de la mort, et l'emmènera avec lui en Afrique, loin du corps et du souvenir de son frère concupiscent. Jean-François de la Plaine renoncera aux faveurs d'Anne Brisseau, la métisse avec qui il s'est d'abord soulagé de son exil africain, pour se consacrer tout entier à sa « fille adoptive », Amélie, future mère de son fils. Beaumarchais lui-même se laissera attendrir, en dernier ressort, par la perspective de l'enfant à naître. Seul le Diderot d'É.-E. Schmitt conservera jusqu'au bout son caractère libertin ; mais c'est un libertinage bien bourgeois, qui tient plus de Feydeau et du boulevard que de Crébillon et des salons—qui a plus à voir, en somme, avec le XIXe (tel qu'il se survit en Guitry) qu'avec le XVIIIe siècle[6].

Le rapport du Philosophe au concret trouve aussi à s'exprimer dans son empirisme, dans sa pratique de l'*expérience* plus ou moins scientifique. Comme pour la dégaine ou l'activisme érotique, un élément « authentique » des Lumières est progressivement décanté, réduit à un rôle de signal. Autrement dit, dans les œuvres dont il s'agit, c'est moins le Philosophe qui fait l'expérience, que l'expérience qui fait (qui habilite, qui note et dénote) le Philosophe. Ainsi le frère d'Honoré Fragonard, Cyprien, pratique clandestinement la dissection des cadavres, y risquant (et, ultimement, y perdant) son poste d'enseignant. Cette pratique macabre est toutefois immédiatement mise en rapport avec un objet plus noble, tout à fait éclairé : Cyprien rêve de fonder un « Cabinet d'anatomie universel », grâce auquel « les hommes sauront enfin qu'ils sont tous semblables ». Ponceludon de Malavoy est ingénieur, et ne monte à Versailles que pour obtenir du Roi les sommes nécessaires à l'irrigation des marais de sa province. Mathilde, sa maîtresse, se consacre à des expériences de botanique et à l'élaboration d'un scaphandre, pour laquelle, véritable femme de science, elle n'hésite pas à s'exposer à la noyade. Combaud, le second progressiste de Jean-François de La Plaine, fait voler une montgolfière sur les plages du Cap Saint-Martin. C'est aussi vers le ciel que se portent les ambitions scientifiques du comte de Kerfadec : à une montgolfière (encore ancrée dans une certaine vraisemblance historique) succèdent une petite machine ailée, propulsée du haut d'un hangar ; puis une grande machine volante, à traction chevaline ; et, enfin, un aéroplane en bonne et due forme, à vapeur et à hélice. C'est d'ailleurs dans cet étonnant engin que le fils et la belle-fille du comte, devançant Blériot d'un bon siècle, quitteront finalement la France révolutionnaire pour rejoindre l'Angleterre.

Cette présence constante et qualifiante de l'expérimentation rend d'autant plus étrange — pour ne pas dire suspecte — le traitement qu'infligent au thème les créateurs du *Libertin*. Le film de Schmitt et Aghion a beau se poser comme un hommage à l'*Encyclopédie* et à ses artisans, comme une apologie de la raison triomphante, l'expérimentalisme des Lumières y est systématiquement tourné en bourrique, ou détourné à des fins purement humoristiques. Le baron d'Holbach, présenté comme un doux rêveur, soumis aux humeurs et aux décrets de la formidable baronne, y perd son temps à calculer la densité des bulles de savon, et à inventer des appareils dont l'inutilité n'a d'égal que la barbarie — ainsi cet « orgue à cochons », variation sur l'orgue à chats de Kircher, par lequel on souhaite manifestement provoquer l'hilarité du spectateur. Sa femme, elle aussi frappée du démon de l'empirisme, consacre toute son activité botanique à la production d'hallucinogènes, aphrodisiaques et autres excitants, et impose à ses invités une série d'innovations culinaires plus ou moins anachroniques (chocolat, loukoums, caviar, ananas, maïs soufflé). On aimerait croire qu'il y a là une critique larvée du positivisme, des excès potentiels de la pensée des Lumières ; on voudrait penser qu'É.-E. Schmitt, fin diderotien, cherche à placarder l'hyperrationalisme du XVIIIe siècle. Tout bien considéré, il ne semble cependant y avoir que matière à rire — plus ou moins jaune, selon l'humeur et le caractère.

Le personnage du Philosophe s'inscrit enfin dans un *réseau*. Il entretient, avec les grandes et les petites figures des Lumières, des relations personnelles ou intellectuelles. Le Philosophe de cinéma est un infatigable *name dropper* ; il se réclame sans cesse des ténors de la Philosophie, dont la simple mention suffit apparemment à le qualifier. Le comte de Kerfadec correspond avec Mirabeau et Lavoisier, et confie à son fils, en partance pour l'Amérique, une lettre de recommandation à l'usage de son « ami Benjamin Franklin » ; il parle ailleurs de Diderot et de « ce pisse-froid de Rousseau » — coup de patte obligé à Jean-Jacques, considéré comme trop près des idéaux et des atrocités révolutionnaires. Les officiers du Cap Saint-Marin discutent, dans leurs temps libres, du *Supplément au voyage de Bougainville*, et mentionnent les noms de Mirabeau, de La Fayette et de Condorcet, parmi les membres de la nouvelle Société des Amis des Noirs. Les Encyclopédistes sont évoqués dans *le Pacte des loups*, ainsi que Buffon, dont Fronsac est l'agent, et qui fait même une furtive apparition, opposant à l'intransigeance de son jeune protégé les principes de la paix civique et de la raison d'État. Voltaire, comme l'exige son statut de symbole et de souverain des Lumières, est toutefois la figure la plus fréquemment évoquée. Son nom suffit à inspirer le respect du Beaumarchais de Guitry et Molinaro, qui prend immédiatement sous son aile un jeune homme recommandé par Ferney. Ponceludon de Malavoy contraste l'*esprit* voltairien, généreux, charitable, avec la mesquinerie de celui qu'on pratique à la cour. Voltaire est nommé dans *Chouans !*, dans *le Pacte*, et n'est pas épargné par *le Libertin*, où il fait l'objet de quelques allusions salaces.

Le Philosophe se définit ainsi à partir de quelques traits, de quelques caractéristiques intrinsèques : le débraillé, le libertinage, l'expérimentation, l'évocation litanique des grands « noms » des Lumières. On pourrait sans trop de peine allonger la liste, pour y inclure des éléments plus intangibles mais non moins signifiants. Il y a une certaine manière philosophique de se porter, de se *presse*r, de courir sans cesse derrière les idées ; il y a une diction du Philosophe, précieuse et « sautillante », tentant de suggérer l'atmosphère légère et spirituelle des salons ; etc. Cette mythologie cinématographique a cependant aussi—comme toute sémiologie qui se respecte–un aspect *différentiel*. Le « philosophe » de Diderot et Dumarsais se définissait déjà par une série d'oppositions (avec le dévot, le pédant, l'ermite, le stoïcien) ; celui du cinéma français se révèle souvent, à lui-même comme aux autres, en se dissociant de figures concurrentes—celle de l'aristocrate, bien sûr, mais aussi celles du clerc, du « poëte », du bourgeois, du paysan, de l'homme du peuple. Il ne s'agit pas de procéder ici à ces mythologies parallèles (relativement marginales, dans la mesure où elles ne s'appliquent qu'aux seconds rôles, aux figures de « soutien », sur lesquelles se détache celle du héros-Philosophe) mais de signaler que ce système de relations et d'oppositions s'exprime souvent sous la forme d'une *confrontation* ; et que cette confrontation intervient généralement, sociabilité « dix-huitième » oblige, dans le cadre d'un *repas*. Les propos et les débats de table permettent aux différents rôles de se définir, en articulant—selon un didactisme lui-même parfaitement caractéristique du film (et du roman) « historique »—les enjeux, les tensions idéologiques ou philosophiques qui structurent à la fois l'intrigue et le personnel du récit. On peut citer, à cet égard, trois scènes (ou cènes) exemplaires. Un dîner offert par Jean-François de La Plaine aux dignitaires du Cap Saint-Martin révèle les conflits qui existent, au sein de la colonie, entre le parti « éclairé », antiesclavagiste (de La Plaine lui-même, ses officiers Combaud et Blanet, le fort libéral abbé Fleuriau), et les éléments plus conservateurs, dont la fortune (ou la survie) est liée au commerce des esclaves (le négrier

Denis, l'ordonnateur de Kermadec). C'est également lors d'un repas—champêtre, celui-là—qu'intervient la dispute précédemment mentionnée entre Diderot et le cardinal d'Holbach, confrontation manichéenne des Lumières et de l'Église, où le Philosophe, par provocation, réitère certaines des propositions les plus extrêmes du *Rêve de d'Alembert* sur l'homosexualité ou la masturbation[7]. Enfin, le somptueux repas donné par le comte de Morangias, dans *le Pacte des loups*, installe les relations sur lesquelles toute l'axiologie du film sera ensuite fondée : rupture entre Fronsac, « Philosophe » et « parisien », et la noblesse provinciale, frileuse et bornée qui l'entravera dans sa mission ; ridicule du poète Des Forêts, rival de Fronsac pour le cœur de Marianne de Morangias ; animosité palpable de Fronsac et de Jean-François de Morangias, qui se détache rapidement de la masse aristocratique pour devenir l'« adversaire », l'incarnation même des forces obscures (et obscurantistes) à l'œuvre dans le Gévaudan.

3. Avènement du Philosophe. *Où l'on voit comment nos héros ont acquis leur nouveau statut*

Il nous reste à déterminer comment cette figure du Philosophe s'est peu à peu imposée, comment elle en est venue à occuper cette position fédératrice dans l'imaginaire cinématographique français. Sur un plan strictement chronologique, on identifiera trois étapes, trois moments, correspondant à une héroïsation toujours plus marquée du personnage philosophique.

Le cinéma de la fin des années 1980, s'il met déjà en scène des personnages « éclairés », garde une attitude sceptique et soupçonneuse envers la Philosophie. Les fêtes du Bicentenaire, alors même qu'elles imposaient une image globalement positive de la Révolution (en mettant l'accent sur ses aspects les plus rassembleurs : tolérance, libre pensée, droits de l'homme), ont sans doute favorisé cette interrogation sur le sens et les conséquences des Lumières. Au grand air national, entonné lors des célébrations officielles, le cinéma populaire s'est plu à opposer une partie discordante et contestataire.

Le comte de Kerfadec s'avère ainsi l'aristocrate dont rêve une certaine droite hexagonale : philosophe certes, mais surtout débonnaire (il emprunte, rappelons-le, les bons gros traits, la voix douce et posée de Philippe Noiret), il aime ses paysans comme le (bon) père de famille aime ses enfants. Il accueille favorablement la nouvelle de la prise de la Bastille, en ordonnant immédiatement l'organisation d'une fête, qui réunira « péquenots et sang-bleus » ; il sera toutefois atterré par la Terreur, et choisira de joindre les rangs de la chouannerie, où l'appelle de toutes manières son esprit de caste[8]. Les films sur le XVIII siècle prennent souvent leurs distances par rapport aux excès de la Révolution : Jean-François de La Plaine est destitué par la Constituante ; le Marquis de Bellegarde (*Ridicule*) est exilé Outre-Manche, où il apprend à goûter l'*humour* anglais ; Thomas d'Apcher, l'assistant de Grégoire de Fronsac dans le Gévaudan, sera ultimement exécuté. Il ne s'agit cependant là que de *codas* ou d'épisodes, n'entachant pas (ou si peu…) un message globalement favorable aux Lumières. *Chouans !* est le seul (ou le dernier) de ces films à prendre aussi résolument parti pour les mouvements contre-révolutionnaires. Le point d'exclamation du titre joue plus qu'un rôle d'emphase rhétorique : c'est l'affirmation tonitruante d'un *credo*. La présence de personnages de « mauvais chouans », d'aristocrates intraitables et sanguinaires, ne change pas la leçon générale du film, que scelle la mort du marquis, transpercé par les balles de la République.

Tout au long de ces développements, le Philosophe reste dans une position difficile. Aux représentants de la Terreur comme aux chouans les plus fanatiques, il oppose un humanisme tolérant. Dans une époque troublée, polarisée, il prêche une impossible modération. Cet apparent retrait intellectuel ou idéologique se double d'un (réel) retrait narratif. L'âge et l'embonpoint du comte l'empêchent de prendre véritablement part à l'action. Durant la plus grande partie du film, Kerfadec assiste, à peu près impuissant, à la confrontation de son fils, général de l'armée catholique et royaliste, et de son ancien protégé Tarquin, commissaire de la Révolution. Le Philosophe, lorsqu'il ne passe pas résolument du côté du Mal (comme Tarquin justement, autre partisan des Lumières), est dépassé par les événements. Pire, par son action ou par ses idées subversives, il est plus ou moins directement responsable de cette fièvre de l'Histoire ; comme tout intellectuel—par définition inefficace, palabreur, sinon tout à fait dangereux—, il ne peut se racheter que par la mort. Tarquin et le comte mourront en effet tous deux ; leur martyre donnera aux « véritables » héros—non Philosophes—la chance de vivre, et de quitter une France devenue folle.

La même ambiguïté persiste dans l'autre opus de l'année « bicentenaire », *les Deux Fragonard*—bien que cette ambivalence ne soit plus ici produite par un retrait, ou par une incapacité à agir sur les événements, mais par une division, un éclatement du type philosophique. Les trois principaux personnages masculins du film se partagent en effet les attributs qui se joindront et se cristalliseront dans la figure du Philosophe. À Honoré Fragonard revient le libertinage et le « débraillé » ; à son frère Cyprien échoit l'esprit empirique des Lumières, dans sa variante monomane et ascétique. Le « méchant » de l'histoire, Salmon d'Anglas, interprété avec une terrifiante froideur par Sami Frey, présente toutefois lui aussi des propriétés « philosophiques ». Tout, de sa cruauté aristocratique à sa préciosité perruquée, tendrait à en faire un scélérat d'opérette, guère différent de ceux qu'affronteront Diderot, Fronsac ou Beaumarchais. Mais les ambitions de Salmon d'Anglas, si elles sont meurtrières, sont aussi scientifiques. Il encourage les expériences de Cyprien Fragonard, et dépasse ce dernier en audace : il propose à l'anatomiste de lui procurer, non plus un cadavre exhumé à la sauvette, mais un corps « frais », nouvellement sacrifié à l'autel de la science (et, qui plus est, un corps beau : celui du modèle même de *l'Escarpolette*). D'Anglas (que l'on montre par ailleurs entouré d'horloges, d'automates, d'éprouvettes et de sabliers—instruments traditionnels du savant, qui composaient aussi le laboratoire d'un Kerfadec) incarne la part d'ombre, la face cachée des Lumières, cette dimension trouble que les incarnations ultérieures du Philosophe prendront le plus grand soin de gommer.

Le mythe du Philosophe s'affirme ensuite dans les trois productions de 1996, lesquelles se situent—à la fois chronologiquement et idéologiquement—à mi-chemin entre l'ambivalence du bloc précédent et le type parfaitement assis du *Libertin* ou du *Pacte des loups*. Un malaise subsiste dans *les Caprices d'un fleuve* : Jean-François de La Plaine affiche un certain mépris pour « l'*Encyclopédie* et les encyclopédistes », qu'il assimile à un rationalisme déshumanisant, et auxquels il oppose l'irréductible « différence » de l'Afrique. S'il cite avec approbation les propos antiracistes d'un Diderot ou d'un Condorcet, il ridiculise les affirmations de Buffon/« bouffon » sur la différence minime séparant le singe du Noir. Le retour en France, à la suite du rappel par la Convention, est qualifié de « véritable exil »—se substituant à l'exil royal, depuis longtemps assumé. Plus romantique que « philosophe », plus impétueux que raisonneur, de La Plaine refuse même le principe de tolérance, et se réserve le droit d'« être intolérant avec ce qui [lui] déplaît ». Le personnage, malgré ces réserves, est cependant un homme d'action : duelliste, coucheur, brillant cavalier, il n'hésite pas à s'enfoncer dans le désert pour retrouver sa fille adoptive, enlevée par des marchands d'esclaves. Le héros-Philosophe, mâtiné de baroudeur et de cow-boy, offert à l'admiration du spectateur, est manifestement déjà en route.

Le Beaumarchais de Guitry et Molinaro—dramaturge, séducteur, agent secret—et le Ponceludon de Leconte ne connaissent plus cette ambivalence. Chez l'un comme chez l'autre, le type philosophique est définitivement posé ; surtout, les camps sont désormais absolument tranchés. Il n'est plus question d'éventuels excès des Lumières, ou de quelque part obscure de la Philosophie. D'un côté se dressent le héros et ses alliés, partisans des « nouvelles idées » ; de l'autre, les forces de l'obscurantisme : la noblesse, le pouvoir politique, le clergé, dont on signale l'insidieuse connivence. Pour Leconte comme pour Molinaro, l'essentiel n'est plus de déterminer la valeur morale des Lumières et de leur contraire (quel qu'il soit), mais bien de savoir *où*, dans ce système figé, se *situent* les différents personnages. Ainsi, parce qu'il espère en tirer profit, Ponceludon « passe à l'ennemi », et fait son chemin dans les milieux frelatés de la cour ; réalisant la profonde incompatibilité des deux sphères, et sa propre appartenance à la première, il reviendra cependant à la pure Philosophie ; tout est affaire d'allers-retours, de déplacement, dans un monde dont les valeurs et les lignes de partage sont clairement établies. Le problème de l'axiologie, définitivement réglé, cède la place aux seules questions de circulation narrative[9].

Le Pacte des loups et *le Libertin* ne font en somme que radicaliser ce modèle, en le poussant jusqu'à la caricature—ou, si l'on préfère, jusqu'à l'épure, jusqu'à la quintessence. Le Diderot du *Libertin* n'est pas un aventurier au sens propre ; il n'est pas, comme Beaumarchais, chargé de missions secrètes et diversement compromettantes. La coterie encyclopédique prend toutefois, dans la vision bédéesque d'É.-E. Schmitt, toutes les allures d'une organisation clandestine, d'un *service spécial* philosophique, avec son quartier général–la crypte d'Holbach, sorte de *Batcave* des Lumières—, ses agents, ses complices et ses réseaux. Le conflit de l'Encyclopédie et de l'Église, plus que celui de deux idées ou de deux systèmes de pensée, devient celui de deux organisations antagonistes, l'une consacrée au Bien, l'autre au Mal—reliquat du film d'espionnage des années 1960 ou '70. Quant à Grégoire de Fronsac, on l'a déjà vu, c'est un panaché de James Bond, de Bob Morane, de Bruce Lee et des personnages taciturnes de Sergio Leone ; le Philosophe, sans perdre l'identité mythique qui est devenue la sienne, attire désormais à lui tous les archétypes de la culture populaire—et ce syncrétisme est peut-être le signe de sa consécration définitive.

Chez G. Aghion comme chez Ch. Gans, l'opposition déjà signalée entre le parti des Lumières et celui de l'obscurité est elle-même portée à l'extrême, éliminant toute possibilité d'équivoque. L'*Encyclopédie* interdite est investie de tous côtés par ses ennemis, qu'il s'agisse des gardes royaux, de l'insidieux cardinal d'Holbach, ou de la peintre Therbouche, espionne à la solde de l'Église, qui sera cependant « convertie » *in fine* par l'énergie sexuelle de Diderot. Fronsac doit pour sa part affronter la société secrète aristocratique et fondamentaliste des « Loups de dieu », dont le but ultime est le renversement des Lumières et le retour à l'ordre ancien. Le manichéisme de cette structure, sa simplicité absolue, son partage sans reste entre « bons » et « méchants », ne sont sans doute pas étrangers à la popularité de la formule « dix-huitiémiste ».

Cette rigidité de la matière philosophique est en tout cas ce qui lui assure, paradoxalement peut-être, son caractère plastique, sa capacité à absorber des éléments thématiques ou narratifs étrangers. Nous avons déjà évoqué la présence, dans les productions du corpus, de *topoi* habituellement associés au western. On pourrait facilement multiplier les parallèles entre les deux « genres »—ou, plus exactement, recenser tout ce que ces films « de Philosophes » (comme on dit un film « de cowboys », « de pirates » ou « de samouraïs ») empruntent au Far-West hollywoodien ou transalpin. On ne s'étonnera pas de trouver des duels dans *les Deux Fragonard*, *Ridicule* ou *les Caprices d'un fleuve* ; la topique cinématographique rejoint ici un usage (trop) bien implanté sous l'Ancien régime. Certains autres emprunts sont toutefois plus surprenants : ainsi de la fusillade entre chouans et soldats, dans le film de Ph. de Broca ; de l'arrivée salutaire de la « cavalerie », à la fin du *Pacte des loups* ; de la séance d'entraînement du *Pacte*, où Fronsac, Mani et d'Apcher liquident un à un tous les potirons d'un potager, à coups de pistolet, d'arbalète et de tomahawk ; ou des chevauchées (plus ou moins) fantastiques qui parsèment *Ridicule*, le *Pacte* et *les Caprices d'un fleuve*[10]. Le western n'est d'ailleurs pas la seule forme qui soit ainsi vampirisée. Sans répertorier les multiples allusions au film de gangster ou au cinéma d'horreur, nous signalerons deux scènes directement calquées sur des séquences hitchcockiennes célèbres. Le combat de Marianne et de Mme Dantès, dans *les Deux Fragonard*, est un renvoi transparent au meurtre raté de Grace Kelly, dans *Dial M for Murder* (*Le Crime était presque parfait*, 1954) ; Ph. Le Guay pousse la coquetterie jusqu'à donner aux deux scènes une même conclusion : au couteau planté entre les omoplates du meurtrier, chez Hitchcock, correspond la broche tout aussi brutalement fichée dans le dos de la perfide Dantès (elle-même fortement inspirée, au demeurant, de la Mrs Danvers de *Rebecca*). Le verre de lait empoisonné qu'on vient porter à Marianne de Morangias, dans *le Pacte des loups*, est par ailleurs le même que celui que Cary Grant servait à Joan Fontaine, dans *Suspicion* (*Soupçons*, 1941). Le clin d'œil cinéphilique ne nuit en rien à l'action, et prouve, s'il en était encore besoin, la malléabilité, le caractère foncièrement hospitalier du film philosophique.

4. Conclusion. *Où l'on s'interroge brièvement sur les raisons et les conséquences de cette héroïsation de Philosophe*

De 1988 à 2001, du taciturne comte de Kerfadec à l'impétueux Grégoire de Fronsac, le personnage du Philosophe est donc devenu l'un des *types* héroïques du cinéma populaire français. Ses traits distinctifs se sont accentués ; l'univers dans lequel il évolue a perdu de sa complexité, pour se fondre finalement en un schéma binaire, opposant les Lumières (modernes, tolérantes, triomphantes) à tout ce qui les combat (l'Église, la Noblesse, l'Obscurantisme sous toutes ses formes). En fait, le XVIIIe siècle philosophique ne fournit plus qu'une armature, un canevas dont le manichéisme garantit l'efficace. Est-on pour autant autorisé à porter un regard sévère—le regard du puriste, du « professionnel »—sur une production qui n'a jamais eu d'autre ambition que celle de divertir ? Il nous semble au contraire que les deux parties (le XVIIIe siècle, le cinéma) sortent gagnants de cette alliance contre-nature. Le XVIIIe y trouve un mode idéal de diffusion ; il parvient même parfois, au détour d'une réplique ou d'une péripétie, à imposer une ou deux idées qui lui sont propres. Le cinéma français, lui, y trouve un modèle particulièrement rentable d'organisation de l'imaginaire—un modèle local, « autochtone », où peuvent être recyclés (et, dans les meilleurs cas, sublimés) l'héritage du western, du film d'espionnage, du thriller, du cinéma d'horreur, du film d'arts martiaux, de la comédie musicale, du cinéma de cape et d'épée, *etc*.

Subsiste (au moins) une question : pourquoi cet investissement populaire des Lumières s'est-il précisément opéré *à ce moment-là*, autour de la dernière décennie du XXe siècle ? Le combat philosophique permet sans doute à une postmodernité inquiète de se ressourcer, de se réapproprier des valeurs qui « vont de soi », face à un ennemi assez caricatural pour en devenir incontestable. La lutte du Philosophe a un caractère d'évidence–caractère d'autant plus marqué qu'on en a systématiquement retranché tout ce qui pouvait apporter une note d'ambiguïté. Le western a été disqualifié par son racisme, son traitement trop léger du génocide amérindien ; la fin de la guerre froide a fait perdre au cinéma d'espionnage son plus important ressort ; le film de terreur s'est perdu lui-même dans la surenchère grand-guignolesque et la spécularité. Le Philosophe peut récupérer ces modèles en voie de liquidation ;

il est, pour paraphraser de nouveau R. Barthes, le dernier héros heureux.

Nous avons par ailleurs déjà évoqué l'influence qu'a pu avoir le Bicentenaire de la Révolution sur cette cristallisation de l'imaginaire français autour du Philosophe. Il serait en effet fort étonnant qu'une telle abondance commémorative n'ait pas agi, de façon à la fois durable et substantielle, sur la construction et la conception contemporaine des Lumières. À bien des égards, le discours « officiel » du Bicentenaire n'a fait que réitérer la *doxa* laïque et républicaine ; il s'inscrit dans la tradition hagiographique qu'a inaugurée la Constituante, le jour où elle a transporté rue Soufflot les mânes de Voltaire et de Rousseau. On n'a pas attendu 1989 pour canoniser le combat philosophique, en l'opposant à un obscurantisme monolithique, monarchiste et religieux ; c'était la vision des Philosophes eux-mêmes, ce sera celle de Michelet, de Paul Hazard, des manuels d'histoire ou de littérature autorisés par la IIIe ou la Ve Républiques. L'importance de la célébration révolutionnaire réside donc moins dans la création d'un savoir que dans sa transmission. Les fêtes de '89 ont garanti aux Lumières une présence médiatique, éditoriale, fictionnelle ; elles leur ont permis de s'infiltrer, plus profondément qu'autrefois, dans le discours et la culture de l'Hexagone. Le XVIIIe siècle a acquis, dans les années de l'après-Bicentenaire, une *visibilité* qui n'a (plus) rien à envier à celle d'époques traditionnellement plus fréquentées, plus investies fantasmatiquement (comme le Moyen Âge, ou le XVIIe siècle louis-quatorzien). Il n'est pas interdit de penser que le XVIIIe a soustrait au XVIIe son statut de « Grand siècle » ; il a en tout cas désormais des prétentions au titre, qui auraient été inimaginables il y a cinquante ou trente ans.

Seule une série de sondages ponctuels pourrait permettre de tester cette hypothèse, de vérifier s'il y a eu, comme nous le pensons, une « dix-huitiémisation » de la culture contemporaine. Il faudrait s'intéresser aux indices « savants » (nombre des rééditions et des publications universitaires, reconfiguration du canon, programmes de l'Éducation nationale), sans négliger les traces des Lumières dans le discours publicitaire, télévisuel, paralittéraire ou cinématographique. Le corpus ici étudié devrait ainsi être complété par les œuvres consacrées (« sérieusement » cette fois) à des figures historiques. Certains écrivains et hommes de lettres du XVIIIe siècle font en effet l'objet de leur *propre* filmographie, parfois extrêmement fournie ; c'est notamment le cas de Sade—personnage à part, évidemment, mais qui participe certainement, lorsqu'il est incarné par un Daniel Auteuil, au mythe du héros-Philosophe. Il ne s'agit pas d'entreprendre ici ces enquêtes (dont l'hétérogénéité exigerait du reste l'apport de plusieurs disciplines, de l'histoire à la didactique, de la sociocritique à la médiologie), mais de remarquer comment l'héroïsation du Philosophe au cinéma, phénomène accessoire, relativement marginal, fort éloigné en tout cas des hautes sphères de la Science et du Savoir, contribue à un mouvement général, dont il est peut-être la forme la plus sensationnelle et la plus ostensible.

Notes

[1] Dans notre lecture, on le constatera rapidement, nous ne nous sommes pas attardé à la question des anachronismes, invraisemblances et autres infidélités. Il serait vain de dénoncer des erreurs flagrantes, et souvent revendiquées, dont on ne peut tout au plus que regretter l'effet délétère sur un public non prévenu. Cet examen du *costume* (au sens que les anciens théoriciens de la peinture donnaient à ce terme) n'est pas pertinent à la définition du type ou du mythe (post)moderne qui nous intéresse ici—lequel, de toutes façons, tient plutôt de la reconstruction que de la recréation documentaire. Nous avons par ailleurs évité, autant que faire se pouvait, d'encombrer ces pages de jugements de valeur intempestifs. Nous nous sommes interdit de poser (et de répondre à) la question de la *qualité* des œuvres en cause, laquelle n'est pas non plus tout à fait pertinente à notre propos. Pour qu'on ne puisse cependant nous accuser de cacher notre jeu, ou—pire encore—de traiter indistinctement d'objets incommensurables, nous déclarerons d'emblée, et une fois pour toutes, que nous trouvons *Chouans !*, *Beaumarchais* et *Le Libertin* désolants ; *Les Deux Fragonard*, intrigant quoique raté ; *les Caprices d'un fleuve*, intéressant, bien que par moments fort naïf ; *Ridicule*, admirable ; et *le Pacte des loups*, tout à fait jubilatoire (cette jubilation s'avérant d'ailleurs plutôt celle de l'amateur de cinéma hong-kongais, que celle du dix-huitiémiste patenté.).

[2] On saura par ailleurs gré au réalisateur d'offrir ici au spectateur (et à la spectatrice) les formes élancées de Vincent Perez, là où l'exactitude historique aurait plutôt suggéré un physique replet. L'héroïsation du Philosophe passe d'abord par une sorte de chirurgie plastique, qui élimine ses rides, raffermit ses chairs, et dote le personnage d'un physique d'athlète. La figure du Philosophe prend aujourd'hui les traits de tout ce que le cinéma français compte de « beaux » jeunes premiers, de B. Giraudeau à V. Perez, de C. Berling à S. Le Bihan. É. Molinaro n'a cependant pas, dans *Beaumarchais l'insolent*, la relative pudeur (ou le relatif bon goût) de G. Aghion : il impose au public insouciant l'image (au demeurant fort improbable) d'un Benjamin Franklin pachydermique, se précipitant hors de son bain pour prendre dans ses bras Beaumarchais médusé. Cette seconde nudité est toutefois plus ambiguë et plus « complexe » que celle du Diderot « libertin » : elle révèle le Philosophe, certes, mais aussi l'« Américain », l'âme simple et « naturelle », peu au fait de la politesse française ou des mœurs continentales. On ne cherchera pas dans ce portrait le Franklin « réel », fils de la puritaine Nouvelle-Angleterre et courtisan consommé, qui serait sans doute mort de honte plutôt que d'apparaître publiquement dans ce simple appareil ; on y décèlera par contre une (plus ou moins) fine note d'antiaméricanisme, laquelle fait écho à la thématique antibritannique développée autrement par le scénario.

[3] La chevelure libérée de Fronsac renvoie au reste autant au type du guerrier « sauvage » qu'à celui du Philosophe. Elle marque le retour à l'« état de nature », à la sauvagerie nécessaire pour affronter les âmes primitives à la solde des « Loups de Dieu ». On peut voir dans cette saine barbarie un hommage à Rousseau, ou au Voltaire de *l'Ingénu*, s'inscrivant ainsi, malgré tout, dans un certain réseau « philosophique ».

[4] « Je ne parle qu'en mon nom propre, selon ma conscience ; à la différence de votre Éminence, je ne fais pas parler Dieu à ma place. » C'est à la réplique suivante que le cardinal—joué par un Michel Serrault somnambulique—traite Diderot de « libertin », justifiant s'il en était besoin le titre du film et de la pièce.

[5] On ne saurait du reste faire une lecture univoque du personnage de l'aristocrate, qui mériterait sans doute sa propre mythologie « positive » (et non essentiellement négative, comme celle à laquelle nous procédons indirectement ici). Il y a en effet de *bons* nobles au cinéma, comme il y en a de mauvais. Certains personnages aristocratiques incarnent manifestement l'« ennemi », la Réaction, l'Antiphilosophie; fidèles à une certaine imagerie populaire, ils concentrent en eux toute la noirceur, toutes les tares de leur classe. D'autres occupent une position axiologique contraire; ils se placent résolument du côté du « bien »—des

Lumières—, en dépit de leurs titres ou de leurs privilèges. C'est le cas, bien sûr, des *héros* aristocrates, comme le comte de Kerfadec, le marquis Ponceludon de Malavoy, ou le chevalier de Fronsac—« petits » nobles, hobereaux de province, proches de leurs gens, et ainsi prémunis contre les vices et les travers des « Grands ». C'est aussi le cas des comparses, des adjuvants titrés—nobles éclairés, réceptifs aux « nouvelles idées », quand ils ne sont pas à leur source même : le duc de Chaulnes (*Beaumarchais l'insolent*); le marquis de Bellegarde (*Ridicule*); le baron d'Holbach (dont É.-E. Schmitt, dans un double mouvement paradoxal, fait à la fois un parfait imbécile et le co-directeur de *l'Encyclopédie*); le marquis d'Apcher et son fils Thomas, le comte de Morangias (*le Pacte des loups*); etc. Ces variations reflètent sans doute l'ambivalence (ou la division) de la France contemporaine face à la figure de l'aristocrate, capable du meilleur comme du pire, à la fois bourreau sous l'Ancien Régime et martyr sous la Révolution, ogre et mousquetaire, terrifiant et magnifique. Il est en tout cas impossible de renvoyer naïvement cette diversité d'opinions à la politique secrète ou revendiquée des différents auteurs : cette vision nuancée de la noblesse n'est pas le propre d'un quasi-légitimiste nostalgique comme Ph. de Broca, mais apparaît aussi chez un ex-soixante-huitard comme P. Leconte.

[6] Dans la mythologie contemporaine du Philosophe, ces qualités amoureuses se doublent de compétences *martiales*. Le Philosophe sait aimer; il sait aussi se battre. De Kerfadec à Ponceludon de Malavoy, de Cyprien Fragonard à Jean-François de la Plaine ou à Beaumarchais, tous se retrouvent, à un moment ou à un autre de leurs aventures, un pistolet ou une épée à la main. À sa maîtrise inégalée de l'arme blanche et de l'arme à feu, Grégoire de Fronsac joint même, on l'a vu, une surprenante connaissance du *kung fu*, dans ses variantes les plus échevelées. Cette aptitude est moins un héritage des Lumières (l'activité militaire étant plutôt, on le sait, une prérogative aristocratique) qu'une conséquence du nouveau statut du personnage : appelé à remplir un rôle héroïque, à combattre (au sens fort du terme) les dévots machiavéliques et les partisans des anti-Lumières, le Philosophe ne peut plus ignorer cette dimension pugnace. Dans la mesure où le corps à corps a remplacé la dispute réglée, où le *débat* a fait place au *combat*, le Philosophe doit joindre à son arsenal traditionnel (la parole, l'écrit, l'argumentation) quelques armes « réelles », qui seules peuvent désormais confondre l'adversaire. On peut du reste y voir une autre manifestation, un autre exemple de cette santé, de cette énergie physique qui caractérise le Philosophe, et qui trouve ici, comme dans les ébats amoureux, une nouvelle occasion de dépense.

[7] À cette première confrontation, essentiellement verbale, fait pendant une seconde, plus « pratique », et ouvertement allégorique, où l'homme de Dieu et le Philosophe prodiguent leurs soins respectifs à un garçonnet malade : aux prières du cardinal, qui voit dans les maux de l'enfant le châtiment du Ciel pour les péchés qui sévissent au château d'Holbach, Diderot préfère l'intervention directe, et prépare, avec l'aide de l'*Encyclopédie* elle-même–dont l'utilité s'avère ainsi spectaculairement démontrée—un remède contre la crise de foi(e).

[8] Il respecte ainsi, jusque dans le détail, le cheminement du personnage de Julien Dandieu, interprété par Noiret lui-même dans *le Vieux fusil* de R. Enrico : même passage d'un homme pacifique à la violence, suite aux méfaits d'un groupe d'« envahisseurs » (ici les robespierristes, là les forces d'occupation nazies) ; même événement, la mort de la femme aimée, qui entraîne la conversion finale à la revanche armée ; même totale absence d'ambiguïté morale, la scélératesse des « occupants » ne connaissant aucune borne. Le parallèle n'est sans doute ni fortuit, ni innocent ; le rapprochement de la Terreur et de l'Occupation, en particulier, entre tout à fait dans le programme révisionniste de Ph. de Broca.

[9] La Révolution, dans ce contexte, n'a plus le caractère tragique qu'elle revêtait encore pour Ph. de Broca ou B. Giraudeau. Dans *Beaumarchais l'insolent*, elle est annoncée par le succès du *Mariage de Figaro*, contre lequel susurre un Louis XVI très « grande folle ». Elle liquide par ailleurs le monde corrompu rejeté par Ponceludon et par Mathilde, lesquels

sont devenus, comme nous l'apprend l'épilogue anglais du film, de bons « citoyens ». Dans les deux cas, l'épisode révolutionnaire est chargé d'une valeur positive, et non plus réduit à ses dérapages terroristes ou régicides.

[10] L'épisode central du film de B. Giraudeau, dans lequel Jean-François de La Plaine part à la recherche de sa fille adoptive enfuie, rappelle fortement le thème et la manière de *The Searchers* (*la Prisonnière du désert*, 1956) de John Ford. On y retrouve la même *obsession* chez le personnage en quête (bien que la figure « paternelle » et celle de l'amant, séparées chez Ford, soient ici réunies en un seul homme), le même *objet* de la quête (une fille / maîtresse enlevée), une même impression progressive d'épuisement, une même explosion finale de violence—dirigée, là contre les Comanches, ici contre les marchands d'esclaves.

FILMOGRAPHIE

Beaumarchais l'insolent, 1996. Réalisation : Édouard Molinaro. Scénario : É. Molinaro, d'après une œuvre inédite de Sacha Guitry. Interprétation : Fabrice Luchini (Beaumarchais), Sandrine Kiberlain (Marie-Thérèse), Manuel Blanc (Gudin), Jean-François Balmer (Sartine), Claire Nebout (le chevalier d'Éon), Michel Serrault (Louis XV), Jacques Weber (le duc de Chaulnes).

Les Caprices d'un fleuve, 1996. Réalisation : Bernard Giraudeau. Scénario : B. Giraudeau. Interprétation : B. Giraudeau (Jean-François de La Plaine), Richard Bohringer (Blanet), Thierry Frémont (Pierre Combaud), Roland Blanche (Monsieur Denis, négrier), Aissatou Sow (Amélie), France Zobda (Anne Brisseau).

Chouans!, 1988. Réalisation : Philippe de Broca. Scénario : Daniel Boulanger, Ph. de Broca, Jérôme Tonnerre. Interprétation : Philippe Noiret (comte Savinien de Kerfadec), Sophie Marceau (Céline), Lambert Wilson (Tarquin), Stéphane Freiss (Aurèle de Kerfadec, fils du comte), Jean-Pierre Cassel (Baron de Tiffauges), Charlotte de Turckheim (Olympe de Saint-Gildas).

Les Deux Fragonard, 1989. Réalisation : Philippe Le Guay. Scénario : Ph. Le Guay, Jérôme Tonnerre. Interprétation: Joaquim de Almeida (Honoré Fragonard), Robin Renucci (Cyprien Fragonard), Philippine Leroy-Beaulieu (Marianne), Sami Frey (Salmon d'Anglas), Nada Strancar (Mme Dantès).

Le Libertin, 2000. Réalisation : Gabriel Aghion. Scénario : G. Aghion, Éric-Emmanuel Schmitt, d'après la pièce d'É.-E. Schmitt. Interprétation : Vincent Perez (Diderot), Fanny Ardant (Madame Therbouche), Josiane Balasko (la baronne d'Holbach), Michel Serrault (le cardinal d'Holbach), Arielle Dombasle (Madame de Jerfeuil), Françoise Lépine (Madame Diderot), François Lalande (le baron d'Holbach).

Le Pacte des loups, 2001. Réalisation : Christophe Gans. Scénario : Stéphane Cabel (adaptation de C. Gans et S. Cabel). Interprétation : Samuel le Bihan (Grégoire de Fronsac), Vincent Cassel (Jean-François de Morangias), Émilie Dequenne (Marianne de Morangias), Monica Belluci (Sylvia), Jérémie Rénier (Thomas d'Apcher), Mark Dacascos (Mani), Hans Mayer (le marquis d'Apcher).

Ridicule, ou les Désordres causés par Grégoire Ponceludon de Malavoy à la cour de Versailles, 1996. Réalisation : Patrice Leconte. Scénario : Rémi Waterhouse, Michel Fessler, Éric Vicaut. Interprétation : Charles Berling (le marquis Grégoire Ponceludon de Malavoy), Jean Rochefort (le marquis de Bellegarde), Fanny Ardant (Madame de Blayac), Judith Godrèche (Mathilde de Bellegarde), Bernard Giraudeau (l'abbé de Villecourt).

(Ré)visions de la période pré-moderne dans l'oeuvre de Philippe Sollers

Séverine Genieys-Kirk (University College Dublin)

Avant-gardiste, poussant les limites de l'écriture romanesque à ses extrêmes, maître funambulesque de la parole qui virevolte de siècle en siècle, Philippe Sollers nous entraîne dans l'univers de ses innumérables références littéraires et artistiques. Dans cette étude, nous nous interrogerons donc sur le statut que l'auteur confère à la référence littéraire et artistique à l'époque pré-moderne. Est-elle un jeu de la part de l'écrivain sans ou avec une fin en soi ?

En se livrant à ce jeu "[du] rassemblement, [des] citations, [des] collages", soit à ce jeu du " roman comme encyclopédie et arche de Noé" (*Fête à Venise*, 228), son art de romancier répondrait, en quelque sorte, sous le signe de la provocation et de l'agressivité, à un désir (pédagogique) d'inviter le lecteur contemporain à réviser ses " classiques" tant méconnus que connus. Pourtant Sollers ne saisit pas seulement à vif (ou devrait-on dire au vol) écrits et témoignages.

En effet, comme nous le verrons essentiellement à partir de ses références à François Villon et à Cyrano de Bergerac, sa "mission esthétique" (Cusset, 190) parvient au contraire, à force d'incessantes reconstructions et déconstructions, associations et identifications, à nous en offrir une vision créatrice et récréative, non dépourvue d'acrobaties verbales et musicales.

> — Trop de références littéraires.
> — Il les faut—relativité.
> (*Les Folies françaises*, 74)

Regard neutre de France sur le scénario que vient de lui lire son père, le narrateur, scénario dans lequel Sollers réinvente le célèbre et mythique personnage de Don Juan ? Ou son jugement est-il un condensé, anodin en apparence, des critiques virulentes qui décrètent l'oeuvre sollertienne absconse, parce que foisonnant, d'une part de citations et d'"allusions érudites" (Cusset, 192), et d'autre part brouillant la clarté de l'intrigue, sans crier garde ? La réplique tout aussi laconique que le constat de France montre un interlocuteur fort de son autorité, au sens large du terme, allant au-delà de la simple paternité, soit au sens d'*auctoritas* ; en d'autres termes elle révèle le caractère inébranlable de l'écriture sollertienne, fidèle à son *modus vivendi*. La référence littéraire, sommes-nous tentée de déchiffrer sous cet elliptique

" il les faut—relativité", serait un devoir (*il les faut*) scientifique (entendons ce terme dans son premier sens etymologique, du latin *scire*), soit un devoir relatif au savoir. En énonçant aussi brièvement la nécessité des références littéraires, Sollers "le brouilleur de pistes" (Fardeau, 1999), le fougueux à la phrase qui " désacralise et provoque" (Kurk, 140), se voulant " railleuse et impudente" (ibid.), devance le critique peu avenant. De romans en romans, il part à la rencontre tout comme à l'encontre de ses détracteurs dont il nous présente lui-même les points de vue sous le couvert de l'ironie. Ainsi dans *Le Portrait du joueur*, fiction autobiographique, Sollers imagine un dialogue avec un personnage sans âme, sans visage, impersonnel se fiant au qu'en-dit-on, sans esprit critique aucun :

> Enfin, il paraît qu'il est un peu connu à Paris — Vous croyez vraiment ? Pas autant que Michel Tournier, tout de même ? Ah, *Les Rois Mages*, j'ai adoré, pas vous ? Et puis on sent qu'il comprend tellement bien les enfants... — Vous savez qu'il a été maoïste ? — Qui Tournier ? Non celui-là... Moi, on m'a surtout dit que ce qu'il écrivait était très superficiel, confus, dégoûtant... (118)

Dans d'autres instances, son sarcasme va jusqu'à dénoncer l'absence de caractère, l'insipidité de ce qui s'écrit et déferle sur le marché du livre, parce qu'obéissant aux lois de ce dernier—lois qu'il résume ainsi dans *Fête à Venise* en prenant pour exemple un genre autobiographique, les mémoires :

> Conseils-informations minitel :
> Vous avez connu des gens connus ou très connus ? Vous voulez écrire vos Mémoires ? Très simple : évoquez des souvenirs *les plus plats possibles* que tout le monde aurait pu vivre, en employant *un maximum de lieux communs* dont n'importe qui pourrait se servir. Résultat : ils sont comme nous, nous sommes comme eux. Succès. (153, *nos italiques*)

Les prosateurs d'aujourd'hui tomberaient ainsi dans l'excès de la fadeur, de l'"inoriginalité", comme le suggèrent notamment les deux expressions superlatives. Cette dénonciation acerbe d'une littérature devenue industrie, produite selon des recettes n'exigeant que peu d'ingrédients, ou du moins des ingrédients accessibles à tous, est ainsi présente dans toute l'oeuvre sollertienne. Aussi ne doit-on pas s'étonner si dans *L'Étoile des amants*, roman récent, il affiche à nouveau son dépit devant l'inanité de la phrase à succès :

> Phrases courtes, vocabulaire courant, pas de jeux de mots, pas de références culturelles, vous êtes moyen dans un univers moyen, vous vous adressez à la lectrice moyenne voulant devenir un

> lecteur moyen. Le tout dépressif, style traduit colonisé, photo, publicité, vieux produit nouveau, changez la photo, même critique toute prête, bingo. (54)

Si le "pas de références culturelles" dans la citation ci-dessus fait écho au "Il les faut [les références littéraires] — relativité", le "pas de jeux de mots" dévoile par la négative ce qui constitue pour Sollers le réel plaisir du texte :

> *L'Évangile selon Philippe.* C'est un document gnostique en copte traduit du grec, avec des lacunes, des phrases interrompues, des enjambements difficiles à saisir, des ruptures de ton continuelles, ce qui rend sa lecture passionnante, un vrai roman comme il n'y en a plus. (*L'Étoile des amants*, 131)

Ici, Sollers nous fournit un joli contre-exemple d'une phrase sans "jeux de mots", sans "références culturelles" : en un tour de plume, il allie les deux. La référence culturelle : *L'Évangile selon Philippe*. Sollers savoure sans aucun doute cette heureuse coincidence : un titre qui tombe à pic ; et comme par magie le signifiant se dédouble. Dans ce cas précis, Sollers, tel un expert de codilogie, attache plus d'importance à la forme qu'au contenu de ce document gnostique. On a donc envie de voir là plus qu'un jugement esthétique, soit le reflet d'une prose narcissique. Philippe/Sollers, l'évangéliste, prêchant non pas comme l'original la bonne parole de Jésus, mais un art d'écrire "comme il n'y en a plus", ou plutôt, comme il le pratique, devrait-on nuancer. Voici une autre instance où, venant de s'insurger contre la léthargie d'une société qui "n'écr[it] plus, [lit] de moins en moins, obéit aux injonctions des images et des chiffres manipulés", soit contre "le programme d'une tyrannie qui s'installe", il décrit la nature cryptique de sa prose :

> Mots couverts, devinettes, scansion entre les lignes : c'est une activité des services secrets. (*La Guerre du goût*, 379-80)

Attaque contre ceux qui le taxent d' "illisible" ; riposte, pourrait-on dire, qui nous ramène à la fin de la citation ci-dessus extraite du *Portrait du joueur*, laissée en suspens :

> Moi, on m'a surtout dit que ce qu'il écrivait était très superficiel, confus, dégoûtant... — Illisible... — Plein de points de suspension... (118)

Ce terme "illisible" que Sollers utilise, comme l'écrit Catherine Cusset dans son analyse d'un autre exemple (188), "à l'insu" du lecteur, est un mot-clef nous menant dans les méandres de son oeuvre critique. Soit à travers ses romans ou ses essais, il semble s'attacher à faire revivre sur la page ces écrivains que les contemporains et la postérité (dans bien des cas) ont jugés d'un oeil suspect et dont ils ont mépris l'oeuvre. Ainsi dans son essai sur Dante, Sollers édifie une grille de lecture précieuse, comme si, en nous guidant dans l'oeuvre d'un de ses auteurs de prédilection, il nous servait de cicérone dans le labyrinthe de ses propres romans: "rien n'est jamais illisible, rien n'est jamais complètement lisible" (*L'Écriture*, 18). La formule est donnée plus loin : "création et critique ne sauraient être séparées" (ibid., 29). Sollers nous invite à une lecture qui n'est autre que décryptage ou déchiffrage (Mortimer, 326). Mais s'il nous guide au détour d'une phrase, il éprouve un certain plaisir à prendre le lecteur au piège et à railler son ignorance[1]. En effet, il exploite la double fonction de la littérature telle que la concevaient notamment les théoriciens du roman au dix-septième siècle, à savoir l'utile et l'agréable. Mais là où les théoriciens définissaient *l'utilitas* selon des critères éthiques, Sollers accorde un rôle différent à sa prose, puisque devant son constat, réitéré en plusieurs endroits de son oeuvre, d'un fléau qui frappe la société, l'inculture, il se fait un devoir, rajoutons ludique, de nous faire réviser nos classiques, en ayant recours au procédé de la référence littéraire, culturelle, et surtout à celui de la citation, composante même de cette écriture codée, "clandestine" (Mortimer, 326)[2]. Un tel procédé d'écriture, on le sait, témoigne d'une adhésion à une nouvelle vision de l'art—vision que l'on pourrait définir à partir de ce constat de Jean-Michel Maulpoix au sujet de la littérature de 1950 à 1990 que cite William Thompson :

> [L'écrivain] devient le metteur en scène de son héritage. Ou son conservateur. Ou son démolisseur. Il procède par citations ou plagiats. Il joue aussi bien avec les oeuvres du passé qu'avec les déchets ou les signes de la consommation de masse. (25)

Ainsi Sollers exhume du passé des noms d'auteurs (Villon, Cyrano de Bergerac, Théophile de Viau, Molière, Sade), d'artistes (Rembrandt, Watteau, Fragonard), de compositeurs (Marin Marais, Couperin, Rameau, Bach) et de personnages (Dom Juan, Célimène) au destin qui le fascine. La liste est loin d'être exhaustive. Mais ce qui nous intéresse ici est qu'il retrace le chemin de la critique, ou du moins le chemin de ce destin survivant à travers maintes adaptations et interprétations des oeuvres auxquelles ces noms se rattachent. Dans *Les Folies françaises*, nous explique Sollers, il "s'est attaché à récrire le mythe [donjuanesque] sous forme de synopsis d'opéra" (*Éloge*, 823). Dans *La Fête à Venise*, il parvient presque à leurrer le lecteur en lui faisant croire à l'existence d'une toile de Watteau, donnant son titre au roman, "redoublement", nous dit le narrateur, des *Fêtes vénitiennes* : y figurent "une deuxième femme-fontaine, explosive de sensualité et une seconde danseuse retenue". Echappant doublement au regard critique, puisqu'elle est un leurre, mais aussi parce dans la réalité vécue du narrateur, elle "n'a jamais été montrée au public" (89), cette toile est pure, non menacée d'être défigurée par une critique s'obstinant, selon Sollers, à "placer [l'oeuvre de Watteau] sous le signe de la mélancolie" (*Éloge*, 815), de la négation :

> Le narrateur a le temps de regarder cette toile, il la connaît bien, il s'intéresse à l'oeuvre de Watteau. Il est ainsi amené à se poser des questions pour savoir comment Watteau a été interprété, depuis sa mort, en 1721. Il va avoir la surprise de constater que l'interprétation de Watteau est presque toujours négative. Comme si ses peintures choquaient un très profond préjugé. Watteau devient le peintre de la mélancolie, de la tristesse, ou, en tout cas, du sentiment... (*Magazine Littéraire*, 99)

Au contraire, à travers le regard du narrateur, elle se décompose et se recompose en un tout vivant, féminine et érotique. Cette recomposition devient une aventure fantasmatique où le référent féminin de ses tableaux s'ancre dans le présent de celui qui les contemple :

> Où te trouver, toi, dans Watteau ? Mais un peu partout. De dos, blanche et svelte, dans le grand pré au bord du lac aux statues, dans *Les Deux Cousines*, à Paris. [...] Accroupie, décolletée en bleu, robe rose, dans la clairière à trouée de nacre de *La Déclaration attendue*, à Angers. [...] Tu peux être aussi dans *L'Eté* de Washington, si tu veux. Tu te lèves sans bruit la nuit, tu sors des tableaux, tu voles jusqu'ici pour attendre une autre de tes apparitions dans *La Fête à Venise* en train de flotter sur l'eau, robe rouge, mouvement chuchoté sur fond d'escalier monumental [...]. (109)

En s'adressant à Luz, en la confondant avec les modèles féminins, en la faisant pénétrer dans et sortir des toiles, l'auteur restitue à l'oeuvre sa fraîcheur et son merveilleux, alors que souvent, sous la plume de la critique, elle devient un " paradis embusqué" (110), et que, selon le narrateur, "ses paysages enchantés sont un leurre" (111). Il réagit, en effet, avec sarcasme devant ces interprétations lisant l'oeuvre à la lumière de la vie psychologique supposée du peintre :

> il y a au moins deux escargots malades dans les bosquets, trois moineaux poitrinaires dans les arbres. Tes personnages dansent sur un volcan, le vide les ronge, ils ont un cancer généralisé quand ce n'est pas une paralysie générale. (111)

Il défie la critique conventionnelle, en plaçant d'emblée l'œuvre, non sous le signe de la négation mais sous celui de l'hyperbole : elle a " quelque chose de plus aéré, de plus détendu, de plus jeté, de plus rouge [...]" (89). Tandis que la critique la présente figée, paralysée, Sollers nous la montre " explosive de sensualité", nous mène au coeur de la création artistique, en imaginant un scénario racontant la vie de Watteau qui sera refusé, parce que sans tragique. En effet il met en scène la frivolité et la jouissance qui caractérisent ses deux vies, sa vie sociale et sa vie d'artiste (qu'il imagine) :

> A moins qu'il ne parte pour Saint-Cloud avec des amis, acteurs, actrices, danseuses, danseurs, musiciens, musiciennes, ils se déguisent, dînent, allument des feux, il les dispose à sa guise, proches ou lointains, leur demande de l'oublier, se mêle à eux, s'écarte, rentre dans le jeu et en sort, dessine, déchire, redessine. (122)

C'est d'une manière identique que Sollers se décrit en pleine écriture : "J'écris. La plume court, glisse, tourne, pénètre, s'arrête, repart, vole, danse, repart." (*La Guerre du goût*, 256). Peinture et écriture se rejoignent. En superposant dans la suite du passage une scène érotique avec celle de l'acte de la création, Sollers pousse la métaphore du plaisir du texte (qui se peint) à ses extrêmes. Cette révision des interprétations négatives de l'univers de Watteau semble donc comme animée de ce même projet qui l'incite à créer un nouveau Dom Juan dans *Les Folies françaises*, celui de faire "entendre enfin le grand air de liberté" (*Éloge*, 825).

A ce processus de déconstruction des interprétations, adaptations, légendes et mythes, s'ajoute celui de la restitution des oeuvres qui peut prendre des allures d'exhibitionnisme érudit, mais qui, comme nous allons le voir dans un instant à travers l'étude de sa référence au *Testament* de Villon[3], aux *Etats et empire de la lune* (1657) et à *L'Empire du soleil* (1662) de Cyrano de Bergerac[4], détermine à la fois un mode d'écriture et de lecture qui défie toute linéarité temporelle et dont Sollers nous fournit la clef à travers une citation de Heidegger :

> L'Histoire n'est pas une succession d'époques mais une unique proximité du Même, qui concerne la pensée en de multiples modes imprévisibles de la destination, et avec des degrés variables d'immédiateté. (*La Guerre du goût*, 10)

Sans aucun doute, c'est ce côté rebelle de François Villon et de Cyrano de Bergerac, qui range ces deux auteurs dans le Parnasse sollertien des libertins au même titre que Sade qui en est la figure de proue. Ils partagent une patrie commune : marginalité, scandale, affront.

Le nom de Villon figure dans *Les Folies françaises*. Il apparaît comme tombé du ciel, hors du temps, aux côtés de Molière le secondant sur l'axe temporel. Cette subite apparition est provoquée lorsque le narrateur propose un choix d'auteurs à France pour ses études supérieures :

> Il faut préparer ton diplôme en fac. Que choisir, dès maintenant ?
> Pour être tranquilles ? Du classique ? J'ai deux idées : Molière
> et Villon. (24)

Il faudra alors attendre quelques pages pour une autre mention du poète, introduisant cette fois une première citation, les huitains qui ouvrent le recueil du *Petit Testament* :

> On reprend Villon:
> " L'an quatre cens cinquante six
> Je, François Villon, escollier
> Considerant, de sens rassis,
> Le frain aux dents, franc au collier... »
> - 1456? Le *Lais*?
> Le Legs, Petit Testament. Il a vingt-cinq ans. Dans une rixe à propos d'une femme, il a tué un prêtre, Phillipe Sermoise. Ça s'arrange, mais il cambriole le trésor du Collège de Navarre. Il est de nouveau en fuite. Écoute bien les octosyllabes, Je, François Villon, escollier, un /deux-trois-quatre-cinq/six-sept-huit. (32)

Mais à la relecture, on ne peut être que frappé par l'allitération fricative faisant écho au nom de François, tout comme au titre du roman : elle annonce l'agressivité de la phrase sollertienne qui s'anime, comme impatiente à la question de France, mêlant anecdotique (l'anecdote que nous devrions tous connaître) et esthétique, passant du nom d'auteur au "corps intérieur"[5], ce corps qui produit un octocsyllabe parfait, mais méconnu, comme l'indique dans la citation suivante ce "bonjour" ironique de l'oralité : "Il traverse les siècles, bonjour" (32). Et le narrateur continue, se radoucissant, croyant en sa fille : "apprends-le par coeur, l'effet viendra peu à peu" (32). Est-ce là un glissement de sens[6], croyance en l'avenir culturel de sa patrie, comme il l'exprime dans un entretien avec Marc Fumaroli dans *Le Débat* (1994) ? Ce dialogue contraste en effet avec celui plus long qu'il tient avec son éditeur Saul, attendant désespérément que le narrateur lui soumette un manuscrit . Saul, l' inculte, le léthargique, qui au nom de Villon posera la vilaine question " C'est récent ?" (48), s'oppose clairement à France, dont la réplique donne, certes timidement, un élément d'information, une date et un titre exacts. Exaspéré par Saul, le narrateur se met à déclamer ce qui par la suite prendra en quelque sorte la fonction d'un refrain, "do-ré-mi-fa-sol-la-si-do", par lequel il attire notre attention à la structure métrique dominante du testament : l'octosyllabe. Mais curieusement, sitôt la gamme scandée, il cite le célèbre dizain carré ouvrant "La Ballade du concours de Blois" faisant non pas partie du *Testament* mais d'une série de poésies diverses. Erreur voulue ? En somme peu importe. Ce qui importe plutôt, c'est la vision qu'il offre de l'œuvre : il fait appel à nos sens et plus précisément, à l'ouïe.

Ce qu'il recherche, semble-t-il, c'est nous faire entendre la musicalité dominante du vers villonien. En effet Villon réapparaît après une série de digressions musicales par le biais de deux autres références culturelles aux compositeurs Marin Marais (1656-1728) et François Couperin (1668-1733). Sollers nous amène à établir une association entre la référence à Marais et celle à Villon, bien que quelques pages les séparent, au moyen d'un jeu de mots tacite : en effet la référence impromptue à l'opéra de Marais, intitulé *La Gamme* (55), appelle sans aucun doute une expression : *chanter sa gamme à quelqu'un* signifiant *réprimander quelqu'un* en français classique. Le mystère du refrain octosyllabique éclate ainsi au simple titre d'une œuvre bien choisie, puisque quelques pages plus tôt, le narrateur exprimait sa colère devant l'ignorance de Saul en lui chantant sa gamme ! Le refrain octosyllabique et le titre de l'opéra feraient donc office de paroles performatives, jouant avec le double sens d'une expression surannée, flottant aérienne. Ce lien n'en demeure pas moins purement analogique, unissant poésie et musique, en accord cependant avec la théorie de l'écriture à laquelle Sollers adhère : la poésie, nous rappelle-t-il, est selon la formule de Jakobson "fictio rhetorica musicaque posita" (*Ecriture*, 23), ce qu'illustre en cette instance même la prose sollertienne. Elle se laisse porter par les sons : le son d'un mot en engendre un autre, comme si de vrille en vrille, la phrase s'identifiait au sujet qu'elle décrit (ici la musique), transportant ainsi le lecteur non dans un de ces palais enchantés comme il en abonde dans les romans du Grand Siècle, où le lecteur est amené à s'imaginer palpant du regard mille curiosités, mais dans un "dictionnaire enchanté", soit un dictionnaire de merveilles sonores :

> Et musique !... La Bourrasque, le Rapporté, le Retour... Tombeau Les Regrets... Passacaille, chaconne, gavotte, menuet, courante, ballet tendre... Les Pleurs... " Joye des Elizées"... Rigodon, forlane en rondeau, musette... Le Rossignol en amour... Guillemette... les vergers fleuris... les calotins et les calotines... les folies françaises ou les dominos... Quoi encore ? Mais les jongleurs, sauteurs et saltimbanques, avec les ours et les singes... Vielleux, gueux, tambourins, bergeries, commères... Et la favorite, les moissonneurs, les gazouillements... Chaque mot disparu pour nous seuls. Dictionnaire enchanté, Chut ! Attention, sorcière ! Ne va pas te confier ! Ne va pas dire que j'écris cette langue maudite !... Les Dominos !... Sept à huit !... Do-ré-mi-fa-sol-la-si-do! (58)

Sollers ne nous donne aucune clef quant au nom du compositeur ; au lecteur d'identifier le Grand Couperin derrière ces titres d'œuvres qui font partie essentiellement du second livre de pièces de clavecin (Paris 1716-17). Sollers nous introduit dans un univers de genres musicaux et de danses méconnues du grand public[7]. En un instant, donc, il "posthume, [il] restaure, [il] montre" (*Fête à Ve-*

nise, 152) dans son moindre détail la richesse de la création artistique du Grand Siècle. Il nous entraîne dans un univers où le sensoriel prévaut, où le nom d'une danse s'identifiant à celui du genre musical éponyme, son et corps se font écho. Si cette énumération est d'apparence hétéroclite, elle est pourtant tissée autour d'un principe d'unité, puisqu'elle désigne l'œuvre d'un homme et nous donne la clef du titre du roman. De même, elle évoque, le temps de quelques mesures, la préciosité du dix-septième siècle (le "ballet tendre"), la sensibilité naissante du dix-huitième siècle (les "pleurs", les "gazouillements"). Elle éveille l'image d'un monde qui pourrait bien être celle du Moyen-Age de Villon, comme le suggèrent le nom de Guillemette et ces autres personnages farcesques ("les jongleurs […] gueux […], commères"). Enfin au terme de cette énumération, Sollers rétablit le lien entre ce monde musical et celui poétique de Villon par le fil sonore conducteur : "Do-ré-mi-fa-sol-la-si-do!". Et en effet quelques lignes plus loin, on lit :

> "Où sont les gracieux gallans
> Que je suivoye au temps jadis,
> Si bien chantans, si bien parlans,
> Si plaisans en faiz et en dis ?
> Les aucuns sont morts et roidis
> D'eulx n'est-il plus riens maintenant :
> Repos aient en paradis,
> (do ré mi fa sol la si!)
> Et Dieu saulve le remenant!" (59)

Nous noterons ici que Sollers semble prendre un malin plaisir à vouloir dérouter son lecteur : la gamme servant de refrain est amputée, pour sans aucun doute sauver la rime, une supercherie par laquelle l'auteur fausse la lecture du vers qui précède le refrain et par laquelle il nous invite à en modifier le rythme original pour lui allouer une cadence moderne : la diérèse dans le verbe "ai-ent", tout comme dans le nom "Di-eu" au vers suivant, devient monosyllabique, perdant ainsi, sous l'emprise de la parenthèse, corps étranger au poème, toute la richesse phonique de la diction médiévale. Enfin, le "je" de la citation discourant avec le temps, avec la mort, se détache, se mêlant à la voix du narrateur, se qualifiant ainsi : "[…] je suis commissaire au temps, reporter spécial en durée, employé au chiffre, spécialiste des fonds secrets" (59-60). Et tel Villon, dans le poème ci-dessus, se rappelant le doux souvenir de ces "gracieux gallans", Sollers enjoint sa fille de ne pas oublier l'essentiel, qui se présente au lecteur pareil à une contre-fugue, tel le souvenir d'un vertige à peine fixé sur la page, saisissable sans l'être, parce que de nature fugitive :

> Mais souviens-toi : Bourrasque! Rapporté! Tombeau Les Regrets!… Sieur de Sainte-Colombe… (60)

Nous remarquerons ainsi le retour soudain de la phrase sollertienne sur elle-même, convoquant avec force, bien que subrepticement, l'œuvre déjà citée du musicien François Couperin, mais aussi Marin Marais à travers la référence à son maître qui lui enseigna la viole, Augustin Dautrecourt, connu aussi sous le nom de Sieur de Sainte Colombe. Cette injonction se lit donc comme l'extraction d'un thème majeur, central non seulement à l'oeuvre de Villon, mais aussi à celle de Sollers, central à l'écriture et à la musique, comme si le reste de l'énumération de l'œuvre de Couperin, analysée ci-dessus, n'était qu'ornement, élan rimbaldien de la plume qui "vole selon…". Et ce thème est celui de la mort, de l'enfouissement du passé, de ces noms (comme *Sieur de Sainte Colombe*) qui survivent à peine au temps, qui appartiennent à "un jadis" que seuls les *happy few* ("le remenant") peuvent scruter.

Par la mise en place d'un système d'échos, la phrase sollertienne dans sa quête de restauration du passé, d'un poète peu lu, se métamorphose, par quelque effet baroque, en écriture miroir : non seulement elle nous invite à relire l'œuvre de Villon, mais elle en reflète et le rythme dansant et l'essence protéenne qu'elle ne cesse ici de célébrer, par l'intermédiaire du refrain octosyllabique. De plus, l'énumération des oeuvres de Couperin pourrait bien être une référence oblique au second huitain de la "Ballade de la bonne doctrine", commençant ainsi : "Ryme, raille, cymbale, fluctes"[8]. Enfin, le "je" villonien dans le texte de Sollers est l'expression d'un "je" subversif et "provocateur" auquel le "bon folastre" qu'est l'auteur peut aisément s'identifier. C'est là un procédé que l'on retrouve dans *Passion Fixe*, nous faisant (re)découvrir l'oeuvre de Cyrano de Bergerac.

Dès lors que notre auteur s'intéresse au libertin en tant qu'homme, le sujet qu'il décrit se transmue en commentaire autobiographique :

> Son nez n'est pas aussi grand qu'on l'a dit (tiens, au fait, pourquoi l'a-t-on dit ?). Voilà un aventurier codé, un anarchiste couronné, un mauvais plaisant, un comploteur, un bateleur, un bretteur, un poète. (109)

> Cyrano, qui n'est pas du tout le hâbleur imaginé par Edmond Rostand, fait quelques pas dans l'île de la Cité, à Paris, avant de rentrer dans son hôtel particulier et sa bibliothèque-laboratoire. Ses livres ont l'air d'avoir été imprimés hier. (284)

Les nombreuses références que fait Sollers à l'oeuvre de Cyrano fournissent ainsi un autre exemple de la nature réflexive de la prose sollertienne s'imprégnant des caractéristiques du sujet qu'elle décrit. Si dans le cas de Villon, ce que recherche Sollers est de nous faire entendre à travers l'orchestration de voix multiples, digne d'un maître d'opéra, la richesse musicale de sa poésie, dans le cas de notre libertin du dix-septième siècle, il s'agirait, si l'on se fie aux deux citations ci-dessus, de démolir ce personnage séduisant qu'Edmond Rostand a légué à la postérité et qui, remportant un succès mérité, écrase de son poids légendaire l'original. Ce programme de déconstruction d'une légende va de pair avec celui de la restitution de la vérité littéraire, soit de l'écrivain derrière l'homme, ou plutôt du livre qu'il s'agit de faire sortir de l'oubli[9]. Et en effet Sollers y réussit subtilement en s'attachant moins à l'anecdotique qu'au contenu même du livre que l'auteur investit d'une réalité physique (50), puisqu'il s'agit d'une édition précise du début du dix-huitième siècle. Sollers nous en donne avec minutie chaque détail (titre, éditeur, endroit et date d'impression) dont subsiste le charme sur la page malgré la typographie moderne :

Les Œuvres diverses de
Monsieur De Cyrano Bergerac
Tome premier
Enrichi de Figures en taille douce
À Amsterdam
Chez Jacques Desbordes, Marchand
Libraire sur le Pont de la Bourse
joignant le Comptoir de Cologne
MDCCX

Toute mention biographique se résume en tout et pour tout à une évocation on ne peut plus succinte de la physionomie et des ennemis de Cyrano, de sa philosophie libertine, sans que le mot ne soit prononcé, et des circonstances étranges de sa mort. Il en est de même du nez de Cyrano qui ne point que très timidement au détour d'une parenthèse pleine de piquant (109). Sollers ne manque pourtant pas de mettre en scène un nez, comme le lecteur pourrait s'y attendre dans un texte qui fait hommage à Cyrano. Mais le lien entre le nez de la digression sollertienne (83-86) et celui de la tirade légendaire de Rostand ne tient qu'à un fil, à un "atome" (89), à un signe englobant à lui tout seul la pensée matérialiste de Cyrano, l'écrivain. Le nez devient alors un embrayeur linguistique appelant une expression puis une autre. Certes, la digression pourrait bien être aussi un pastiche de la neuvième scène du second acte de la pièce de Rostand, où le rival de Cyrano, Christian, s'amuse à interrompre et finir les phrases de ce premier au moyen d'expressions nasales idiomatiques pour mieux se moquer de lui. Mais dans le cas de la digression sollertienne, l'auteur, d'un coup de baguette, dissout la synecdoque cyranesque en un véritable exercice de style, effaçant toute référence à la difformité du célèbre nez. En écartant tous détails biographiques et légendaires, Sollers nous présente son oeuvre sans partialité aucune. Et en utilisant une édition précise, il opère un renvoi au réel qui donne ainsi la suprématie non seulement au livre, l'objet, mais aussi à la lecture de celui-ci, ou plus exactement, comme nous le verrons dans un instant, à l'aventure, l'expérience physique de "la lecture et [de] sa voix".

Nous assistons de nouveau à l'effet miroir, anamorphotique de l'écriture sollertienne s'identifiant obliquement à l'oeuvre de Cyrano. L'aventure (32-34) que décrit ici Sollers a quelque ressemblance avec l'aventure extraordinaire que nous relate Cyrano au commencement de son livre :

> Quoy, disois-je en moy mesme, apres avoir tout aujourd'huy parlé d'une chose, un Livre qui peut-estre est le seul au monde où cette matiere se traicte, voller de ma bibliotecque sur ma table, devenir capable de raison pour s'ouvrir justement à l'endroit d'une avanture si merveilleuse [...] : Sans doubte, continues-je, Les deux vieillards qui apparurent à ce Grand homme sont ceux la mesme qui ont desrangé mon Livre et qui l'ont ouvert sur cette page pour s'espargner la peine de me faire cette harangue qu'ilz ont faicte à Cardan. (*L'Autre monde*, 360)

Alors que Sollers ouvre le livre sciemment, il n'en demeure pas moins que la raison pour laquelle il "prend" ce volume est sans justification rationnelle, tout comme l'aventure qui vient d'arriver à Cyrano : celle du narrateur est le fait, nous dit-il, du " hasard ou de l'instinct", tout comme elle est le fait du "miracle ou [d'un] accident [de la] providence ou [de la] Fortune" (359) dans le cas de Cyrano. Mais ce dédoublement ne s'arrête pas là. Tout comme le narrateur nous dit être "arrivé au passage où Cyrano raconte son aventure", l'aventure de ce dernier est similaire : la page à laquelle est ouvert ce livre de Cardan relate une anecdote autobiographique, similaire à ce qui vient d'arriver à Cyrano. Si Sollers réécrit cette aventure tout en la rendant crédible et en y laissant toutefois une petite pointe de "hasard", il dit s'identifier avec ce que ressent Cyrano à la vue de ce livre :

> J'ai toujours cru, moi aussi, que les livres étaient des instruments magiques, indiquant quand il faut à qui il faut l'attitude à avoir, le chemin à suivre. Ils font semblant d'être inertes, mais ils agissent en sous-main. Le papier renferme des atomes non encore connus, l'encre secrète des particules invisibles. (33-34)

Nous décelons ici une référence oblique à l'épisode célèbre de *L'Autre monde* où Cyrano, arrivé, dans les états et empires du soleil, observe un arbre composé de fleurs, de branches et de fruits, finissant par se détacher et se transformer en êtres humains microscopiques s'assemblant alors pour se métamorphoser en homme. Penchons-nous un instant sur la première étape de cette métamorphose :

> tous les fruits, toutes les fleurs, toutes les feuïlles, toutes les branches, enfin tout l'arbre, tomba par pieces en petits Hommes voyans, sentans et marchans, lesquels [...] au moment de leur naissance mesme, se mirent à danser à l'entour de moy. (457)

La référence oblique que nous semble faire Sollers à ce passage nous est suggérée par un déplacement lexical, l'association bien usitée entre livre/feuille/arbre[10]. L'inertie du livre, de la page, est ainsi comparable à celle de l'arbre cyranesque ; tous deux secrétant mille vies possibles. En d'autres termes, ces "atomes non encore connus", ces "particules invisibles" sont tels les composantes de l'arbre dont Cyrano admire la beauté mais dont il ne soupçonne pas qu'elles sont prêtes de se métamorphoser en humanoïdes, en êtres sensibles doués de perception à l'égal des humains. Et en effet si l'on file plus avant la métaphore, ces "atomes non encore connus" ne sont-ils pas là ces mêmes " Hommes voyans, sentans et marchans", une fois que les signes typographiques s'assemblent et prennent sens, s'animent d'une vie intérieure en la présence d'un lecteur, sans laquelle le texte ne peut exister ? De même apprend-on de la bouche de la "pomme raisonnable, ce petit bout de Nain" (456) que la métamorphose miraculeuse de l'arbre n'eût pu avoir lieu sans la présence de Cyrano :

> Animal humain [...] apres t'avoir long-temps consideré du haut de la branche où je pendois, j'ay crû lire dans ton visage que tu n'estois pas originaire de ce Monde ; c'est à cause de cela que je suis descendu pour en estre éclaircy au vray. (457)

D'abord spectateur d'un monde inanimé, il devient le spectateur d'un monde qui, sous l'effet de sa présence, se meut tel un corps :

> Aussi-tost que ces petits Hommes se furent mis à danser, il me sembla sentir leur agitation dans moy, et mon agitation dans eux. Je ne pouvois regarder cette danse, que je ne fusse entraisné sensiblement de ma place, comme par un vortice qui remuoit de son mesme bransle, et de l'agitation particuliere d'un chacun, toutes les parties de mon corps, et je sentois épanouïr sur mon visage la mesme joye qu'un mouvement pareil avoit étendu sur le leur. (458)

L'expérience corporelle et sensorielle que vit le spectateur cyranesque nous semble comparable à la définition que donne Sollers de la lecture dans *Éloge de l'infini* : "La lecture met en mouvement le corps tout entier" (372). Ainsi l'image du "vortex" (tout comme celle de la danse) est au coeur de la conception sollertienne de l'écriture et de la lecture :

> La bibliothèque tourne lentement sur elle-même, l'espace s'ouvre avec elle, et aussi le temps des volumes, chacun sa date significative rejoignant les autres dans un même pli, le même creuset brûlant. Je sens les pages tassées vivre dans le feu comme des *salamandres*, elles sont en train de composer ensemble, *braises*

et cendres, une seule histoire pleine de bruit, de fureur, mais aussi de plaisir, de gaieté. *"Une soudaine joie s'empara de mon âme..."* [...]. *"Mon âme éternelle, observe ton voeu, malgré la nuit seule et le jour en feu ..."* Et la joie attire l'espérance, et l'espérance de secrètes lumières dont la raison est éblouie. Oui, oui, la raison éblouie, quel titre. (103, *nos italiques*)

Ce passage confirme la référence oblique que nous venons d'analyser. Les petits hommes du "Balet" cyranesque sont en effet ici les livres, les volumes ; quant au "vortex", il se traduit par un tourbillon à la fois imagé (*la bibliothèque tourne*) et lexical (comme l'indique le terme *creuset*). Cette description de l'expérience de la lecture n'est toutefois pas seulement un écho voilé à l'épisode du "Balet des petits hommes". L'image du "vortex" imprègne tout le passage et crée un effet de mise en abyme : le terme "salamandre" nous ramène quelques pages en arrière (51), où Sollers cite la description du "Fleuve de l'imagination" que fait le personnage Campanella à Cyrano. De même, la citation (que nous avons matérialisée en caractères gras) fondue dans le texte (sans guillemets) est mentionnée un paragraphe plus tôt. Ces doubles renvois (au texte de Sollers et à celui de Cyrano) détiennent l'essentiel de ce qui fait, en plus de son adhésion à la théorie atomiste de Lucrèce, l'originalité de la pensée de Cyrano, se caractérisant par son héliocentrisme, théorie copernicienne selon laquelle le soleil, soit le feu constitue le principe de toute création tout comme celui de la destruction (Harth, 162). Cependant la phrase sollertienne, décrivant la métamorphose des pages au contact du regard humain, s'accompagne d'un tourbillon de références quasi insaisissables que soulèvent deux mots "bruit" et "fureur" : Shakespeare ? Fulgurance du vers rimbaldien ? Faulkner ? C'est Rimbaud qui gagne. En effet, cette réécriture de l'épisode cyranesque souligne la modernité d'un texte comme *L'Autre monde* que Sollers nous fait lire à la lumière du célèbre poème de Rimbaud, "Elle est retrouvée ! / Quoi ? L'éternité [...]", se trouvant dans "Délire II" d'une *Saison en enfer*. Il opère tout d'abord un emprunt lexical (" braises"), dont il confirme la source de façon déviée quelques lignes plus loin en citant non le second vers du cinquième quatrain où se trouve le terme mais le second quatrain du poème en question. A travers ces deux emprunts lexicaux (*salamandres* et *braises*), Sollers instaure un dispositif ludique d'associations que le lecteur doit seul déchiffrer. L'écrivain et le poète à travers cette réécriture de l'épisode cyranesque se font donc écho sur la page — un écho qui vibre à l'infini, puisque ces deux emprunts lexicaux appartiennent à deux textes que l'on pourrait lire comme se reflétant l'un l'autre, comme animés d'un même principe, eau et feu, contenu à la fois dans l'image rimbaldienne (ici omise par Sollers) de la "mer mêlée/ Au soleil", et celle du "fleuve d'imagination" (à laquelle nous renvoie le terme "salamandre" comme nous venons de le voir), qui n'est autre que " liqueur légère et brillante étincelle", "couche de pur or potable" (50). Si Cyrano et Rimbaud partagent donc un même lexique, celui de l'alchimie, ils partagent aussi ces mêmes sentiments que Sollers identifie au coeur de la bibliothèque en pleine métamorphose, soit au coeur de l'écriture en train de s'écrire, de se dire sous le regard du spectateur : "plaisir et gaieté"[11]. Bien que Sollers ne cite pas le vers de Rimbaud en question ("ô bonheur, ô raison, [...] étincelle d'or [...]. De joie, je prenais une expression bouffonne"), cette joie rimbaldienne, inscrite en exergue du poème "Elle est retrouvée! [...]", se fond dans la voix sollertienne qui, à son tour, la fait éclater sous la référence cyranesque. C'est ainsi, toujours et encore, au lecteur de poursuivre plus avant la comparaison arachnéenne que Sollers tisse entre Cyrano et Rimbaud et dont il nous laisse élucider la pertinence. Feu et joie: voilà ce qui rapproche nos deux hommes, se comparant tous deux à Prométhée. C'est ainsi que Cyrano s'exprime, alors qu'il décide de monter jusque sur la lune pour "s'esclaircir" de ce qu'il vient de lui arriver :

> Et pourquoy non ? me respondois-je aussi-tost : "Prométhée fut
> bien autrefois au Ciel dérober du feu." (360)

Quant à Rimbaud, dans sa lettre à Paul Demeny (1871) où il y définit le rôle du poète, il écrira la célèbre formule :

> Donc le poète est vraiment voleur de feu. (347)

Ce voyage fantastique imaginé par l'écrivain savant et la quête poétique rimbaldienne (celle de " Trouver une langue" [347]) procèdent d'un même désir scientifique: "arriver *à l'inconnu*" (346), "faire sentir, palper, écouter ses inventions", être "*un multiplicateur de progrès*" (347).

Voilà donc ce qui fait la modernité de l'écriture cyranesque, et non la phrase suivante, comme s'en plaint Sollers, phrase qui le fascine, puisqu'il l'a déjà citée, mais dont une interprétation courante, selon lui, ferait de Cyrano un précurseur de la technique moderne.

> "C'est un Livre, à la vérité, mais c'est un livre miraculeux, qui
> n'a ni feuillets ni caractères ; enfin c'est un Livre où pour apprendre
> les yeux sont inutiles... Ainsi, vous avez éternellement
> autour de vous tous les grands Hommes, en morts et vivants qui
> vous entretiennent de vive voix..."
>
> Je ne vois pas le rapport avec la radio ou le disque, mais là-dessus
> Dora me demande si on sort dîner. (175)

Ainsi donnée, elliptique, la citation ne nous permet de comprendre qu'à mi-voix l'amusement de l'auteur dont il occulte la portée par l'omission de ce qui précisément à ses yeux a mené à une mauvaise appréciation concernant la vraie modernité de Cyrano :

> Quand quelqu'un donc souhaitte lire, il bande avec une grande quantité de touttes sortes de clefs cette machine, puis il tourne l'esguille sur le chapitre qu'il desire escoutter, et au mesme temps, il sort de cette noix, comme de la bouche d'un homme ou d'un instrument de musicque, tous les sons distincts et differens qui servent entre les grands lunaires à l'expression du langage.
> (*L'Autre monde*, 414)

En occultant ce passage d'une imagination débordante pour l'époque à laquelle il est écrit, Sollers lui confère un nouveau sens. Privée d'une partie de sa matière, cette phrase a un air de famille : elle rappelle la phrase de Voltaire que cite Sollers dans son essai "La lecture et sa voix" : "quoiqu'il y ait beaucoup de livres, croyez-moi, peu de gens lisent ; et parmi ceux qui lisent, il y en a beaucoup qui ne se servent que de leurs yeux" (*Éloge*, 374). Tronquée, elle appelle cette autre formule que forge Sollers, s'inspirant de celle de Debord[12], "tempo, tympan : savoir vivre, savoir écouter, savoir parler, savoir lire" (ibid., 375). Ainsi l'image sollertienne de la lecture, "mouvement du corps entier", se double d'une métaphore vocale : lire une phrase, c'est savoir entendre son tempo, son pulse ; c'est savoir écouter la voix, vivre les vibrations de l'écriture. En nous renvoyant donc à l'expérience de transformation, d'élévation de Cyrano qu'il nous invite à interpréter comme anticipatrice de la quête rimbaldienne, Sollers fait sienne la langue du libertin et du poète maudit pour décrire l'expérience (méta)physique même de la lecture, de l'alchimie du Verbe sur la page blanche.

Leçon d'éveil, leçon de lecture, l'écriture de Sollers est, certes "sur un mode agressif", un(e) véritable "geste esthétique" (Cusset, 192) : la référence littéraire, culturelle, artistique n'est donc pas pur exhibitionnisme savant, mais elle sert un dessein poétique et ludique. Au fil de la phrase, elle se liquéfie tout en devenant le lieu d'une crystallisation, celle du plaisir du texte, des mots et des sons. En faisant de la référence sa matière première, son univers se déploie ainsi tel le palimpseste d'une mémoire associative qui confère à la vision qu'elle nous offre de la période pré-moderne une coloration parfois toute surréaliste, en provoquant des rencontres inédites : Villon, Marais, Couperin ; Cyrano, Rimbaud. En effet, Sollers ne fige pas la référence dans l'espace temporel qui lui est propre ; il la fait, comme nous l'avons vu avec la poésie de Villon et le récit fantastique de Cyrano, "traverser les siècles" de façon fantaisiste. Enfin, à travers la référence littéraire ou artistique, la prose sollertienne ne cesse de parler d'elle-même : fugues, contre-fugues, variations, comme le rappellent les incessantes références à Bach, elle est, comme le dit lui-même Sollers à la première personne dans *La Guerre du goût*, "un corps-plume. Rien d'autre que l'ouverture du présent et du passé et de tout le futur." (256).

NOTES

[1] Dans *Voir/Ecrire* (104), dialogue entre Christian de Portzamparc et Phillipe Sollers, ce dernier nous parle amusé de l'emploi qu'il fait de la poésie de Lautréamont sans donner aucune indication quant à la source de ses citations qui se fondent ainsi dans sa prose, incognito, et que les moins avertis, soit la majorité, croient être de son propre cru.

[2] Voir aussi les remarques de Léon S. Roudiez dans son analyse de *Nombres* sur l'utilisation de la citation par Sollers (363).

[3] Sollers, dans *Les Folies françaises*, cite à partir du *Petit Testament* (1456), du *Grand Testament* (1461) et des *Poésies diverses* figurant souvent dans les éditions modernes à la suite de ces deux premiers ouvrages.

[4] Nous ferons référence à ces deux textes à partir de l'édition (1977) de Jacques Prévot, intitulée *L'Autre monde*.

[5] Sur son concept de "corps intérieur", voir *Éloge*, 837.

[6] Katherine C. Kurk, à ce sujet, note que son prénom France est "all-encompassing, past and future, but consumedly the present: "Tu es ma fille et tu es ma langue" (56) " (136).

[7] Certaines de ces danses pourraient cependant être tout aussi un clin d'œil à l'œuvre du claveciniste et organiste, Louis Couperin (1626-1661), oncle de François...

[8] L'analyse que fait Jane H. Taylor de cette ballade est d'autant plus intéressante qu'elle définit la poétique villonienne en des termes qui correspondent parfaitement à la poétique sollertienne: "It is lexical exhibitionism that most characterises this ballade: the words emerge in a gleeful free-associative riff. Villon skips with what seems like limitless poetic versatility from verse to music […]" (83).

[9] Ici nous nous référons à ce commentaire de Sollers observant, sarcastique, ce qu'est devenu le rôle de l'écrivain : "Un écrivain, aujourd'hui, sait bien qu'il sera jugé de plus en plus sur sa "correction morale" et politique, comme s'il n'existait pas. Ce qu'on lui demande, en somme, est d'oublier ses livres" (*Éloge*, 374).

[10] Association exploitée plus loin dans le roman par le narrateur qui, tel un personnage des romans pastoraux (nous pensons à *L'Astrée*), "grave Cyrano sur le tronc d'un tulipier" (345).

[11] Dans *La Fête à Venise*, le narrateur vit une expérience similaire alors qu'il contemple la toile éponyme : "La planète tourne pour moi autour de ce pinceau, il s'est faufilé partout, c'est une pieuvre, un envahissement parachuté posthume, les villes n'ont plus d'existence que par ces improvisations placées en leur coeur, ces dimensions, ces sujets toujours les mêmes et jamais les mêmes" (140). Ainsi d'un roman à un autre, Sollers établit, fidèle à la tradition littéraire, un lien de parenté entre roman et peinture. De plus à travers les termes "plaisir", "gaieté" qui nous ramènent irrésistiblement par simple association au tout début du paragraphe où l'auteur parle de l'existence d' "un Dieu de l'écriture", d' "un Dieu silencieux" (103), l'on pourrait voir ici une référence à l'œuvre de Nietzsche, à laquelle Sollers fait aussi hommage.

[12] "Pour savoir écrire, a dit une fois Debord, il faut avoir lu, et pour savoir lire, il faut savoir vivre". (*Éloge*, 375).

Works Cited

Barthes, Roland. *Le Plaisir du texte*. Paris: Seuil, 1973.

Cusset, Catherine. "Philippe Sollers: après moi le déluge, ou le roman comme encyclopédie et arche de Noé". *Stanford French and Italian Studies* 80 (1992) : 187-94.

Cyrano de Bergerac, Savinien. *L'Autre monde*, in *Oeuvres Complètes*, édité par Jacques Prévot. Paris : Eugène Belin, 1977.

Fardeau, Patrice. " Sollers, un tigre et toutes ses dents". *Regards 47*, Juin 1999, http://www.regards.fr.archives11999/199906/199906cre04.html.

Fumaroli, Marc et Sollers, Philippe. " Literature between Past and Present : An Exchange". *Partisan Review*, 64 : 1 (1997) : 63-75. Traduit du français par Tess Lewis. " La littérature entre son présent et son passé : un échange", in *Le Débat* (March-April 1994).

Harth, Erica. *Cyrano de Bergerac and the Polemics of Modernity*. New York : Columbia University Press, 1970.

Kurk, Katherine C. " Philippe Sollers", in *The Contemporary Novel in France*, édité par William Thompson. Gainesville : University Press of Florida, 1995. 127-44.

Mortimer, Armine Kotin. " Philippe Sollers, Secret Agent". *Journal of Modern Literature*, 23 : 2 (Winter 1999-2000) : 309-27.

Portzamprac, Christian de; Sollers, Philippe. *Voir / Ecrire*. Paris : Calmann-Lévy, 2003.

Rimbaud, Arthur. *Oeuvres*, édité par Suzanne Bernard. Paris : Garnier, 1960.

Roudiez, Léon S. *French Fiction Today : A New Direction*. New Brunswick, NJ : Rutgers University Press, 1972.

Sollers, Philippe. *L'Écriture et l'expérience des limites*. Paris : Seuil, 1968.

———. *Portrait du joueur*. Paris : Gallimard, 1984.

———. *Les Folies françaises*. Paris : Gallimard, 1988.

———. *Le Lys d'or*. Paris : Gallimard, 1989.

———. *La Fête à Venise*. Paris : Gallimard, 1991.

———. *La Guerre du goût*. Paris : Gallimard, 1996.

———. *Passion Fixe*. Paris : Gallimard, 2000.

———. " Philippe Sollers: Contre la grande tyrannie". Propos recueillis par Jean-Jacques Brochier et Josyane Savigneau. *Magazine Littéraire* 285 (Février 1991) : 96-103.

———. *Éloge de l'infini*. Paris : Gallimard, 2001/2003.

———. *L'Étoile des amants*. Paris : Gallimard, 2002.

Taylor, Jane H. *The Poetry of François Villon*. Cambridge : Cambridge University Press, 2001.

Thompson, William (ed.). *The Contemporary Novel in France*. Gainesville : University Press of Florida, 1995.

Villon, François. *Poésies*, édité par Louis Thuasne. Paris : Auguste Picard, 1923.

———. *Poésies complètes*, édité par Claude Thiry. Paris : Lettres Gothiques, 1991.

Between Freedom and Memory: The Early Modern in Barthes's *Le Degré zéro de l'écriture*

Jeffrey N. Peters and Todd W. Reeser

In a little-discussed early essay titled "Plaisir aux Classiques" (1944), Roland Barthes stages his encounter with what he calls *les Classiques* as a love affair. This is not merely a sober form of intellectual admiration, but a passionate, even erotic courtship in which classical writers are cast, Echo to his Narcissus, as lovers. They shoot him with Cupid's arrow, they respond to *him*, they seek *him* out: "je me sens choisi; l'artiste me découvre; il me chante, il chante ma peine, ma joie, ma curiosité; il la chante bien; il en a tout vu, tout senti, et d'autres choses encore que je ne voyais ni ne sentais" (45). The objects of an infatuation, classical writers have seen everything, they know and have felt more than the enamored Barthes. If classical writers speak about "me," it is because their writing does not. The grammar of the classical text privileges the personal pronouns "ils" or "on," leaving open, at the site of the paradigmatic third person, a space for the reader's desire: "[p]lus le lecteur aura de passion, plus il se retrouvera dans les Classiques" (45). The reader is required by the mysterious "obscurity" and apparent indeterminacy of the classical text to find passion in the creation of meaning: "[l]es Classiques se sont offerts à nous avec un tel mépris de s'expliquer qu'ils nous laissent libres de tout leur supposer.... Enfermées dans les limites de la perfection, les oeuvres classiques sont...des trames, des ébauches, des espoirs où l'on peut indéfiniment ajouter" (47). The pleasure of *les Classiques* thus derives from a basic freedom to "love" the classical text, to submit it to "our" own hermeneutic desires, and to understand our present as a secret anticipated by our (classical) past.[1]

As he portrays it in "Plaisir aux Classiques," classical writing is the sign of a doubleness fundamental both to Barthes's conception of *écriture*, developed during the 1940s and published in book form in his 1953 *Le Degré zéro de l'écriture*, and to much of his subsequent thinking about the problem of *littérarité*. Because, in Barthes's early view, classical writers require their readers to participate in the creation of meaning, they offer their work to history as a possible site of individual freedom. Through the expression of their own desire, through the recognition of their own pleasure as constitutive of the text, readers are liberated from the constraints of meaning passively received. At the same time, Barthes suggests, classical writing is a constraint. It is necessarily remembered in the present as a point of origin that may be either assumed or rejected, but never forgotten, by a literary posterity whose parameters it inevitably defines. In fact, Barthes begins "Plaisir aux Classiques" by establishing a continuity between the modernist present and the classical past, citing links between Proust and Sévigné, Gide and Montaigne, Valéry and La Fontaine, and asserting that to emphasize classical writing exclusively or to ignore it defiantly is to misunderstand equally the nature of the literary in France.[2]

Barthes's description of classical writing in "Plaisir aux Classiques" as the simultaneous expression of a freedom and a constraint anticipates the principal terms through which he will soon after frame his crucial notion of *écriture*. In *Le Degré zéro de l'écriture*, Barthes defines *écriture* as a writer's "compromise" in matters of form between freedom and memory:

> Ainsi le choix, puis la responsabilité d'une écriture désignent une Liberté, mais...[i]l n'est pas donné à l'écrivain de choisir son écriture dans une sorte d'arsenal intemporel des formes littéraires. C'est sous la pression de l'Histoire et de la Tradition que s'établissent les écritures possibles....[A]u moment même où l'Histoire générale propose–ou impose–une nouvelle problématique du langage littéraire, l'écriture reste encore pleine du souvenir de ses usages antérieurs....L'écriture est précisément ce compromis entre une liberté et un souvenir. (148)

The concept of *écriture* defines a writer's critical relation to the institution of literature and to the question of *littérarité*, or the formal and ideologically marked qualities that make writing literary, as these are defined through (often unexamined) social agreement at a given moment in history. Unlike language in its grammatical sense ("langue") and style, both of which according to Barthes are "objects" prescribed by nature (147), *écriture* provides a writer the opportunity to choose the political and aesthetic position to be assumed with respect to the social institution of literature. But such a choice, Barthes emphasizes, is never really freely made. Even Camus's famous *écriture blanche*, which Barthes cites at the end of *Le Degré zéro de l'écriture* as one possible effort to reject all formal signs of literary tradition, is condemned to repeat the history of literature (179). The proposed lack of *écriture* in Camus's work is transformed by social ideology into an *écriture* of lack; it ends up reemphasizing the very notion of *écriture*, firmly established since the mid-seventeenth century, according to Barthes, through the elements that assert a formal perspective, even if it is a perspective of neutrality or absence.

In *Le Degré zéro de l'écriture*, Barthes returns time and again to what he calls "classicism" as the originary point of a literary-historical trajectory that emphasizes ruptures rather than continuities. Here, Barthes casts classicism as the aesthetic that literary modernism must oppose as it liberates itself from the confining instrumentality of the sign. Classical writing becomes an emblem of the collusion between literary practice and monolithic authority that emerges with the appearance of *écriture*. And yet, although it is rejected by a modernist and avant-garde literary tradition, which Barthes demonstrates to be the expression of a search for political freedom through aesthetic choice, classicism always returns in his discussion as the seminal term that gives, through its negation, coherent meaning to any literary history of France. Its rejection liberates even as its persistence in memory constrains.

What is less clear, however, and what is, we believe, in need of scrutiny, is the theoretical move that transforms "les Classiques," broadly construed, into a narrowly, and often stereotypically, defined "Classicism" between the 1944 essay and *Le Degré zéro de l'écriture*.[3] In "Plaisir aux Classiques," Barthes's discussion of a "Littérature Classique" appears to correspond in historical terms to what we might today call the "early modern" period.[4] In 1947, however, Barthes published an article titled "Responsabilité de la grammaire" in the journal *Combat* that responded to critics of his earlier 1947 article "Qu'est-ce que l'écriture?" (which later became the first chapter of *Le Degré zéro de l'écriture*).[5] Here, the emergence of a "high" classical period corresponds both to the invention of *écriture* and to the division of literary history into two discrete early modern periods: the classical and what Barthes calls the preclassical, defined as everything preceding the appearance of *écriture* in 1660. Working through Vaugelas, Barthes argues that between 1647 and 1660, the date commonly cited as the beginning of a specifically classical era in France, the linguistic value of *clarté* was defined only as a quality of speech at court. After 1660, however, this value based on the usage of the few was justified on new grounds: "la clarté, qui dix ans auparavant n'était que l'usage avoué du plus fort, se pose comme universelle: la Grammaire de Port-Royal justifie les règles non plus par l'usage mais par l'accord logique entre la règle et les exigences de l'esprit" ("Responsabilité," 96). In Barthes's view, a universal language creates the conditions necessary for the appearance of *écriture* wherein literary usage expresses uncritically the ideological values of absolute monarchy. Simultaneous to this development is the disappearance of the preclassical. Literary history, for Barthes, now begins with classical writing, restrictively defined as that writing which signals its alliance with absolutist, and, later, bourgeois, culture. Preclassical writing, often described as multiple and socially various, becomes, in Barthes's history, that which is rejected with the invention of *écriture*. It no longer has a role in the history of modernism, which Barthes will define as a product of the rejection of a purely classical unity.

Given Barthes's preoccupation with what he would later call the obsessive "classico-centrisme" of French literary history, it makes sense to ask why his own definition of *écriture* so often depends upon classicism as a descriptor of historical and theoretical divisions, repetitions, and oppositions.[6] In other words, it would appear that even as he develops in *Le Degré zéro de l'écriture* a theory of specifically modernist writing which depends upon the nineteenth-century rejection of classical aesthetics, Barthes is himself seduced by the persistent memory of an apparently unitary classicism. If classicism functions for Barthes as the sign of the freedom available through the problematic of *écriture*, as that which allows the modern writer's potential liberation through its negation, it also signifies as the point of origin for the concept of *écriture* itself. In this essay, we explore the "early modern" in Barthes's presentation of French literary history in *Le Degré zéro de l'écriture* and suggest that the theory of *écriture* depends upon the construction, and thus recurrent memory, of a classicism that may only be rejected by modernism once it has itself harnessed and rejected a preclassical "lack" invented at the moment of its own foundation. Modernism is thus founded not only upon an opposition to a classical past, but upon a division within the "early modern" that prefigures the modernist oscillation between freedom and memory.

CLASSICISM AND THE ORIGINS OF THE MODERN

Although the extent to which Barthes was responding directly to Sartre's 1948 *Qu'est-ce que la littérature?* in the early essays that would become *Le Degré zéro de l'écriture* is not entirely clear,[7] there can be no doubt that the historical orientation and primary theoretical preoccupations of Barthes's 1953 work owe much to Sartre's example, as well as to that of Marx.[8] In addition to being a confirmed "Sartrian" in this period of his intellectual development, Barthes appears to have been interested in the possibility of tracing a literary history that retained the basic chronological design of Sartre's book while at the same time challenging Sartre's definition of literature, as well as his discussion of its social utility and potential for being deployed in an engaged politics. In fact, Barthes's adherence to a fairly conventional notion of periodization found in Sartre is of particular interest in the present context given the originality of his overall approach to an ideological analysis of the institution of literature. In a chapter from *Qu'est-ce que la littérature?* called "Pour qui écrit-on?," Sartre lays out a history of literature that begins with a brief look at medieval writing in the twelfth century. Moving through the centuries, from the seventeenth to the twentieth (though with almost no attention given to the Renaissance), Sartre argues that literature represents over time humanity's emancipation from the ruling classes. Literature, in fact, has always been fundamentally about freedom, even in the seventeenth century where the emancipatory potential of literary practice was veiled from authors who were blinded by the power which their work merely reinforced.[9] For Sartre, literature *is* the discovery of a potential freedom:

> s'il est vrai que l'essence de l'oeuvre littéraire, c'est la liberté se découvrant et se voulant totalement elle-même comme appel à la liberté des autres hommes, il est vrai aussi que les différentes formes de l'oppression, en cachant aux hommes qu'ils étaient libres, ont masqué aux auteurs tout ou partie de cette essence.

(155)

As it will for Barthes in *Le Degré zéro de l'écriture*, the year 1850 constitutes for Sartre a turning point in the literary history of freedom because by the mid-nineteenth century "men" can no longer ignore the nature of their subjection, and literature can no longer serve simply as the instrument of communication through which a writer must uphold social values of the state (125). Literature may only ever be an expression of alienation, in Sartre's view, until it becomes aware of its own autonomy, until, having passed through the rationalist experiments of the *philosophes* in the eighteenth century and the rise of industry in the nineteenth, its self-reflexive nature signals its opposition to the values of bourgeois ideology.[10]

Although, for Sartre, literature liberates once it becomes self-reflexive, once it functions as an end rather than merely as a means, it is precisely the issue of form that constitutes for Barthes a major area of disagreement with Sartre and the starting point of his own theoretical project. Predictably, Sartre is specifically interested in the historical conditions surrounding the relations of writers and society: whom does, and should, a writer address? How can writing operate as a political act? But if writers become, in Sartre's view, conscious of their own freedom through the practice of writing, they are always dependent on a conceptualization of language as instrumental. As Sartre describes it, words are not, at least as used in prose, themselves objects. Rather, they communicate objects in the world transparently.[11] As such, an engaged use of literature is one in which language functions to reveal to readers the world as it is.[12] Barthes's initial insight in *Le Degré zéro de l'écriture* is to suggest almost precisely the opposite: if literature can be said to have an explicitly political function, it is because writers have recourse not to, in Susan Sontag's words, a Sartrian "morality of ends" (xix), but because they are specifically engaged with, as Barthes defines it, "la morale de la forme" (147-48).[13] Whether attention to such formal preoccupations on the part of a writer can ever constitute real political engagement must necessarily be a matter of some debate,[14] but Barthes clearly believed that, at least as a politically "utopian" project, it could.[15] Moreover, Barthes's most fundamental difference with Sartre is located precisely in the issue of language and form. If Sartre believed that literature could express the progressive awakening of humanity to its own freedom, Barthes argued that the specific issue of literary form was the site of the writer's inevitable subjection. Barthes thereby suspended the problem of form between the poles of freedom and memory. Like Sartre, Barthes believed that an engagement with the problematics of form could express the possibility of an ideological freedom, but only insofar as any freedom defined through a choice of *écriture* was constrained by the memory held within the institution of *littérarité* itself.[16]

In light of the critical scrutiny that he would apply to the notion of literature throughout his career, it is striking that Barthes should maintain in *Le Degré zéro de l'écriture*, at least upon first glance, the positivist model of literary history that French tradition had inherited from Gustave Lanson.[17] In "Réflexions sur un manuel" (1971), his statement on literary history as it is portrayed in school anthologies, Barthes describes what he calls "[les] monèmes de la langue méta-littéraire," the language of literary history that is defined by authors, schools, movements, genres, and centuries, each exemplified by aesthetic characteristics representative of the period (1241-42). This conception of history as defined by divisions and oppositions is directly related in Barthes's thinking to what he calls the censure of literature, or the notion that literature is not open to ontological challenge. The purpose of *Le Degré zéro de l'écriture* is largely different from that of "Réflexions sur un manuel," and yet, the preliminary theoretical principles that will found Barthes's later thinking are already firmly in place. It is notable, then, that even as he radically questions the classifications that constitute a mythology of the literary institution, Barthes continues to have recourse to a basic classicism-to-modernism dichotomy. In fact, Barthes's concern is not to challenge an ultimately Hegelian version of history. It is instead to change the object of historical analysis from the style and content of literary writing to "[les] Signes de la Littérature," or the relation between writing and society that gives social meaning to writing as specifically literary. The myth of literature—as that which always already exists unproblematically—tends in fact to take literature *out* of history, to make it essential and transcendent.[18] But as Barthes writes, "c'est là où l'Histoire est refusée qu'elle agit le plus clairement" (139).

Most significant for our specific purpose is the importance that the problem of classicism assumes for Barthes in his theoretical interrogation of the signs of literature. In an opening passage of the introduction to *Le Degré zéro de l'écriture* that clearly signals the common polemical ground he shared with Sartre, Barthes sets forth the initial elements of the chronology that will govern his discussion:

> On verra, par exemple, que l'unité idéologique de la bourgeoisie a produit une écriture unique, et qu'aux temps bourgeois (c'est-à-dire classiques et romantiques), la forme ne pouvait être déchirée puisque la conscience ne l'était pas; et qu'au contraire, dès l'instant où l'écrivain a cessé d'être un témoin de l'universel pour devenir une conscience malheureuse (vers 1850), son premier geste a été de choisir l'engagement de sa forme, soit en assumant, soit en refusant l'écriture de son passé. L'écriture classique a donc éclaté et la Littérature entière, de Flaubert à nos jours, est devenue une problématique du langage. (139-40)

Here, as in Sartre's *Qu'est-ce que la littérature?*, humanity becomes aware of its social and political alienation in the mid-nineteenth century, choosing an *engagement* of form as its expression. The notion of *écriture* becomes the primary term through which literary history must be understood in its diachrony: "[p]artie d'un néant où la pensée semblait s'enlever heureusement sur le décor des mots, l'écriture a ainsi traversé tous les états d'une solidification progressive: d'abord objet d'un regard, puis d'un faire, et enfin d'un meurtre, elle atteint aujourd'hui un dernier avatar, l'absence" (140). The writer chooses an engagement with form when he or she comes to recognize the ideological bonds that tie subjectivity to history through the practice of art. Like Sartre, Barthes cites 1850 as a convenient year to mark the birth of capitalism and the division of bourgeois society into distinct classes, as the historical moment when *écriture* is exploded, multiplied until the aesthetic decisions made by writers take on the characteristics of choice. For Barthes, each *écriture* becomes the sign of a political act through which writers assume or reject their bourgeois condition.[19]

But this engagement depends entirely on the construction of a version of classicism whose highly specific nature in Barthes's theory allows for the ruptures that will come during the nineteenth century. A number of qualities predominate in Barthes's portrayal of classicism: unity, transparency, economy, neutrality, superficiality (in its etymological sense), horizontality, and instrumentality. These notions are employed by Barthes primarily to distinguish between *langue* and *écriture*. In "Qu'est-ce que l'écriture?," Barthes explains that writing (*écriture*) is not language (*langue*). This is an important distinction because *langue* can never be the site of a choice, and thus of a possible engagement, for a writer. Rather it is a form of nature, a host of habits and requirements that resemble, in Barthes's metaphorical language, the sky and the earth, a horizon of intelligibility which a writer cannot escape: "[n]ul ne peut, sans apprêts, insérer sa liberté d'écrivain dans l'opacité de la langue, parce qu'à travers elle c'est l'Histoire entière qui se tient, complète et unie à la manière d'une Nature" (145).[20] By contrast, *écriture* is the product of a relation between artistic creation and society, an explicit reflection by a writer on the social intention of his or her formal decisions. *Ecriture* must thus be located within *parole* (which Barthes often seems to conflate with *langage*, as distinct from *langue*), the individualized use of a certain language whose *ethos* derives from a critical perspective on the institution of literature and its social value and meaning. Writing after 1850, the artist engages with the problem of the literary institution either by multiplying within language the signs of literature, the various forms of which Barthes chronicles throughout *Le Degré zéro de l'écriture* (Flaubert is exemplary here), or by inventing, or more radically disinventing, a language that redefines literature as impossible (Barthes emphasizes Mallarmé in this context).

Barthes's ultimately highly teleological history of *écriture* therefore requires a point of origin where *écriture* is invented as a form of singularity with respect to the social institution of literature, which can in turn be dismantled by the multiple *écritures* of modernity. Barthes situates this originary moment in 1650 (ten years earlier than in "Responsabilité de la grammaire") when language took a form that allowed the foundation of an initial moment of *écriture* and that consecrated literature as a unified expression of the social.[21] After 1650, according to Barthes, writers were no longer able to reflect upon the nature of language (*langue*) in its capacity to investigate and reveal the world. Thereafter they were caught within a history of language from which they could not escape and which they could not challenge because the only possible *use* of language (*parole*) was kept within the boundaries of a history established as a universal *value* of the emergent absolutist monarchy: *écriture* as the relation that holds between language—understood as universal history—and "une idéologie triomphante" (180). If *écriture* is the sign of a social pact, classical *écriture* can only ever be its confirmation because, as Barthes describes it, there is no possible use of language that is not the unified expression of either a restricted social environment (the court) or an ideology of universality.[22] Literary language is thus indistinguishable from any acceptable form of social discourse; one can only be the confirmation of the other. It is not until the nineteenth century, when Victor Hugo first applied pressure to the *alexandrin* by endowing the relational design of verse with, in Barthes's terms, a density of the word (163), that literature becomes recognizable as a problematic of *écriture* which either justifies or destroys itself through a use of language and which engages with the problem of *littérarité*. Classical art, writes Barthes, "ne pouvait se sentir comme un langage, il était langage, c'est-à-dire transparence, circulation sans dépôt, concours idéal d'un Esprit universel et d'un signe décoratif sans épaisseur et sans responsabilité" (140).

Once language (*langue*) becomes inserted into history as a kind of nature, as Barthes suggests it was with the invention of classicism in the mid-seventeenth century, *écriture* also comes into existence as the expression of the writer's engagement with its form. But the specific purposes for which language is put to use in the classical period, according to Barthes, are never threatening to the nature of language in any way that would challenge its relation to the social institution of universality as this is described in literary practice. Language use as of 1650, Barthes writes, is only ever superficial and neutral. The priority of rhetoric in this period is merely testament to the "decorative" function of poetic language: "[t]oute poésie n'est alors que l'équation décorative, allusive ou chargée, d'une prose virtuelle qui gît en essence et en puissance dans n'importe quelle façon de s'exprimer" (161). Unlike modern writing, in which words can become their own nature and can create their own identity as substance, classical language is a kind of translucent layer spread over the body of thought. Words are not the site of invention or creation where thought is progressively embodied in poetic procedure. Rather, they are the neutral, instrumental, and superficial expression of thinking that is pre-formed: classical words "ne reproduisent pas comme plus tard, par une sorte de hauteur violente et inattendue, la profondeur et la singularité d'une expérience; ils sont aménagés en surface, selon les exigences d'une économie élégante ou décorative" (163).

By virtue of its primarily metonymic character, as well as its fundamentally relational function, classical language use does not fulfill the conditions necessary for the appearance of an *écriture* capable of challenging the nature of *langue* and the basic social and literary values that it expresses. Barthes's early modern is thus limited to a form of classicism that made possible the differentiating revolutions of modernism through a definition that emphasized traditional notions of clarity and universality. This curious return to "classicism" throughout *Le Degré zéro de l'écriture*, a work which insists precisely upon the ideological construction of literary periods and traditions, appears to suggest that the "early modern" anachronistically implied in the 1944 term "les Classiques" was too indistinct a period to serve as a proper foil for the modernism that lies at the heart of Barthes's essay. As we will see, the brief invention and rejection of the preclassical that opens Barthes's history of writing in the chapter "Triomphe et rupture de l'écriture bourgeoise" fixes the classical into place and in turn enables the renunciations characteristic of modernism.[23]

Uses of the Preclassical

In "Réflexions sur un manuel," Barthes notes that in the positivist—and "classico-centric"—model of French literary history, what comes before classicism necessarily foresees it: "Ce qui est avant le classicisme annonce le classicisme—Montaigne est un précurseur des classiques" (1244). Similarly, what follows classicism cannot avoid an association with its aesthetic principles and is forced to respond to it in some way, even if only to reject it: "ce qui vient après le récupère ou l'abandonne" (1244). Barthes's rehearsal of the stereotype according to which the preclassical "announces" classicism as a kind of literary John the Baptist serves as a critique of traditional French literary histories that do not study preclassical periods on their own terms. But, surprisingly, this approach to "la Littérature préclassique" (169) may also be found to inform Barthes's own discussion of the period in *Le Degré zéro de l'écriture*. Although classicism generally functions as a stable point of origin for modernism, Barthes opens his history of writing (Part II of the text) with a description of the preclassical. But the opening of his history of writing in no way substitutes the preclassical for classicism as point of origin in his trajectory. In fact, it focuses on discounting the possibility that the preclassical is anything but a "precursor" to classicism. Barthes does not focus on how elements of classicism are already present in the preclassical, as he believes a traditional literary history might do. Instead, the preclassical is employed as classicism's foil–not only because of its non-classical characteristics, which are emphasized, but also because it does not belong in Barthes's classical-to-modern trajectory in the first place. As we will see, then, the disappearance of the preclassical from Barthes's literary history "announces" classicism's presence through its negation.

Although Barthes appears to isolate the preclassical as a point of origin for his history of writing, the main point of the brief section (169-70) is not to consider the specificity of the period's relation to *écriture*, but to evoke and then remove it from any association with his history. The central issue is the perceived plurality of the period: "Il y a, dans la Littérature préclassique, l'apparence d'une pluralité des écritures; mais cette variété semble bien moins grande si l'on pose ces problèmes de langage en termes de structure, et non plus en termes d'art" (169). Barthes's opening sentence appears to be a response to a traditional view of the preclassical as a period defined by a plurality of "art"—a term he does not explain, but which suggests a linguistic *copia*, presumably including the proliferation of genres (e.g. essay, *nouvelle*, sonnet, novel, drama, pastoral) and a variety of linguistic styles (e.g. Rabelais's multilingualism, Montaigne's bilingualism, Corneille's *préciosité*). But whatever Barthes means here by "art," the main characteristic ascribed to the period is its freedom, a manifestation of the traditionally assumed *volonté* of the preclassical (and especially Renaissance) writer. By discounting the period 1500-1650 from his discussion, Barthes transforms the preclassical into classicism's absent other. The central issue for Barthes is that when language is described in terms of "structure," language in the grammatical sense (*langue* as opposed to *langage*) does not exist in the preclassical. The period before 1650 gives the modernist reader "l'impression de variété" since "la langue paraît encore essayer des structures instables" and "elle n'a pas fixé définitivement l'esprit de sa syntaxe et les lois d'accroissement de son vocabulaire" (169). As a result, Barthes's notion of *écriture*, dependent on a certain stable notion of *langue*, cannot apply to the preclassical period. If language is "un corps de prescriptions et d'habitudes, commun à tous les écrivains d'une époque" (145), the preclassical is a kind of bodyless mass. Since writing is held between freedom and remembrance, and since *langue* is the central aspect of remembrance (and sometimes synonymous with it), the preclassical threatens the formal principles of his historical project by risking a collapse into freedom. Perhaps more importantly, however, the non-existence of *langue* also suggests that class, its close correlate, is also absent and in this sense implies a view of the preclassical as a society in which class ideology has not yet formed.

As this view implies, class ideology—one of the central aspects of Barthes's history of writing—bears significantly on the exclusion of the preclassical. The only discussion of the preclassical in *Le Degré zéro de l'écriture* is found in the first section of Part II. Ostensibly the most historical section of the work, the chapter traces Barthes's trajectory of writing from the preclassical to "la modernité." Because there is no "class" per se in "the preclassical," at least not in Barthes's history, it is impossible to fit any discussion of the period into the chapter. If class, or at least the bourgeoisie, has not yet come to hegemony, then in Barthes's schema there can as of yet be no constraints on writing. The title of the chapter itself ("Triomphe et rupture de l'écriture bourgeoise") already positions the discussion of the preclassical in a classed context, even though Barthes does not enter into a detailed discussion of class itself in this chapter. If "[c]ette écriture classique est évidemment une écriture de classe" (170), the non-writing of the preclassical is defined as the anti-classed text and, from there, the preclassical text easily falls into the implied category of the ideologically free text, outside the constraints that arise only in a bourgeois-centered classicism.

Barthes's depiction of the preclassical is largely related to his implicit and explicit response to the construction of this crucial period in previous histories. Barthes might need classicism as his origin, but the preclassical—or at least the Renaissance—was the standard originary moment of Lansonian French literary history. In his essay "La Méthode de l'histoire littéraire" (1910), for example, Lanson remarks, "[s]i mes réflexions regardent principalement la littérature française depuis la Renaissance, c'est que je la connais mieux et j'y pense constamment" (31).[24] In his "Avertissement" to his book on Montaigne, Lanson describes one of the objects of his introduction: "atténuer la difficulté de la première rencontre, qui résulte autant de la liberté d'allure de l'écrivain" (7). Because he is working within a rubric of a national history of signs in which the Renaissance cannot "remember" the ancients and in which plurality is not yet a viable option for a trajectory that ends in the plurality of modernism, Barthes will avoid considering the Renaissance, and by extension the preclassical, as a period whose multiplicity could serve as an origin.

Also pertinent in this regard is Sartre's view of the preclassical in *Qu'est-ce que la littérature*? In the chapter "Pour qui écrit-on?," Sartre comments on the move from the dominance of a medieval Church ideology (and thus of an ecclesiastical reading public that destroys the writer's freedom) to a secular ideology in the seventeenth century, which asserts an attempted control over writing. Working within the traditional century-divisions of French literary history, Sartre comments on this shift from one kind of ideology to another: "A cette époque la laïcisation de l'écrivain et de son public est en voie d'achèvement. Elle a certainement pour origine la force expansive de la chose écrite, son caractère monumental et l'appel à la liberté que recèle toute oeuvre de l'esprit" (111). Although Sartre does not incorporate the Renaissance per se in his discussion, the lacuna in his version of literary history implies the presence of the period and, consequently, removes the possibility that it might correspond to his existential theoretical apparatus. The "force expansive de la chose écrite" would seem to refer to the printing press and to the proliferation of the physical book, and the "appel à la liberté" to preclassical texts. Rabelais's linguistic freedom and freedom from the constraints of ideology in the Bakhtinian mode, for instance, might come to mind as one aspect of the question.[25]

Sartre thus reduces the Renaissance to a period of increasing secularization, a literary bridge that destroys the ideology of the Middle Ages and enables the appearance of an ideology specific to the seventeenth century. The shift in ideology corresponds to a shift in the reading public, transforming how and for whom the writer writes but nonetheless still restraining the writer's freedom. The very absence of a Renaissance in Sartre's literary history, however, implies its presence as a possible contrast to the two periods that surround it. The Renaissance was not a period in which the writer was the protector of a literary ideology or a definition of the writer that, for Sartre, defined the previous and following periods as periods of stasis.[26] The sixteenth century, then, poses a problem for this simplified trajectory of French literary history since for Sartre it does not correspond to an approach in which the writer is imbued with class ideology, and in which some kind of clear ideology (e.g., of the Church or monarchy) can fully define how one writes. The Renaissance would appear to be construed in Sartre's schema as the missing exception that confirms the rule, a pause in a premodern literary trajectory in which the writer is not guilty of a kind of literary bad faith that would cause one to write for a given audience and thus to give up any claim to existential freedom.

For Barthes, however, whatever freedom is attributed to this period is not freedom at all. Preclassical writing might *look* free, might resemble the pedagogical stereotype of the sixteenth century, which he terms "la vie débordante" (1242) in "Réflexions sur un manuel," but it is only so for those (like Sartre) who do not situate the institution of writing itself at the center of their analysis. Without an ethic of writing, the preclassical writer cannot consciously "engage" in language. As a result, what looks like freedom is in fact something else: it is the writer "engaged" in knowing Nature:

> à ce titre l'écriture encyclopédique de Rabelais, ou l'écriture précieuse de Corneille—pour ne donner que des moments typiques—ont pour forme commune un langage où l'ornement n'est pas encore rituel, mais constitue en soi un procédé d'investigation appliqué à toute l'étendue du monde. C'est ce qui donne à cette écriture préclassique l'allure même de la nuance et l'euphorie d'une liberté. (169)

Barthes's choice of "langage" to refer to preclassical discourse here suggests an attempt to reduce the freedom ascribed to the period. Even before invoking again his distinction between *langue* and *écriture*, Barthes describes the period as composed of "langages": "Esthétiquement, le XVIe siècle et le début du XVIIe siècle montrent un foisonnement assez libre des langages littéraires" (169). Since his style/language/writing triad does not apply to the period, one might expect Barthes to use the term "parole" here to designate an individual act of textual *volonté* for this period, with *parole* serving as a term often conceived of as about free expression and thus potentially implying the very freedom that Barthes rejects. The use of "langage" here, then, implies the restraint that Barthes will impose on preclassical freedom by applying his *écriture/langue* dichotomy and by discarding what appears to be the period's "euphorie de la liberté." Instead, as we will see, it is modernism that will play the role of euphoric text.

If *langue* is the world that one sees, "un horizon, c'est-à-dire à la fois une limite et une station" (145), it does not then equal the world, but rather examines the world. Like Foucault's Renaissance man in *Les Mots et les choses*, Barthes's preclassical writer seeks to explore and understand the cosmos, writing the world rather than actually inhabiting it.[27] It is classicism, however, that corresponds to the theoretical and poetic world of *Le Degré zéro de l'écriture*, as represented in part by the use of geometric metaphors. The initial articulation of style and language in Barthes's discussion of writing graphs itself around horizontal and vertical axes, a volumetric space in which writing is mapped: "L'horizon de la langue et la verticalité du style dessinent donc pour l'écrivain une nature" (147).[28] Since "l'écriture est une fonction" (147), it is mapped onto the grid composed of *langue* and *style*. The writer who links "la forme à la fois normale et singulière de sa parole à la vaste Histoire d'autrui" (147) in effect graphs his or her own text. These images correspond to comparisons of classical language to mathematics. After describing the relational nature of the economy of classical language, Barthes proposes the following: "Un regard sur le langage mathématique permettra peut-être de comprendre la nature relationnelle de la prose et de la poésie classiques" (162). And when discussing the differences between prose and poetry, Barthes evokes what he calls the "double équation de M. Jourdain" in Molière (Poésie = Prose + a + b + c // Prose = Poésie – a – b – c [161]). Graphing a function aptly represents Barthes's notion of classical writing as caught between freedom and memory. On the one hand, the writer has the freedom to graph a function as he or she sees fit, but, on the other hand, the very act of graphing is already predetermined by the possibilities of a (historical) grid.[29]

As its exclusion in Barthes's discussion suggests, the preclassical serves no direct purpose except to perform its own erasure as a founding gesture of classicism's unity. If, as we have seen, its erasure is carried out by virtue of its position exterior to *écriture*, the preclassical is also situated outside the freedom/memory dyad that defines writing for Barthes. Consequently, whereas the memory of classicism is central to how modernist writing defines itself, the preclassical simply cannot be remembered by classicism. When Barthes moves from the preclassical to the classical, he sees only rupture and difference: "Sans doute les écrivains classiques ont-ils connu, eux aussi, une problématique de la forme, mais le débat ne portait nullement sur la variété et le sens des écritures, encore moins sur la structure du langage" (170). The characteristics of the previous period are completely erased as "seule la rhétorique" takes over as object of debate. In the same way that Barthes dispels "artistic" languages representative of freedom in his version of the preclassical, he dispels "[l]a diversité des 'genres' et le mouvement des styles à l'intérieur du dogme classique" as "des données esthétiques, non de structure" (169). This holdover, this possible memory of preclassical plurality "within" ("à l'intérieur") classical dogma, has to be written out in favor of "une écriture unique." But it also has the effect of expunging the potential for a preclassical memory within classicism, thereby preserving classicism as an embodiment of memory. If the modernist writer can read the classical writer, the classical writer cannot engage the preclassical writer. In Barthes's schema, Proust can have a textual relation with Sévigné, but Pascal cannot read or "remember" Montaigne. By expelling the preclassical, by casting memory as stable and univocal, Barthes constructs a classicism of remembrance which prepares, subsequently, a remembrance of classicism.

THEORY AS PERFORMANCE

One of the signal ironies of Raymond Picard's 1965 critique of *Sur Racine* (1963) is that it accuses Barthes, a writer who described his own relation to literature as a relation of passionate reverence, of cold-heartedness and irreverence.[30] The entirety of *Critique et vérité* (1966), Barthes's response to Picard's book, is a paean to literature not without similarities in tone to the 1944 "Plaisir aux Classiques." Barthes responds here to Picard by suggesting that if one is going to take literature seriously, one must recognize that literary texts open themselves to the probing desire of the reader.[31] But Picard's comment, intended to be derisive, that Barthes's method in *Sur Racine* amounts to "une sorte de critique métaphorique" which "n'est d'ailleurs pas dépourvu d'un certain charme poétique" (25, 76) in fact locates a crucial dimension of Barthes's thinking. We would propose that *Le Degré zéro de l'écriture* exemplifies in an inchoate state Barthes's claim, increasingly explicit throughout his career, that literary criticism is finally, itself, a form of poetic *écriture* wherein critical endeavor becomes dramatic narrative.[32] In *Le Degré zéro de l'écriture*, the presentation of literary history is transformed into a tragedy of form in which both the preclassical and the classical are, in different ways, forgotten and remembered, killed off and resurrected in what becomes for Barthes a play of passion.[33] We suggest that the ultimately poetic nature of *Le Degré zéro de l'écriture* is Barthes's response to a theoretical and historical impasse achieved at the end of the essay. If *écriture* was destined to remain suspended between freedom and memory, even after the experiments of the avant-garde, as Barthes suggests, the only critical response that did not merely proclaim the failure of literature to have political import had to be a kind of dramatic essay. *Le Degré zéro de l'écriture* concludes with a discussion of the necessarily utopian nature of language which is itself a utopia of language. Barthes's essay, in the end, is a form of (critical) poetry.

We have already seen how Barthes's own writing forgets the preclassical even as it organizes a theoretical history around its absence, in a sense killing it off and then letting its ghost (but not its "memory") haunt the modern. For even as the preclassical is written out of literary history, modernism is shown, in the final section of "Triomphe et rupture de l'écriture bourgeoise," to resemble its aesthetic principles. In this way the preclassical and modernism function as bookends to this key chapter of Barthes's text. Picard's notion of a "metaphorical" criticism appears particularly appropriate here since Barthes implies that the preclassical is a kind of modernism *avant la lettre*. Specifically, plurality returns, in a different guise, around 1850, although this time within the history of *écriture*.[34] In the passion play that is his history, the multiplication of modernist writing is reborn as it returns to an absent period.

In this way, modernism gestures toward (but does not fully effect) a remembrance of the preclassical. Barthes's suggestion that "une mémoire seconde . . . se prolonge mystérieusement au milieu des significations nouvelles" (148) appears particularly important in this context where the multiple *écritures* of modernism necessarily remember the past, even a past that is cast as absent. Barthes's main interest, of course, is how modernism "remembers" classicism, how it is its "prisoner" (148), caught in the "tragedy" of classicism. If, as he writes in "Responsabilité de la grammaire," "[l]e problème pour les écrivains d'aujourd'hui, c'est donc de couper l'écriture dès ses origines historiques, c'est-à-dire, en fait, politiques" (80), the rejection of classicism, the "origine" par excellence, would suggest that the preclassical is not implicated in this break, ironically allowing for the possibility that modernism has the option of returning to its preorigins and imitating some version of its plurality. In this way, then, the preclassical becomes a second-order memory of modernist writing. It is that which should constrain, but which turns out instead to be potentially liberating since the primary elements of the preclassical, initially cited by Barthes to erase them, return transformed. Barthes remarks that "on sait que tout l'effort de Mallarmé a porté sur une destruction du langage, dont la Littérature ne serait en quelque sorte que le cadavre" (140). But to destroy language is, on one level, to return to an unstable prelife. Chateaubriand's writing might reveal "le poids léger d'une euphorie du langage, une sorte de narcissisme où l'écriture se sépare à peine de sa fonction instrumentale et ne fait que se regarder elle-même" (140), but one might say the same thing of the auto-reflexive and explosive language(s) of Rabelais. This remembrance, or, more properly, "de-forgetting," of the preclassical is one way in which Barthes's criticism is indeed "metaphorical," to use Picard's word, for the rejected literary period ends up implicitly resembling the modern.

Several of the formal characteristics that Barthes assigns to the preclassical often seem to describe *Le Degré zéro de l'écriture* itself. As Réda Bensmaïa has suggested, the later Barthes is in the process of becoming another Montaigne, of reformulating a genre–the essay–defined by narrative engagement with other texts.[35] But it is precisely the near-absence of Montaigne from Barthes's work–here and elsewhere–that is as significant as any similarity that might be discovered between the founder and the rewriter of the *essai*. It is striking that Barthes only occasionally mentions Montaigne; that he wrote nothing devoted to a precursor with whose writing practice he had much in common; and that he does not directly acknowledge his influence. But as he later states in a 1964 interview ("Je ne crois pas aux influences"), Barthes does not believe in "influences" or in the transmission of ideas, but rather in the transmission of "'langages', c'est-à-dire des formes que l'on peut remplir différemment" (1451). Montaigne's "form" – in this case a performative, poetic approach to the essay genre, an "essai sans la dissertation," as Barthes calls one category of the *texte scriptible* in *S/Z* (11)–may be what is passed on, but only as a form to be filled in, not to be written about. Montaigne's *Essais* do not "influence" Barthes, for whom "la notion de circulation" is a more appropriate term than "influence," but they instead function as what he calls "monnaies," unstable and unpredictable elements of writing opposed to stronger and more stable "forces" (1451). Borrowing his image, we could say that Barthes repeatedly acquires and spends Montaigne, but that he cannot save him long enough to write about him.[36]

For it is the dramatic death and return of classicism that exemplify the critical drama of *Le Degré zéro de l'écriture*. What begins as a theoretical history of French writing becomes, as a poetic spectacle performing in its procedure the very conclusion of the text, an attempt to save, through what to Picard would look like destruction, the literature he loves–the *idea* of literature, whose real challenges to the reader, as Barthes explains in *Critique et vérité*, he sought to accept and explore and whose ideological monumentality he was not interested in defending. With the "éclatement de l'écriture française" (148-49) that Barthes identifies in the mid-nineteenth century comes the Sartrian *prise de conscience* of both the entailment of *écriture* in bourgeois ideology and the potential power of literary writing to resist its social reach. Writers who, during classicism, could not choose among historically possible *écritures* because language was fully implicated in the authority of monarchy, or who, after 1850, were required to justify literature by making it the product of work (Flaubert) found themselves at an impasse of *écriture* in the late nineteenth century. If *écriture* is, as Barthes writes, a "morale de la forme," it is because the writer under capitalism is forced to realize that, unlike in Sartre's discussion, writing is never freely undertaken. There is of course an important element of choice in *écriture* that is not available to the writer in matters of language and style, as we have seen, but even at the level of *écriture*, the writer is held in a position of tension between creative freedom and the memory of a confining past. The recognition of the historicity of *écriture* reveals not merely the writer's potential freedom, as Sartre would have it, but the impossibility of getting outside of the ideological bonds of literature without renouncing it.

For Barthes, the representative figure is Rimbaud. The institution of literature, with its conventions and requirements, was unacceptable to Rimbaud; so too was the choice of an original form of writerly practice that would itself become an entrenched form of *écriture*, with all of its links to social acceptability. The only possible response for Rimbaud, as articulated in his poem "Adieu," is the abandonment of literature altogether (the product of Rimbaud's work is, in Barthes's words, a "silence de l'écriture"). For Barthes, ultimately a profound lover of the literary word, Rimbaud's response was itself unacceptable. *Le Degré zéro de l'écriture* is an effort to push beyond Rimbaud, and the impasse of *écriture*, to locate a form of literary art that would be simultaneously aware of the social and ideological constraints of *écriture*, and sufficiently subversive of literary convention to signal a real liberation from bourgeois ideology.[37] Mallarmé points the way here, through what Blanchot has called the "regard d'Orphée" whereby the writer saves what he or she loves by renouncing it.[38] Mallarmé, Barthes writes, uses silence and empty space graphically in order to liberate language from its social entrapment. They make words, when they appear, explode, "moins comme le lambeau d'un cryptogramme que comme une lumière, un vide, un meurtre, une liberté" (179). Mallarmé's solution–one example of what Barthes calls "le degré zéro de l'écriture"–is similar to Camus's *écriture blanche*, but its principal characteristic is absence rather than whiteness.

What is surprising and revealing, at the end of *Le Degré zéro de l'écriture*, is Barthes's equation of the zero degree of writing in Camus with classical writing:

> l'écriture neutre retrouve réellement la condition première de l'art classique: l'instrumentalité. Mais cette fois, l'instrument formel n'est plus au service d'une idéologie triomphante; il est le mode d'une situation nouvelle de l'écrivain, il est la façon d'exister d'un silence. (179-80)

Classical writing has here come full circle. It has passed through a "tragedy" of art according to which literature can only be saved through a recognition of its impossibility. In its basic design, however, the form of modernist *écriture* idealized by Barthes is precisely one that serves merely to convey, in a classical sense. Avant-garde language is once again surface and translucence. It no longer even invents its own essence, as under modernism, because such invention only reformulates the historical signs of literature in which *écriture* is irrevocably caught. And yet, in a final reversal and final statement of the impossibility of literature, Barthes notes that even a practice of the zero degree is doomed to become its own *écriture*.[39] Barthes is forced to conclude that "un chef-d'oeuvre moderne est impossible, l'écrivain étant placé par son écriture dans une contradiction sans issue" (185). The impasse of writing is, finally, the impasse of the social itself, a utopian dream for a classless society, a nonhypocritical realization of the classical claim that the values conveyed through a universal grammar really were available to and representative of everyone.

Le Degré zéro de l'écriture becomes in these respects the performance of a tragedy in which the aesthetic conventions of classical writing are a lover who must be killed in the name of a higher principle: literature itself. Classical writing, the beloved of "Plaisir aux Classiques," is established as the origin of *écriture* so that it may be rejected as a mode of false consciousness when modernist, and then avant-garde, writing is multiplied and distorted by social subjects trying to be free. *L'écriture blanche* is a utopian project, a memory of the classical dream of linguistic instrumentality reformulated within the terms of a (relative) freedom. Barthes's essay thus does two things simultaneously: first, it mirrors in a performative mode the avant-garde writing that he defined in his concluding chapters by effecting an Orphic gesture of renunciation (of a beloved classicism) in order to achieve an artistic liberation; second, and by doing so, Barthes transforms the critical activity into the creative act that he will describe, in varying degrees of explicitness, in much of his subsequent writing.[40] As he writes in the early 1960s, the critic "prête l'oreille au naturel de la culture, et perçoit sans cesse en elle, moins des sens stables, finis, 'vrais', que le frisson d'une machine immense qui est l'humanité en train de procéder inlassablement à une création du sens, sans laquelle elle ne serait plus humaine" ("L'Activité structuraliste," 1332). If Barthes had discovered, along with the writers whose work he admired, literature to be impossible once the nature of its subjection was revealed, once *écriture* was revealed to be permanently unresolved in its suspension between freedom and memory, his solution appears to have been to seek a dialectical and readerly–critical, creative, poetic–response to writing. The rejection of classicism in *Le Degré zéro de l'écriture* thus emblematizes a renunciation of capitalist ideology by making reading and criticism a utopian act of love in the present (a participation in the free invention of meaning) rather than an act of consumption of the past (in the form of determinate meaning that has to be remembered as a literary monument).[41]

Through its specific handling of the problem of classicism, then, *Le Degré zéro de l'écriture* dramatizes at the start of Barthes's career the theoretical gesture that would define the arc of his subsequent work. Classical writing, the mythological sign of a socially coercive practice of literary passivity (reception as consumption), is rejected in a utopian statement of the final impossibility of literature. And although he does not call explicitly in 1953 for a reinvention of reading as a form of creation, reading as, itself, poetic, Barthes makes an important move in this direction by sacrificing his beloved *Classiques* in the essay. The rejection of classical *écriture* is followed by a theoretical impasse achieved at the end of the book which will occur simultaneously with the reappearance of a covert, transformed classicism, not as a defeated return to the past, but in memory of an earlier passion. The theoretical situation at the end of *Le Degré zéro de l'écriture* suggests that literature will have to be saved not by the discovery of formal conventions freed from the strictures of history, but by a creative performance, which *Le Degré zéro de l'écriture* reveals itself ultimately to be, akin to an act of love. In late works like *Le plaisir du texte* (1973) or *Fragments d'un discours amoureux* (1977), in which the transactions between texts and their readers are cast as an exchange of love, the postulation of reading as *eros* returns Barthes to his beginnings, both to classicism, where the mystery of the text encourages a passionate *construction* of meaning, and to *Le Degré zéro de l'écriture*, where the notion that an ideologically normative definition of literature must be rejected is first proposed.[42]

NOTES

[1] From the very beginning of his career, then, much of Barthes's theoretical project as it would develop later on is already apparent in this essay as an initial statement of the desire that the Barthesian reader brings to literature. As he would later write in *S/Z*, "l'enjeu du travail littéraire (de la littérature comme travail), c'est de faire du lecteur, non plus un

consommateur, mais un producteur du texte" (10). The reader, already in 1944, is not a consumer, but a consummator who is, to use Barthes's word in the essay, "seduced" by the obscurity of the classical writer.

[2] "Ceux qui ne lisent que les Classiques et ceux qui ne les lisent pas du tout ont l'esprit également fermé" (45). In a text published before "Plaisir aux Classiques," "Notes sur André Gide et son 'Journal'" (1942), Barthes already comments on the relation between the modern and the early modern: "Rien de plus propre à la littérature française, rien de plus précieux que ces duos qui s'engagent, de siècle à siècle, entre écrivains de même classe: Pascal et Montaigne, Rousseau et Molière, Hugo et Voltaire, Valéry et Descartes, Montaigne et Gide" (25).

[3] This shift appeared decisive, defining *Le Degré zéro de l'écriture* with its emphasis on the historical break that opposed classical to modern writing, and underpinning the fundamental distinctions made by Barthes in later work such as *S/Z* (between *le texte lisible* and *le texte scriptible*) and *Le plaisir du texte* (between *le texte de plaisir* and *le texte de jouissance*).

[4] Barthes speaks of authors ranging from Montaigne to Rousseau, and, in a short addendum to the essay, establishes a list of quotations taken from various authors that exemplify, for Barthes, the mysterious pleasures to be found in the "classical" text. In addition to writers such as Corneille and Bossuet, Barthes cites the eighteenth-century writers Voltaire, Montesquieu, Vauvenargues, and Chamfort to support the preceding arguments of the essay. "Plaisir aux Classiques" thus emphasizes historical continuity, eschewing any precise notion of literary periodization within the early modern period. Classical writing is fully pertinent in and to a modernist present with which it enjoys a relationship of "solidarité" and which reinvents conceptual problems already confronted by earlier thinkers: "l'attention qu'on accorde aux problèmes présents n'est fructueuse que si l'on ne s'imagine pas trop qu'ils sont nouveaux" (46).

[5] "Responsabilité de la grammaire" was the title Barthes gave to his essay. It was published, however, as "Faut-il tuer la grammaire?," the title given to it by Maurice Nadeau, the editor of *Combat*, in an effort to remove possible references to Sartrean *responsabilité*. On the early history of Barthes's *Combat* essays, including those that would be grouped in *Le Degré zéro de l'écriture*, see Stafford, 17-33, and Calvet, 70-83.

[6] On the *classico-centricisme* of French literary history, see Barthes's "Réflexions sur un manuel."

[7] On the relations between Sartre's thinking and his own, see Barthes's "A propos de Sartre et l'existentialisme;" see also, Stafford, 20-33, and Calvet, 58-83.

[8] On Barthes's relation to Marxism (especially in connection with theater), see Roger, who considers Barthes "in the 1950s as accompanied by Marx, rather than following his teachings" (174). Roger points out that Barthes was introduced to Marxism late in 1944 by his friend Georges Fournié in Switzerland, and that in 1971 Barthes proclaimed that he had been "a Sartrian and a Marxist" when the Armistice was signed (175). Though a Marxist inflection is apparent in the early Barthes (and in *Le Degré zéro de l'écriture*), the extent to which he can be considered a Marxist is unclear.

[9] Sartre, 94-105.

[10] "Je dis que la littérature d'une époque déterminée est aliénée lorsqu'elle n'est pas parvenue à la conscience explicite de son autonomie et qu'elle se soumet aux puissances temporelles ou à une idéologie, en un mot lorsqu'elle se considère elle-même comme un moyen et non comme une fin inconditionnée" (156).

[11] "L'art de la prose s'exerce sur le discours, sa matière est naturellement signifiante: c'est-à-dire que les mots ne sont pas d'abord des objets, mais des désignations d'objets" (25).

[12] "[L]a fonction de l'écrivain est de faire en sorte que nul ne puisse ignorer le monde et que nul ne s'en puisse dire innocent" (29-30).

[13] Distinguishing between the positions of Sartre and Barthes, Sontag writes, "[a]s a mor-

alist–Puritan or anti-Puritan–might solemnly distinguish sex for procreation from sex for pleasure, Barthes divides writers into those who write something (what Sartre meant by a writer) and the real writers, who do not write something, but, rather, write" (xxi).

[14] For a discussion of this question, see Martin. On *Le Degré zéro de l'écriture* as "the sketch of an ethics of writing," see Wiseman, 18-23.

[15] On the centrality of the concept of utopia to Barthes's work, as well as the notion that utopia is itself a kind of writing, see Knight, *Barthes and Utopia*.

[16] Kristeva explains how, for Barthes, art is always situated between the present and the past, culture and nature: "[art] weaves into language (or other 'signifying materials') the complex relations of a subject caught between 'nature' and 'culture,' between the immemorial ideological and scientific tradition, henceforth available, and the present, between desire and the law, the body, language, and 'metalanguage'" (97).

[17] On Barthes's relation to Lanson, and the notion that he confirmed and extended, rather than merely rejected, the Lansonian paradigm, see Champagne, "The Task of Clotho Redefined" and *Literary History in the Wake of Roland Barthes*.

[18] It makes sense to describe *Le Degré zéro de l'écriture* as a "myth" of literature since Barthes is interested in the ideological connotations that derive from the notion of literature. The famous opening sentence of the essay–"Hébert ne commençait jamais un numéro du Père Duchêne sans y mettre quelques 'foutre' et quelques 'bougre'–puts the notion of *écriture* in the terms that Barthes will use to describe the "mythe" in the 1957 *Mythologies*. Hébert's "foutre" and "bougre" do not, as Barthes writes, signify. Rather, they "signal" "une situation révolutionnaire." Similarly, the ideological formation of Literature derives from a secondary order of signification: words denote, but they connote "literariness." On the opening line of *Le Degré zéro de l'écriture*, see Miller.

[19] "C'est alors que les écritures commencent à se multiplier. Chacune désormais, la travaillée, la populiste, la neutre, la parlée, se veut l'acte initial par lequel l'écrivain assume ou abhorre sa condition bourgeoise" (171).

[20] Similarly, style, for Barthes, is a metaphor, "c'est-à-dire équation entre l'intention littéraire et la structure charnelle de l'auteur" (146). Again, there is no choice available to the writer in questions of style. It is the product "d'une poussée, non d'une intention" (146).

[21] Literature did not of course mean in the seventeenth century what it would come to mean in the nineteenth. One need only look at Naudé's *Advis pour dresser une bibliothèque* (1644) to recognize how much *littérature* was attached still in the seventeenth century to the ancient concept of the *studia humanitatis*. For a discussion of the emergence of literature into an early form of modernity during the later seventeenth century under the influence of its civilizing mission, see Bury.

[22] Barthes describes this alternative in "Responsabilité de la grammaire" in terms of an evolution from ideological cynicism to hypocrisy: "en 1647, d'après Vaugelas, être clair, c'est parler comme on parle à la cour; la clarté, c'est le bon usage, c'est-à-dire l'usage du groupe social qui se tient directement autour du pouvoir; mais dès 1660, l'autorité monarchique est suffisamment forte pour passer du cynisme à l'hypocrisie, selon une transformation bien connue dans l'Histoire" (79).

[23] To be sure, even the most cursory survey of seventeenth-century literary culture would serve to reveal the limitations of Barthes's portrait of classical *écriture*. It would be a fairly straightforward matter, for example, to examine the effect that the precise political situation of the classical period might have had on *écriture*. If Barthes's theory calls for a homogeneous court society unaware of the normative nature of the discursive practices that bind it to an "idéologie triomphante," would it matter that the nobility under Louis XIV felt itself to be increasingly alienated from the sphere of real power? In a different register, it would seem pertinent to explore the very substantial arguments in the seventeenth century over the

rhetorical problem of *imitatio* and *inventio*, the extent to which language was meant to repeat or innovate. These were central questions during the *Querelle des anciens et des modernes*. See, for example, Levine, Highet, and R. Duchêne and G. de Donville.

[24] The collection of essays includes "Comment Ronsard invente," "La Vie morale selon Les Essais de Montaigne," and "Sur Montaigne."

[25] Similarly, the opening paragraph of *Le Degré zéro de l'écriture* on Hébert (see note 18) would suggest Bakhtin's subversive Rabelais in addition to the revolutionary Père Duchêne.

[26] As Sartre states: "Il suffit qu'ils [les écrivains] baignent dans l'idéologie des classes privilégiées, qu'ils en soient totalement imprégnés et qu'ils n'en puissent même pas concevoir d'autres. Mais, dans ce cas, leur fonction se modifie: on ne leur demande plus d'être les gardiens des dogmes, mais seulement de ne pas s'en faire les détracteurs" (110).

[27] See Foucault, 45-59.

[28] On these spatial images with respect to Saussure or to Jakobson, see Wiseman (25-26). In "Responsabilité de la grammaire," it is more specifically classical French which is considered horizontal: "cette communicabilité tant vantée de la langue française n'a jamais été qu'horizontale; elle n'a pas été verticale, elle ne s'est jamais profilée dans l'épaisseur du volume social" (79).

[29] For Barthes, writing is also mapped onto the gridded space of the nation: "tant que la langue hésite sur sa structure même, une morale du langage est impossible; l'écriture n'apparaît qu'au moment où la langue, constituée nationalement, devient une sorte de négativité, un horizon qui sépare ce qui est défendu et ce qui est permis, sans plus s'interroger sur les origines ou sur les justifications de ce tabou" (169). In this sense, langue functions as a kind of Nature that holds its cultural past within it. The nation is the "society" par excellence in which the writer must be located to function as a moral agent, and consequently, not to have a "society" against which writerly "creation" is opposed (147) is not to be able to produce writing. If *écriture* is defined in part as "le language littéraire transformé par sa destination sociale" (147), an absence of *langue* cannot but forestall any possibility of class transformation.

[30] In *Nouvelle Critique ou nouvelle imposture*, Picard suggests that Barthes's "dangerous" book could only be of interest to those "qui ne s'intéressent pas vraiment à la littérature" (85).

[31] For example, "[l]ire, c'est désirer l'oeuvre, c'est vouloir être l'oeuvre, c'est refuser de doubler l'oeuvre en dehors de toute autre parole que la parole même de l'oeuvre: le seul commentaire que pourrait produire un pur lecteur, et qui le resterait, c'est le pastiche (comme l'indiquerait l'exemple de Proust, amateur de lectures et de pastiches). Passer de la lecture à la critique, c'est changer de désir, c'est désirer non plus l'oeuvre, mais son propre langage. Mais par là-même aussi, c'est renvoyer l'oeuvre au désir de l'écriture, dont elle était sortie. Ainsi tourne la parole autour du livre: lire, écrire: d'un désir à l'autre va toute littérature" (79).

[32] Susan Sontag captures the "dramatic" quality of Barthes's writing: "[d]rawn to hyperbole, as all aphorists are, Barthes enlists ideas in a drama, often a sensual melodrama or a faintly Gothic one. He speaks of the quiver, thrill, or shudder of meaning, of meanings that themselves vibrate, gather, loosen, disperse, quicken, shine, fold, mutate, delay, slide, separate, that exert pressure, crack, rupture, fissure, are pulverized. Barthes offers something like a poetics of thinking, which identifies the meaning of subjects with the very mobility of meaning, with the kinetics of consciousness itself; and liberates the critic as artist" (xiii).

[33] Stephen Heath calls this approach to literary criticism Barthes's strategy of "déplacement": "Comment lire Barthes sinon en reconnaissant à cette oeuvre multiple sa force de déplacement? Partout s'esquisse un même geste, se rencontre un même souci de changer de niveau, de produire une configuration nouvelle, de déplacer. L'enjeu est toujours une

autre histoire" (19). Any literary "history," then, will necessarily become another, possibly undermining, history.

[34] He also states here: "ce que la modernité donne à lire dans la pluralité de ses écritures, c'est l'impasse de sa propre Histoire" (171). In the first chapter, Barthes writes: "L'unité de l'écriture classique, homogène pendant des siècles, la pluralité des écritures modernes, multipliées depuis cent ans jusqu'à la limite même du fait littéraire, cette espèce d'éclatement de l'écriture française correspond bien à une grande crise de l'Histoire totale, visible d'une manière beaucoup plus confuse dans l'Histoire littéraire proprement dite" (148-49). He begins his last chapter with the statement: "La multiplication des écritures est un fait moderne qui oblige l'écrivain à un choix" (184).

[35] See Bensmaïa 24-25, who cites and discusses Barthes's remarks on this notion in *Le Plaisir du texte*. Bensmaïa focuses on the role of the fragment in Barthes's later essays (e.g., 24-25). The fragment serves the reflective function in a way somewhat different from the more teleological *Le Degré zéro de l'écriture*, in which the fragment is not really employed as a means of auto-reflexion or subversion.

[36] On this subject, one might also recall Gide's interest in Montaigne, one that Barthes may have increasingly shared over the course of his career.

[37] Of Rimbaud, Barthes writes, "[c]ette écriture sacrée, d'autres écrivains ont pensé qu'ils ne pouvaient l'exorciser qu'en la disloquant; ils ont alors miné le langage littéraire, ils ont fait éclater à chaque instant la coque renaissante des clichés, des habitudes, du passé formel de l'écrivain; dans le chaos des formes, dans le désert des mots, ils ont pensé atteindre un objet absolument privé d'Histoire, retrouver la fraîcheur d'un état neuf du langage. Mais ces perturbations finissent par creuser leurs propres ornières, par créer leurs propres lois. Les Belles-Lettres menacent tout langage qui n'est pas purement fondé sur la parole sociale. Fuyant toujours plus en avant une syntaxe du désordre, la désintégration du langage ne peut conduire qu'à un silence de l'écriture" (178).

[38] See, for example, *L'espace littéraire*, 225-33. See also Blanchot's hopeful comments on Barthes's *Le Degré zéro de l'écriture* in *Le livre à venir*, 275-85.

[39] "Malheureusement rien n'est plus infidèle qu'une écriture blanche; les automatismes s'élaborent à l'endroit même où se trouvait d'abord une liberté, un réseau de formes durcies serre de plus en plus la fraîcheur première du discours, une écriture renaît à la place d'un langage indéfini" (180).

[40] On Barthes's performative writing as paradigmatic of the rise of theory in the American Academy in the 1960s and 70s, see Henry M. Sayre.

[41] Julia Kristeva points out that Barthes does not speak about writing. He speaks to writing, thereby introducing his own desire. "As for the 'critic,' he takes on the task of pointing out heteronomy. How? Through the presence of enunciation in the utterance, by introducing the agency of the subject, by assuming a representative, localized, contingent speech, determined by its 'I' and thus by the 'I' of its reader. Speaking in his name to an other, he introduces desire" (115).

[42] On Barthes's relationship to beginnings, see Diana Knight, "Where to Begin?".

Works Cited

Barthes, Roland. "L'Activité structuraliste." Vol. 1. In *Oeuvres complètes*, ed. Eric Marty, 1328-33. Paris: Editions du Seuil, 1993.

———. "A propos de Sartre et l'existentialisme." *Magazine littéraire* 314 (October 1993): 51-53.

———. *Critique et vérité*. Paris: Editions du Seuil, 1966.

———. *Le Degré zéro de l'écriture.* Vol. 1. In *Oeuvres complètes*, ed. Eric Marty, 135-87. Paris: Editions du Seuil, 1993.

———. "Je ne crois pas aux influences." Vol. 1. In *Oeuvres complètes*, ed. Eric Marty, 1450-52. Paris: Editions du Seuil, 1993.

———. "Notes sur André Gide et son 'Journal'." Vol. 1. In *Oeuvres complètes*, ed. Eric Marty, 23-33. Paris: Editions du Seuil, 1993.

———. *Oeuvres complètes.* 3 vols. (1: 1942-1965; 2: 1966-1973; 3: 1974-1980) ed. Eric Marty. Paris: Editions du Seuil, 1993-95.

———. "Plaisir aux Classiques." Vol. 1. In *Oeuvres complètes*, ed. Eric Marty, 45-53. Paris: Editions du Seuil, 1993.

———. *Le plaisir du texte.* Paris: Seuil, 1973.

———. "Réflexions sur un manuel." Vol. 2. In *Oeuvres complètes*, ed. Eric Marty, 1241-46. Paris: Editions du Seuil, 1993.

———. "Réponses." Vol. 2. In *Oeuvres complètes*, ed. Eric Marty, 1307-1324. Paris: Editions du Seuil, 1993.

———. "Responsabilité de la grammaire." Vol. 2. In *Oeuvres complètes*, ed. Eric Marty, 79-81. Paris: Editions du Seuil, 1993.

———. *S/Z.* Paris: Seuil, 1970.

Bensmaïa, Réda. *The Barthes Effect: The Essay as Reflective Text.* Trans. Pat Fedkiew. Minneapolis: University of Minnesota Press, 1987.

Blanchot, Maurice. *L'espace littéraire.* Paris: Gallimard, 1955.

———. *Le livre à venir.* Paris: Gallimard, 1959.

Bury, Emmanuel. *Littérature et politesse. L'invention de l'honnête homme, 1580-1750.* Paris: PUF, 1996.

Calvet, Louis Jean. *Roland Barthes. A Biography.* Trans. Sarah Wykes. Bloomington: Indiana University Press, 1995.

Champagne, Roland A. *Literary History in the Wake of Roland Barthes: Re-defining the Myths of Reading.* Birmingham: Summa, 1984.

———. "The Task of Clotho Re-defined: Roland Barthes's Tapestry of Literary History." *L'Esprit créateur* 22, no. 1 (1982): 35-47.

Duchêne, R., and G. de Donville, eds., *D'un siècle à l'ature: anciens et modernes.* Marseille: CMR 17, 1987.

Foucault, Michel. *Les Mots et les choses. Une archéologie des sciences humaines.* Paris: Gallimard, 1966.

Heath, Stephen. *Vertige du déplacement: Lecture de Barthes.* Paris: Fayard, 1974.

Highet, Gilbert. *The Classical Tradition: Greek and Roman Influences on Western Literature.* New York: Oxford University Press, 1949.

Knight, Diana. *Barthes and Utopia. Space, Travel, Writing.* Oxford: Clarendon Press, 1997.

———. "Where to Begin?" *The Yale Journal of Criticisim* 14, no. 2 (2001): 493-501.

Kristeva, Julia. "How Does One Speak to Literature?" In *Desire in Language. A Semiotic Approach to Literature and Art*, 92-123. New York: Columbia University Press, 1980.

Lanson, Gustave. *Essais de méthode de critique et d'histoire littéraire*. Ed. Henri Peyre. Paris: Hachette, 1965.

———. *Les Essais de Montaigne*. Paris: Librairie Mellottée, 1929.

Levine, Joseph. *The Battle of the Books: History and Literature in the Augustan Age*. Ithaca: Cornell University Press, 1991.

Martin, Christian. "Roland Barthes ou l'engagement en question." *The French Review* 75, no. 4 (March 2002): 730-41.

Miller, D. A. "Foutre! Bougre! Ecriture!" *The Yale Journal of Criticism* 14, no. 2 (2001): 503-11.

Picard, Raymond. *Nouvelle Critique ou nouvelle imposture*. Paris: J.-J. Pauvert, 1965.

Richman, Michèle. "Foreward." In Bensmaïa. viii-xxi.

Roger, Philippe. "Barthes with Marx." In *Writing the Image after Roland Barthes*, ed. Jean-Michel Rabaté, 174-86. Philadelphia: University of Pennsylvania Press, 1997.

Sartre, Jean-Paul. *Qu'est-ce que la littérature?* Paris: Gallimard, 1948.

Sayre, Henry M. "Critical Performance. The Example of Roland Barthes." In *The Object of Performance. The American Avant-Garde since 1970*, 246-64. Chicago: University of Chicago Press, 1989.

Sontag, Susan. "Writing Itself: On Roland Barthes." In *A Barthes Reader*, vii-xxxviii. New York: Hill and Wang, 1982.

Stafford, Andy. *Roland Barthes, Phenomenon and Myth. An Intellectual Biography*. Edinburgh: Edinburgh University Press, 1998.

Wiseman, Mary Bittner. *The Ecstasies of Roland Barthes*. London: Routledge, 1989.

The Cyber-Baroque:
Walter Ong, The History of Rhetoric,
and an Early Modern Information Mode

Jean-Vincent Blanchard

How can we have a modern perspective of the early modern? What is at stake when we attach that adjective, *early*, to what designates our own times, the *modern*? The early modern is a curious concept that signifies both sameness and difference in history, allowing historians to understand their own times by practicing genealogies. However, rather than focus here on the well-worn Foucauldian methods for signaling the past, I wish to examine the significance of the early modern in regard to pedagogy. For teachers of the early modern, it is a continuing challenge to make older texts matter in the classroom. The aesthetic aspects of an early modern work are not necessarily obvious and appealing to students. The reality of the teaching experience is that most students are interested in a given topic when they can relate to it, that is, when they can establish a connection between an unfamiliar past and their personal present. But not all works offer the kind of psychological and ethical content that permit ready identification. Indeed an increasingly large number of early modern texts seems destined to the exclusive attention of specialists, in spite of their historical importance.

In this essay, I suggest that studying early modern cultural productions in the context of larger epistemic shifts may be a fruitful way to draw interest toward difficult material. In that perspective, there are many scholarly works that draw comparisons between the present and the seventeenth century, such as Omar Calabrese's *Neo-Baroque: A Sign of the Times* (1992), or the volume *Résurgences baroques* (2001). I argue that one important way to teach the early modern is to practice rhetorical history in the spirit of Marc Fumaroli's and Nancy Struever's work.[1] By focusing both on style and on the logical structure of speech, the history of rhetoric provides concepts that are more precise, accurate, and specific than, say, the categories of *baroque* or *classicism*. The history of rhetoric, among other topics, includes the study of the idea of memory, and thus characterizes the work of Paolo Rossi and Lina Bolzoni, whose recent translations into English have been met with great interest. Furthermore, following Kathleen E. Welch's insight in *Electric Rhetoric: Classical Rhetoric, Oralism, and a New Literacy* (1999), I propose that history of rhetoric is an appropriate method to practice a genealogy of mediation.[2]

One important gesture in the reassessment of rhetoric in the curriculum is to critically examine scholarly works that have provided useful propositions on early modern rhetoric in the perspective of contemporary culture. Walter Ong's contribution on the general history of orality and literacy, which Struever describes as "ground-breaking," is a useful point to begin (93).[3] On the basis of his landmark study on Renaissance methodology titled *Ramus, Method, and the Decay of Dialogue: From the Art of Discourse to the Art of Reason* (1958), Ong developed a compelling, although controversial interpretation of the evolution of human consciousness in relation to technologies such as the printing press. As a result, he is often quoted as a source of inspiration by scholars of contemporary media, especially by those concerned with the technological developments of the Internet.

Many commentators have already remarked on the analogies between Renaissance media modes and the Internet revolution (Landow, 29). Some, more pointedly, state that this historical comparison concerns the opposition between orality and literacy (Hobart, 2, chap. one; Lévy, 98). Hence it is not surprising to see many scholars of contemporary media invoke Ong's work as a primary source of inspiration in their attempt to make sense of the Internet's revolution (Gurak, 13; Kellner, 155; Landow, 82; Lister, 58; Welch). As Landow writes: "These observations about hypertext suggest that computers bring us much closer to a culture some of whose qualities have more in common with those of preliterate man than even Walter J. Ong has been willing to admit" (82). In turn, a few point to the artificial memory tradition, and especially the Renaissance, as the true site of a historical comparison (Brody, 142; Lister, 56). For Steven Johnson, the memory palaces of the classical rhetoricians were "the original information-spaces" (12).

This essay critically examines Walter Ong's work on the French Renaissance with a view to how his historical study illuminates contemporary media theory on technologies such as radio, television, and computers. My goal is not to suggest that his theory be stretched to a complete explanation of the Internet. But we can make his insights relevant to this new field, I propose, by reexamining and extending the historical material that he surveyed in his work on Ramus. By elaborating on Ong's history of rhetoric in the French early seventeenth century, and specifically in relation to the rhetoric of emblems as defined by the Jesuits, I show that there is still much to gain from his work when we tackle the nature of new media forms. Finally, I return to how, in spite of the strong religious grounding of his work, Walter Ong's propositions on the history of consciousness and technology have much in common with pedagogy, if not with genealogy. In this process we will have defined the specific stakes of practicing rhetorical history for conjuring up the past. One will forgive us, in the meantime, for using such catchy words as *baroque*.

1. ONG ON RAMIST RHETORIC AND THE LEGACY OF ITALIAN HUMANISM

In *Ramus, Method, and the Decay of Dialogue*, Walter Ong examined the works of Pierre de La Ramée, also known as Petrus Ramus, a Regius professor of rhetoric and philosophy born in 1515 and assassinated on the Saint-Barthélémy day in 1572 (see also Bruyère, Vasoli).[4] Ramus's work concerned the distinction between logic, dialectic, and rhetoric, that is, the definition and purpose of types of discourse as originally defined by Aristotle. According to Ong, Ramus provided an original contribution to the Renaissance renewal of the arts of discourse spearheaded by the Dutch Humanist Rodolphus Agricola (1443-1485; on Agricola and Ramus, see Bruyère, *Méthode*, 112-14).[5]

In Aristotle's system, ways of knowing were divided according to their object, but also with regard to their ends.[6] Yet as a method, Aristotle proposed different ways of speaking that did not necessarily depend on the nature of the object. Most of these tenets were still valid in Ramus's times, especially in the view of the Scholastics. What distinguished logic, dialectics, and rhetoric was the type of truth that they adopted as their standard. In the second part of the *Analytics*, logic is defined as a demonstrative practice that allows certain knowledge (1: 33). Logical deduction tackles concepts of substance, and enunciations, that is, elements understood through the grid of categories and predicables (a grid for which Porphyry's *Isagoge* provided a working standard). Dialectics was an art of using arguments in disputation ("intellectual training, casual encounters, and the philosophical sciences"; *Topics* 1: 2), relying on a body of formulas called topics, to quickly find ideas.[7] Topics, which were loosely based on predicables and the categories, later came to be seen at once as the patterns for finding arguments, and as the arguments themselves. Dialectics considered the propositions that were most likely to be true, and was thus founded on probability, on what was universally accepted, or what satisfied common sense, or wise men's opinion. Finally, rhetoric was an art of discourse that studied human psychology and particular circumstances to define what could best persuade, notably in courts of justice or in the public forum. The proximity of rhetoric to disciplines such as ethics and politics shows well how Aristotle viewed this discourse as being adapted to judgments in a contingent world. The criterion of truth was verisimilitude, and it was entirely within the speaker's prerogative to use all the resources of language to act on the audience's affects and passions. For Aristotle and his Scholastic followers, whose opinions still held sway in Ramus's times, the object did not necessarily determine the type of discourse to be used: both the preacher and the metaphysician could speak of God, but they did so in completely different terms.

Against scholastic formalism, men such as Rodolphus Agricola advocated a pedagogical theory of communication that doubled as a method. In this perspective, the Ciceronian concept of method can arguably be seen as having had a most important role in the evolution of Western thought because it exerted such a profound influence on the thought of the Humanists (Gilbert, Vasoli). Cicero viewed language as unified. Good speech can only be *one* in achieving a perfect exteriorization of thought in the beauty of words, proclaims Crassus, a protagonist in the dialogue *De oratore* (3.5.19, 20). There are many reasons that explain such a tendency, including the influence of Academic skepticism on the thought of Cicero (Michel). This resulted in a general concept of topical invention that was even more adapted to practical situations. Cicero never intended the art of discourse to be sophistical, though, and he placed the burden of truth on the ethics of the speaker.

Renaissance Humanists sought a way of thinking that would take into consideration the reality of human nature, one that was at once rational and embodied, subject to affects. Thus Cicero's ideas concerning discourse were extremely appealing to them. *Docere* was not incompatible with *movere* and *delectare*. Discourse was somewhat always concerned with action, and could take particular circumstances into consideration. As Ong puts it, "from the point of view of subsequent intellectual history, the most central operations in Agricola's *Dialectical Invention* are his building up of the old notion of *topoi* (topics) or commonplaces at the expense of the predicament or categories" (*Ramus*, 104). "Aristote a voulu faire deux logiques, l'une pour la science, l'autre pour l'opinion, en quoi [...] il a très grandement erré" says Ramus (*Dialectique*, 18). Gone was the reverence toward the metaphysical straightjacket of the categories and the predicables, and generally to an Aristotle that the Humanists viewed as *"argutulus et spinosus."*

Because dialectics also absorbed the modes of invention and proof that belonged to rhetoric, Agricola and Ramus came to view rhetoric as its mere ornament.[8]

> Dialectic is the theory of reason. Therefore whatever is the property of reason and mental ability and can be handled and practised without speech, attribute this by right to the art of dialectic.
>
> Dialectic has three parts—invention of stratagems and arguments, arrangement of these through the syllogism and method, and then memory [...]. Yet what will be left for rhetoric? Not only styles in tropes and figures, which you consider here the only property of the orator, but also delivery. This alone is the proper virtue of rhetoric, its ability to diversify through the brilliance of tropes, to embellish with the beauty of figures, to charm with the modulation of the voice, and to arouse by the dignity of gesture.[9]
> (*Brut. Quaest.*, 16-17)

What makes Ong's analysis of these methodological changes in the Renaissance distinctive is the way in which he binds them with changes in the human sensorium. He notices that when thought uses ready-made arguments, judgment is a process of arrangement, a *dispositio*.

> "Collocation" or assembly or arrangement represents an attempt to deal diagrammatically with the second part of the art of dialectic, that is, with utterance itself. The attempt will soon result in the substitution of the term *dispositio* or arrangement for that of judgment. (*Ramus*, 184)

Indeed, in the pedagogical and topical framework favored by the Humanists, finding the best way to explain something was most often about finding the right order. Agricola writes in his seminal *De inventione dialectica*:

> For just as no one would call a painter or story-teller accomplished who, though he exactly expressed all the parts individually but knew not how to join them and set them in such a relationship that they conveyed the image desired of someone's movements or actions, so he will not earn the title of dialectician who knows how to discover everything with which to produce belief, but knows not how to arrange and set them in order so that they produce the belief for which they are intended. This therefore will be the end of dialectic, to teach in accordance with the potential of the subject of discourse: that is to discover what will produce belief, and to arrange what is discovered aptly, so arranging them that they are as suited as possible for teaching. (McNally, "*De Inventione*," 409)

According to Ong, Ramist judgment necessarily equates the acquisition of knowledge with visual perception, as opposed to aural perception, which is time bound insofar as it cannot be "reversed" (*Presence*, 42). Reversing an audio recording produces an entirely different sound, whereas one can reverse the order of various ideas that have been spatialized in thought without necessarily changing their meaning. There is something specific about *saying* "this is" or "this is not." Hence judgment as arrangement is akin to a visual operation. Underlying Ong's interpretation is the idea that enunciation pertains to orality because it confers an essential quality to a statement when it is uttered in a specific performance, while Ramus saw enunciation as the first degree of a process of arrangement.

> Alongside the term *iudicium*, there is observable in the dialectical tradition a marked tendency to think of this second part or its equivalent not as a judgment of predication or as anything less so overtly suggestive of the oral and existentially-oriented world of sound, but rather as arrangement [...], a concept accommodated to the visualist notion of places, so that the operation which follows after drawing the arguments out of the loci is considered to

be that of deploying them in a new order adapted to the purpose at hand. (*Ramus*, 114)

There are many judicious observations in this commentary. However, contrary to Ong's view, the Ramist inventive part of discourse does have an affinity with oral communication. Ramus never contended that communication was to be strictly visual.

> For the way in which rhetoric, just like dialectic and any other art, should be practiced is explicitly twofold—that is, analysis and genesis. For first of all we must understand the use of the art in representative examples, and then we must fashion our own like them. Just as the precepts of the art are therefore better learned by *listening* to a diligent erudite teacher than by reading his book, so the practical application of the precepts is at first better achieved by *listening* than by reading. A new and hesitant knowledge of an art develops much more easily when someone else leads and points the way, rather than when it advances on its own. (*Brut. Quaest.*, 155, emphasis added)

As this passage shows, *analysis* is grounded in aural perception, for example in a dispute, and being thus faithful to the notion of the Aristotelian dialectical *quaestio* (*Prior Anal.* 1: 1). Nelly Bruyère explains that on the other hand, method as *genesis*, the pedagogical ordering of places in the clearest manner (from the general to the particular), is cast in metaphysical terms. In contrast to the Thomist realism of the scholastics, there is an epistemological break between invention and judgment in the thought of Ramus. In her view, method is "haunted" by a Ramist Platonism that understands it as guided by an inner and natural light.[10] Art is the prerogative of humanity. The truth of method as order does not coexist with the products of sensual and oral perception (invention). As Ong contends, then, method can be thought of as a visual processing. Observation and experience, which Ramus places in the sphere of orality, are at once necessary and devalued, being also the lot of inferior creatures.

For Ong, this visuality of method represents a decisive break with the features of discourse associated with oral communication, notably the circumstantial and practical nature of language.

> By its very structure, Ramist rhetoric asserts to all who are able to sense its implications that there is no way to discovery or to understanding through voice, and ultimately seems to deny that the process of person-to-person communication play any necessary role in intellectual life. (*Ramus*, 288)

These would be the traits of a literate and script-oriented culture that eschews the performative nature of speech.

Thus, as appealing as Ong's interpretation may be, it proves on close examination to be problematic because it oversimplifies the complex interrelation of orality and visuality in Ramus's system. First, there is evidence that much of this visual drive in Ramus's thought stems from the memory tradition, even Lullism. This aspect was overlooked by Ong in his description of print culture's epistemic injunction.

Following the teaching of the great Roman rhetoricians, artificial memory constituted the fourth part of discourse theory, after invention, arrangement, and ornament. It advised on how to remember an elaborate speech by using means related to visuality and imagination, because it is easier to remember something under a visual form than as an oral message. For example, one could imagine a place such as a gallery, or a basilica, and then arrange various figures such as statues in the chosen building. The process could be further refined by associating these speech elements with various symbols to provide more detail. Actual delivery of the speech consisted in an imaginary walk.

Ramus equated the art of memory with his own concept of arrangement. This surely suggests how he thought of *dispositio* in terms of visuality (Yates, 231-40; Rossi, 101). Let us remember as well that in the passage from Agricola quoted above, there is a strong emphasis on visuality. For his part, referring to Cicero, Ramus writes:

> "The art of memory," he says, "resides completely in division and structure." If we therefore inquire into what the art of order is, and what is the art which divides and structures things, then we shall discover the art of memory. Of course my teachings have already laid out carefully this theory of order in the dialectical instructions on the syllogism and method. It is clear therefore that the art of memory is entirely the property of dialectic. (*Brut. Quaest.*, 159)

This influence of memory does not preclude that the print medium might have been a contributing factor in Ramus's spatialization of discourse (Vasoli, "Enciclopedia," 727; *Dialettica*, 254).[11] However it does cast a doubt on the notion of technological determinism. Also, this raises the issue of the place of persuasion in Ramist method, and hence of the loss of a "process of person-to-person communication," given that memory was the traditional fourth part of oratory.

Ramus's theory of discourse marked a departure from the Italians. As Cesare Vasoli has observed, Humanists such as Agricola viewed style as an important part of communication, to the extreme point where verisimilitude could become a satisfying criterion of truth (*Dialettica*, 178). In the same regard, James R. McNally speaks of the "age of humanism" as a "third sophistic" ("*Dux*," 340). Ramus was much more circumspect with his assessment of the significance of rhetoric. He did reduce the ancient art of persuasion to its ornamental part. But let us note also that he distinguished two types of method. The first, that of teachers, was to follow the clearest and most rational order (genesis). The *second*, relying on prudence, was used by orators and poets to determine the proper order of thoughts with a view toward generating affect.

> S'ensuit la méthode de prudence [...]. Elle est nommée par les Orateurs disposition de prudence, parce qu'elle réside grandement en la prudence de l'homme plus qu'en l'art et les préceptes de doctrine, comme si la méthode de nature était jugement de science, la méthode de prudence était jugement d'opinion. (*Dialectique*, 79)

Beginning *in medias res* is an example of the devices used in this second method, a method which places discourse in the realm of opinion. Ramus favored a plain style in rhetoric, signaling how he recognized the potentially irrational effect of ornament on thought.[12] He wrote a book, the *Ciceronianus* (1573; see Fumaroli, *L'âge*, 454-60), which argued for Attic style in the pan-European debate on how one should follow Cicero's example. He also invokes Demosthenes as a proper model of orator. At the opposite end of the stylistic spectrum, he found *Asianism* (or *baroquism*) of the same Cicero, with its digressions, repetitions, and displays of the self, to be highly distasteful (*Rhet. Distinct.*, 125, 157; *Brut. Quaest.*, 74, 86). It is important to note how the type of style also defined a matter of order. The methodical beauty of poets and orators was to be founded in reason, that is, it was the logical part that contributed to the sense of *decorum* (*Rhet. Distinct.*, 125, 157; *Brut. Quaest.*, 74, 86). This rationality should not obscure the fact that the method of prudence, while still being located within the orb of arrangement, could be seen as circumstantial and performative, features that Ong's system confines to orality.

Unfortunately, Ong does not elaborate on the ambiguous status of the *méthode de prudence*, as far as it related to oratory. As we will see now, much of the opposition that he starkly defines in Renaissance rhetoric grounds his wider ranging historical account of the relationship between oral and script cultures up to our contemporary times.

2. ONG ON ORALITY AND LITERACY, HUMAN CONSCIOUSNESS, AND MODERN MEDIA

Ong's work on the characteristics of oral and script cultures can be approached by focusing on the idea of mediation. He remarks on the simple fact that communication as mediation is not necessary and natural: it is a distinctly manmade mode characteristic of print, alphabetic, and script-oriented cultures. It is a mode characterized by analysis, abstraction, disjunction, and referentiality. Certain modes of knowing tend to organize the human sensorium in ways that privilege one particular sense over the other. "Growing up, assimilating the wisdom of the past, is in great part learning how to organize the sensorium" (*Presence*, 6). Ways of knowing are embodied.

In print culture, knowledge of the world is mediated by technologies that separate the knower from the known with visual technologies. Before the work of Elizabeth Eisenstein and Roger Chartier, Ong points out that indices, titles, and typographic layouts are ways of managing information that pertain to visual cognition. On this basis, Ong argues that mediation can alienate subjects by creating "new interior distances within the psyche" (*Interfaces*, 17), that bear on their freedom, the quality of their everyday life, and their relations with others. "While they seem to humanize by increasing knowledge, technologies of the written word also alienate man from the real world, the living spoken word, and thus from himself" (*Interfaces*, 47). Script and print culture is a culture of efficiency and utility, and ultimately of control (*Presence*, 45, 194). In Ong's theory, orality is not a form of mediation. It can thus make the human experience fuller and more authentic. This idea is laid out in *The Presence of the Word* (1967), as well as in subsequent works.

That it requires a serious conceptual effort to think of orality shows well how we take for granted our largely visual/script contemporary mediation mode. But societies without script and print had a completely different relation to knowledge. They could not store it and retrieve it at will. The human memory has limited capacities. In oral societies, "every time an old person dies, a library goes up in flames" (Lévy, 144; 94). Thus the word in oral societies is an *event*, and not a record, a mere representation. Characteristic of oral communication modes is the idea that knowledge is by nature circumstantial, bound to a specific setting.

> Although sound itself is fleeting [...] what it conveys at any instant of its duration is not dissected but caught in the actuality of the present, which is rich, manifold, full of diverse action, the only moment when everything is really going on at once. (*Presence*, 129)

Oral knowledge was transmitted by allegorization because it required the aid of artificial memory. There were devices that allowed memory to be extended beyond the average human capacity. Oral performance relied on mnemonic devices, commonplaces, and formulas to recall the past, "means shaped for ready oral recurrence" (*Presence*, 34). It was by nature aggregative and additive, if not redundant and digressive. Thus the primordial literary form of oral cultures was the oratory, and most importantly the epic, which concerns allegories of values and the addition of plot twists. "If we take the climatic linear plot as the paradigm of plot, the epic has no plot" (*Orality*, 144; also; *Presence*, 57, 87). So the very notion of history must be put in question when one considers how oral cultures related to the past. As one commentator puts it: "The oral tradition [...] did not analyze history in terms of cause and effect, factors and forces, objective and influences" (Farrell, 32). In other words, narrating history was only conceivable in terms of a literate culture (*Orality*, 141-47). A bard sang the past to conjure it up, to commemorate by creating anew.

Oral cultures are deemed by Ong to have favored more authoritarian relations. In cultures where knowledge is passed from generation to generation, where it is dependent on the circumstance of the utterance, and as such is always a renewed performance with opportunities of originality, there is a reverence for the spoken word. Ong views print culture as more conducive to questioning and innovation. The topical invention of orality led to an emphasis on explaining, rather than on discovering.

Perhaps one of the most crucial aspects of this oral *epistémè* as described by Ong is its ethical and polemical aspect. In oral cultures, because knowledge depended on mnemonic devices, like those permitted by epic narration, there was a drive to conceive of things in terms of ethical values. Truth was a matter of deliberating on good and evil. Indeed, truth in oral cultures remained bound by its goal and its circumstances. Fundamentally, it aimed at acting, and its practice was polemical.

> In brief, the movement from oral through typographic culture, as we shall see, corresponds in great part in a shift from a more polemically textured culture to a less polemically textured one, from a culture in which personality structures are expressly organized quite typically for combat, real or imaginary, to one in which hostilities are less publicly exploited and personality structures become expressly organized for greater "objectivity" and, ultimately, for decision making under maximally quantified, neutralized control (decision making based on massive command of data such as computers implement). (*Presence*, 194)

With a special interest toward the world of Renaissance pedagogy, Ong defines the crucial role of adversarial relations in the long tradition of Latin teaching, when jousts and dialectical tournaments were the staples of an orally based classroom instruction (*Rhetoric*, chap. 5). Consequently, truth pertained to probability, since ethical deliberation was not an exact science. The shift from an oral culture to a script one represented a change from the "logic of disputation" to the "logic of private inquiry" (*Presence*, 211).

Yet the ambiguity that we have located in Ong's account of Renaissance rhetoric is still at play. Because it relied on commonplaces, discourse in oral culture was characterized by an emphasis on arrangement, a feature that Ong associates with script. This becomes quite unsatisfactory because it provides us with a rather rigid, if not useless (because contradictory), model of mediation. There are other passages where Ong recognizes that a visually oriented culture does necessarily exclude elements pertaining to orality.

> The fantastically organized memory systems explicated by Miss Yates deal with knowledge with a still highly oral framework insofar as they imply that knowledge is unrecorded and thus must be memorized even at exhausting cost to assure accessibility. (*Presence*, 26)

Moreover, this difficulty in precisely defining the respective sensorium spheres of orality and literacy also appears when Ong tackles the issue of contemporary media, characterized by the use of computers and script, and its so-called secondary orality (*Presence*, 89-90; *Rhetoric*, chap. 6). While Ong sees the spread of computer use as another stage in the dominance of script, he also remarks that technologies such as television have also brought back the popularity of sound as a means of communication. This new presence of the voice would be manifest in the ritual gathering around certain television shows such as quizzes. As Gunther Thomas remarks, Ong's analysis is seriously wanting, and falling short of its goals: how could the perception of television's images be dissociated from its sound?

Actually, it seems to us that it is less pressing to supplement Ong's work with new thoughts on the nature of televised media, since there are questions that are more urgent now when new forms such as the World Wide Web are available and gaining popularity. But what remains crucial is to clarify the ambiguity that we have located in both his Renaissance and general assessment of oral and script cultures. Perhaps a slight displacement in the locus of historical questioning could provide us with pertinent elements to understand our contemporary mediation modes, by providing a communication model that would avoid grounding its theory in a rigid binary definition of orality and literacy. In her masterful study of Ramus, Nelly Bruyère sees the tendency of Ramus to lay out knowledge in a diagrammatic fashion as reminiscent of the art of memory which she associates closely with the art of the emblem: "Jamais constitutifs du savoir, ni point de départ pour de nouvelles recherches, comme chez Bacon, ces schémas dichotomiques relèvent d'un art de mémoire dépouillé de son ancienne enveloppe d'images et d'emblèmes" (*Méthode*, 121). Would an inquiry into this specific iconic mediation provide us with a fruitful perspective to critically elaborate on Ong's insights?

3. Post-Reformation Information Mode: A Rhetoric of the Emblem

There are many important elements of Ong's interpretation of Ramist method that can be found in Jesuit culture.[13] Tackling methodological practices of these religious men is significant, for across the early modern period, they were Europe's intellectual elite and the educators of Catholic Europe. Before we tackle a specific aspect of this method, the *rhétorique des peintures*, let us define some key elements that pertain to the Society intellectual practices at a more general level.

METHOD AND MORALS

The founding fathers of the Society of Jesus adopted many of the Humanistic tenets that informed Ramus.[14] This meant recognizing Ciceronian rhetoric as their standard of discourse (Dear). The Jesuits certainly did not reject Aristotelian logical and demonstrative discursive practices, as shown in the *Commentariorum Collegii Conimbricensis e Societatis Iesu in universam dialecticam Aristotelis Stagiritae* (1607). But persuasion became an important aspect of their method. Rhetoric did bear on discourse not only as a matter of style, but also with its standard of truth, verisimilitude. In another important treatise on the art of discourse, Pedro da Fonseca's *Institutionum dialectarum libri octo* (1564), dialectical argumentative techniques are confused with those of rhetoric. Without specification, Fonseca writes on the subject of arguments: "Dividi solet hoc genus in syllogismum, enthymema, inductionem, et exemplum" (*Inst. Dial.*, 330; cf. Aristotle, *Post. Anal.* 1: 1, *Rhet.* 1: 2, 7-8).[15] In Gérard Pelletier's *Palatium reginae eloquentiae* (1641), the example is listed as a kind of proof under the heading of induction, while both induction and example can also be found next to comparisons and fictions in the chapter on similes (55-58, 145).

There are many reasons that explain such an important shift in the scientific method of the Jesuits, including the rise of probabilistic ethics and casuistry in moral theology. Fumaroli remarks: "It is accepted today that their contextualized and narrative description and evaluations of sins had its epistemic model, if not its neo-classical style, in the ethico-rhetorical investigations of the Humanists ("Jesuit," 97). This orientation in method also involved defining important anthropological tenets. Consequently, arrangement and visuality came to define the nature of judgment in the method taught by the Jesuits as well.

In the wake of the Reformation, Catholic religious authorities reaffirmed the crucial role of free will of individuals on the path to salvation. Theologians such as Luis de Molina recognized the infinite variety of human moral situations, and therefore the contingent and probable nature of the judgments called for in these situations ("Probabilisme"). Probabilistic ethics admitted that when facing two probable but contrary solutions to a problem, one could legitimately opt for the least certain, to Blaise Pascal's indignation: "C'est une fausseté horrible de dire qu'on peut se sauver aussi bien par l'une que par l'autre de deux opinions contraires et dont il y en a par conséquent une fausse" (942). This allowed bodily affect to be taken into consideration in finding moral truth, within the range of more or less plausible choices. For a given moral case, truth was a balancing act between reason and bodily needs, because the theologians found the good in the moderation of passions, and not in a rejection of all affect. Theirs was a theology of the incarnate

God, in the sense that if God had seen fitting to take human form, they thought that he must have been benevolent toward the flaws of that nature.[16]

Not every opinion, however, could be elected as moraly valid. Any option had to be provided by an authority. Thus probabilistic morals gave rise to casuistry to reconcile personal needs and standard moral tenets. The study of each moral case was the natural result of a contingent view of truth. In spite of the benevolent character, not to say complacency, of moral theologians such as Antonin Diana, the art of casuistry certainly remained the hallmark of a culture of authority and tradition.

Curiously, these theological tenets spread in the domains of practical and speculative sciences, fostering a climate of skepticism with regards to the certainty of human knowledge.[17] While the entire body of Jesuit science can not be qualified as probabilistic and sophistical, the work of Rivka Feldhay and Giovanni Baffetti has shown that this rhetoricization came to represent, quite rightly and in the view of many rationalists, the nature of their method. The rules governing the world adapted to the freedom of human judgment. Explanations of nature were moving. The crux of the matter was the fact that understanding the world was seen as *praise to God*, as the first words of Ignatius of Loyola's *Spiritual Exercises* commanded. Truth, then, was defined by its goal, and belonged to those who could move souls toward faith. Searching for pleasure in describing the world with rhetorical ornaments such as allegories, quoting traditional sources, or allowing probability and verisimilitude to function as criteria of an argument, were all acceptable means in scientific procedure. The scientific understanding and description of reality was not only enhanced by fiction, but could also fit the poetic needs of a given context. Nature could be read as a great book of witticisms.

Memory and the Discipline of Knowledge in Jesuit Early Modern Culture

What brings us closer to our concern in this paper is an important intellectual function that the Jesuits brought forward: memory, or the art of visual arrangement, a notion that I consider to be a correlate of probabilistic method. There are many Jesuit texts that serve the purpose of praising memory. Its preeminence was related to the choice of Ciceronian rhetoric, over Seneca's style, as a standard of linguistic persuasion in the Jesuit curriculum, a choice which also entailed a specific anthropological understanding of the somatics of human intelligence. Memory was close to imagination and the visual sense because it was understood as a capacity to keep images in time (see Aristotle's *De anima*, or *Post. Anal.* 2: 19; Bolzoni, 130-78).

Antonio Possevino's (1533-1611) book *Bibliotheca selecta de ratione studiorum* (1593) is here an important source of information. The book was conceived as a treatise on knowledge acquisition, a guide to the curriculum of schools, and a sum of present knowledge. The first chapter of the book, titled "De cultura ingeniorum," was successful enough to be published separately, and was also translated into Italian. The text aims to answer a basic question: how can human intelligence develop to its full potential? For this, Possevino tackled the ideas of two physicians, Girolamo Cardano (1501-1576), and Juan Huarte (1529-1588). The first affirmed that human nature was principally governed by heat and humidity. He also claimed that these qualities were most influential in superior minds, which made such persons particularly immoral. Since studying was seen as having a drying effect, Cardano suggested that long reading and writing vigils, and hence a rather solitary lifestyle, was beneficial to scholars (314). Huarte was a Spaniard who defined various relations between temperaments, rhetorical styles, and intellectual aptitude. In an important treatise titled *Examen de ingenios para las ciencias* (1575; translated in French), he explained that florid style was the product of minds governed by the powers of imagination and memory.[18] What disturbed Possevino in Huarte's theory was his affirmation that very few intellects reunite both memory and intelligence. For Huarte, it was principally the melancholic types, with their body types marked by dryness, who were true geniuses.

> Ceux-là qui ont ensemble l'imagination avec la mémoire, et qui travaillent à recueillir le grain de tout ce qui a été dit et écrit en leur faculté le savent bien mettre en avant, quand l'occasion se présente avec un grand ornement de paroles, et gracieuses nuances de parler, desquels l'industrie en toutes sciences est si grande, qu'il semble à ceux qui ignorent cette doctrine, qu'ils sont fort profonds et haut: mais aussi quand ils viennent à fonder les fondements de ce qu'ils disent et affirment, ils découvrent leur imperfection. Ce qui vient de ce que l'entendement (auquel appartient savoir la vérité des choses dès leur racine) ne peut se joindre à l'ornement du langage et abondance de paroles. (243)

Copia is here seen as antithetical to intelligence. This opinion could only scandalize the Jesuits who championed Cicero's eloquence, characterized by abundance, notably in the form of brilliant visual ornaments. Huarte's theory was predictably bound with a positive assessment of Senecan rhetoric, a concise style marked by the work of *ingenium* rather than memory. There are many texts by religious figures such as Giulio Negrone and Nicolas Caussin who advocate the preeminence of memory in the production of discourse. They affirmed that all types of intelligence could successfully attain true knowledge. Caussin, for example, warned against excesses of melancholy. The crux of the matter appears in the following passage, where Possevino challenges Cardano's contention that humoral theory actually determines intellectual capacities:

> Non è sicuro fondamento quello di Galeno, e molto meno quell di persone, le quali sendo dotte, e Christiane si lasciano abbagliare

> la vista da quelle, che piu sono apparenze, che raggioni. Dalla volonta nostra dunque, e dal libero arbitrio procedono l'azioni. Ne la malinconia, ne gl'altri humori ci tolgono quella giurisdizione, laquale da Dio stesso ci è lasciata libera. (*Coltura*, 25)

By giving a crucial role to memory, the teachers of Catholic Europe's elite affirmed not only that everyone could freely and successfully cultivate their intellect, but they also signaled that knowledge should happen within the limits of a defined curriculum, a body of commonplaces. Melancholics were viewed as solitary and individualistic types, whereas those who cultivated their memory skills were prone to follow traditions. Ciceronian rhetoric, by uniting thought and rhetorical expression, was by definition the style of orthodox knowledge, in the context of probabilism. This is why it was fiercely defended.

There is a tight relation between the ideas defended in Possevino's chapter "De cultura ingeniorum," and the book that contains it. The *Bibliotheca selecta* is a sum of all knowledge available at the time, properly selected, "digested," and ordered. In the late Renaissance, many books of commonplaces were published to facilitate the acquisition of knowledge in the context of an ever increasing printing activity. These huge books provided tools to discipline human intelligence.

A Method of Artful Arrangement

In this culture of memory and the commonplace, arrangement could only be considered to be the most important intellectual operation. Because memory provided the means of invention, treatises and textbooks of logic by Jesuits such as Jean Voellus stated that judgment was a matter of *dispositio*: "Iudicium, sive usus iudicativus, est ille, quo ratio iam inventas et apprehensas disponendo iudicat, et de iis, velut iudex, in alterutram partem fert sententiam: num illae inter se iam dispositae ac combinatae, ita sint aut non sint" (4). Truth was a matter of finding an order, much as Walter Ong found out about Ramus. This was a method characterized by a ready-to-think attitude toward the acquisition of knowledge.

In the perspective of storytelling, one could say that such a concept of discourse favored adding plot twists over building a narrative climax, that is, its preferred genre was the epic. Art as a product of human imagination, as Guido Morpurgo Tagliabue as shown in what is arguably one of the most insightful texts on the baroque rhetorical epistemology, was also conceived as an artful disposition. Figures of speech, such as metaphors, allegories, chiasms, and especially antitheses, were all seen as results of finding an ingenious order to provoke feelings of marvel in the audience (see also Frare). For a *concettista* like Emanuele Tesauro, one could provide a comprehensive theory of tropes by viewing them in the perspective of logical discourse. For Tesauro, witticisms are enthymemes, that is, truncated syllogisms. At the same time, this gave a dignity to art and justified its use in teaching: *delectare* was *docere*.[19]

Dispositio, by being the characteristics of both scientific judgment and art, was the point of contact between these aspects of discourse, and ultimately allowed them to be the same under the rule of ethics, imagination, and *ingenium*. For that, the Baroque rhetoricians were truly the heirs of the Humanists and their pedagogical ideals. Yet they pushed this stylistics of method to its extreme by allowing artfulness to reign in all domains of knowledge. As we have seen, this was not a controversial proposition in the context of a religious view of the world, since knowledge was praise to God.

VISUALITY AND EMBLEMATIC COMMUNICATION

To complete this assessment of *Asianist* method, let us remark on its visual nature. Such rhetoric can be understood in the larger context of the Council of Trent's aftermath. Religious authorities, in defining a strategy to counter the rise of Protestantism in Europe, had prescribed the use of images as a means of communication, provided that they would not be worshiped as idols. Many treatises were then written to define the rules of a proper Catholic art of painting (Paleotti). In churches, theaters, and urban landscapes, images multiplied to propagate the faith. Jesuit colleges were of course at the vanguard of this iconic communication. Students were taught in specially designed classes on how to create and decipher images (Montagu). Above all, the teachings of Ignatius of Loyola, who proposed in his *Spiritual Exercises* to meditate on visual representations to convert the soul, greatly contributed to this trend. Images were valued because they have the power to move human passions with great effect. To those who remarked that the very point of religious teaching was to tame those passions, the proponents of images replied that God had brought his own image to humankind as Christ. Moreover, Christ had left several images, called *achéropoiètes*, as a reminder of his presence on earth: the veil of Veronica, the holy shroud, and a portrait sent to the king of Edessa.

We have already commented on the specific anthropological tenets that underlined this tendency to visualize the *dispositio* of communication. But there are also important aspects pertaining to method that explain this emphasis. In Fonseca's essential treatise, an example is deemed to be a form of argument, equivalent to induction. Following Aristotle, examples could be invented, being then "subdivided into comparisons or fables, such as those of Aesop and the Libyan" (*Rhet.* 2: 19, 20). These fables were often the subject of emblems or *ekphraseis*, which sought to communicate a moral message by presenting vivid renditions of the story. Let us note also that Fonseca considered the process of definition to be a way of speaking, and not simply a source of invention.[20] It is then interesting to remark, following Gombrich and Fumaroli ("Définition") that rhetoricians tended to construct visual emblems on the basis of scholastic definition. Images were proofs. All this made sense in a rhetorical context: proving, especially when the subject is divinely revealed truth, did not necessarily require a syllogism; it could also consist of an addition of vivid images, capable of moving affects in view of persuasion.

No wonder then that amplification (*copia*), whose principal resources stem from the definition and the example, is a crucial element in the demonstrative mode of baroque discourse. In important rhetorical treatises such as Nicolas Caussin's *De eloquentia sacra et humana libri XVI* (1619), or Gérard Pelletier's *Palatium reginae eloquentiae*, amplification is given a prominent place, if not together with demonstration, then between invention and deduction. Overwhelming the mind by adding elements in a sequence of ready-made arguments was the Post-Reformation information mode.[21] In Fumaroli's analysis, the importance given to definition and description in rhetoric shows the permanence of Platonism and hermeticism in the discursive tenets of the Jesuits ("Définition," 39-40). But one can also claim that this emphasis was motivated by a skeptical, if not sophistical, view of speech. Indeed, Albert R. Jonsen and Stephen Toulmin remark that amplification was an essential feature of casuistry.[22]

Such a drive toward proof by the sensory means of visualization would explain why Pascal protested against the sophistical procedures used by Étienne Noël in his arguments against the existence of the void. Pascal writes about his opponent's experimental proofs:

> Il les propose néanmoins avec une hardiesse telle qu'elles seraient reçues pour véritables de tous ceux qui n'ont point vu le contraire; car il dit que les yeux le font voir; que tout cela ne se peut nier; qu'on le voit à l'œil, quoique les yeux nous fassent voir le contraire. Ainsi il est évident qu'il n'a vu aucune des expériences dont il parle. (Lettre de Pascal à M. Le Pailleur, 388)

Rhetorical visibility and *evidentia* had taken over the burden of scientific proof.

The tendency toward visualization in its ethical, methodical, anthropological, and political values explains the crucial importance of Ciceronianism, which, much more than Seneca's style, was characterized by florid ornaments including visual figures. But perhaps the best way to understand this visual culture of communication is to study the immense success of the emblem, an iconic form which, I argue, is an important paradigm of communication in this context.

The Jesuits produced an impressive quantity of emblematic books, particularly between the years 1607 and 1650, in the wake of Blaise de Vigenère's *Les images, ou Tableaux de platte-peinture*. Among these religious works, the *Imago primi saeculi Societatis Iesu* (1640) stands out: it is a monumental celebration of the Society's achievements, published for its centennial anniversary.[23] The French were not left behind in this trend. Specifically, Marc Fumaroli has documented the success of a *rhétorique des peintures*, with its privilege given to ekphrasis and hypothyposis, under the reigns of Henri IV and Louis XIII.[24] Louis Richeome's *Tableaux sacrés* (1601) and *La peinture spirituelle* (1611), or Pierre Le Moyne's *Les peintures morales* (1640) testify to the widespread existence of a culture of iconic communication. While these works are concerned with teaching a moral message, one should not restrict the importance of emblems to religion or ethics. For example, the political works of Claude-François Menestrier, such as his descriptions of princely festivals, or his history of Louis XIV, can only be understood on the background of the emblem form.[25] Such a field of inquiry presents us with many opportunities to understand in a novel way the constitution of modern political power in relation to visual mediation.

Typical subjects of emblems were fables and allegorical stories. The emblem's text, usually a short poem or a *narratio*—the entire emblem being then called *emblema triplex*—stands in duplicate relation to the image and its motto, as Menestrier puts it in his *Art des emblèmes*: "La différence est que les paroles de l'emblème ne servent qu'à expliquer la figure au lieu que la sentence de la devise ne fait qu'un tout avec les figures, et explique plutôt la pensée de l'auteur, que le corps de la devise" (23). In the Renaissance tradition of symbolic images, emblematic communication was purposely enigmatic, and its deciphering involved a complex back and forth movement between text and image. For the purpose of religious teaching aimed at a general public, the Jesuits proposed emblems that were considerably simpler. Their value consisted chiefly in the witty and visual nature of their mediation.

Another crucial characteristic of the emblematic image is that it was widely viewed as standing on its own as a unit of meaning. First, it carried the idea of something detachable, akin to an element of mosaic, or a marquetry. It was thought to be something decorative and ornamental, to be removed from its support, and possibly borrowed and grafted on another support. Rhetoricians also designated discursive ornaments as emblems to express the idea that these were borrowed from other sources. Jean Baudoin, for example, explains that according to the Greek origins of the word, the emblem properly describes an embedded ornament. For Silvestro Pietrasancta, antique emblems were inlays, or seals, set on furniture, vases, and vessels (157-59). Emblematic discourse thus pertained to the notion of *amplificatio*, of an additive nature of visual elements. It called for judgments of arrangement.

Much of these emblematic concepts of discourse must be understood within the tradition of artificial memory. As the studies of Frances Yates, Paolo Rossi, and Lina Bolzoni have documented, such mnemonics were often associated with strains of Neoplatonic thought and hermeticism. It also incorporated elements of Lull's combinatory. Yet there was an essential difference between late scholastic memory systems as practiced by the Jesuits and the conceptions of Giulio Camillo (1480-c.1544), to name one of the better known Humanists in the memory tradition. Camillo invented a memory theater that represented human knowledge in its entirety, thus making the human mind a reflection of the cosmos. Speech, in this context, was not a mere representation, but a subjective and unique recreation, an argument for the dignity and prerogative of the human creature. Humanist thinking was fiercely anthropocentric.

When erudite Jesuits taught their pupils how to use emblems and commonplaces, such as those proposed in Possevino's *Bibliotheca*, they invited them to use knowledge in a public, that is to say, controllable way. Memory and mentalism, while still deriving from the fundamental belief in human freedom, could serve quite different purposes, from the enchanted world of the Renaissance, full of analogies, to the conservative and militant world of the Catholic Reformation. As Jean-Marc Chatelain puts it, baroque speech is fundamentally skeptical: "La vogue des livres d'emblèmes ne se comprend pas en dehors d'une problématique générale de la connaissance dont le mode de questionnement se rapporte à la séparation des mots et des choses" (25). Probabilism is at once the recognition of man's freedom, and, in a theological perspective, of his bodily and fallen nature. It brought about a mediation that participated in both orality and literacy, as a performance of *dispositio*.

The emblem appears to be the privileged medium of *Asianist*, or baroque, communication. First, this communication concerns visual signs. It is emblematic as artful arrangement, both within the emblem itself and in the way it arranges these emblems. This arrangement also conveys the notion of digression, accumulation, and repetition. The context of this discourse is rhetorical, as it tends to consider an allegory of values as a logic. Finally, such a discourse appears to be grounded in thomistic philosophical realism, in a theology of the Fall, in various anthropological notions of mentalism, and in politics. It is a discipline of the mind.

To conclude this section, let us say that Ong's model of communication, by ascribing strict sensory values to the opposition between orality and literacy, can only lead to many shortcomings. Baroque discourse displays many visual elements that are characteristics of rhetorical performance. As far as Ong's work is concerned, a strict association of visual communication with the literate is a reification of the sensorium that participates in the same strategy of knowledge discipline that he wished to denounce. What our research in the history of rhetoric suggests is that one should rather qualify changes in mediation modes as shifts between the poles of invention and arrangement, and between the poles of certainty and verisimilitude, gestures which entail different modes of embodiment. In such a history of mediation, it remains to be seen whether previous configuration of information modes are not analogous to ours, thus allowing a critical understanding of how mediation bears on contemporary human relations.

4. Cybernetics

"The Internet is the specific name of the communication network that is composed of interconnected computers that fully exchange information with each other worldwide," writes Burnett (46). A true revolution in the history of media, the Internet, through e-mail and the World Wide Web, has increased the speed, availability, and quantity of data that individuals can access. The effects of the Internet's invention have been felt rapidly, down to the most banal aspects of everyday life; one can wonder how such change would compare with the print revolution. As I have outlined in the introduction, there are many scholars who have pointed out the similarities between the early modern media revolution and our contemporary one.

What is at stake in this convergence of interest toward the early modern is the assessment of the true emancipatory and progressive potential of the Internet. Indeed, the new modes of information brought about by the Internet raise important issues because they define new relations between subject, the body, and technology in everyday life and social relations. While some have hailed the advent of the Internet as a powerful means to foster and improve human relations in view of social justice, others have been more circumspect in their assessment. On the one hand, some see e-mail and the Web as constituting the ideal forum for political discussion, in line with Jürgen Habermas's concept of the public sphere. Others in this same group emphasize how the Web, with its apparently limitless possibilities of linking and associating, has rendered mediacentric modes of communication obsolete by blurring the traditional author/reader distinction.[26] One does not passively receive information in front of a web browser like a television viewer does.

On the other hand, some have taken a rather grim view of technology's capacity to foster human freedom. This pessimistic assessment pertains to the notion of determinism, that is, the idea that technology delivers information, notably by extending the human sensorium in ways that alter human consciousness and its ability to judge freely. Technological determinism has been frequently associated with the media theories of Marshall McLuhan, and with Ong's, which is not surprising given that McLuhan was his teacher. As we saw previously, Ong's critique of literacy is grounded in the opinion that mediation is a form of alienation, distancing the subject from the authenticity of objects.

But as Burnett and Marshall remark in the perspective of these debates: "Closer to reality is that cybernetics produces a dialectic of constraint and innovation" (28; see also 43, and D. Bell). Technologies, while they inform data and their meaning, are also created by human agents. Hence we should accept a more balanced view in assessing the impact of technologies on human freedom, by recognizing that the Internet, and particularly the Web, is a "contested territory" (Burbules, "Web," 76). The Internet has some remarkable features, capable of fostering better communication and knowledge, thus enhancing lives with self-care and social relations. Yet like other media, it also has the potential to alienate and subjugate with its particular means of communication, beyond the political economy of its deployment.

The Web's mode of operation, then, seems quite remote from what is considered its prototype, Vannevar Bush's Memex system (Johnson, 116-23). In a 1945 issue of the *Atlantic Monthly*, Bush proposed the project of a communication machine that would have allowed its user to navigate freely from document to document by free association. Indeed, there is much that evokes the Internet in this original project. Yet there was a crucial diffference:

> Bush's Memex owner *builds* that "trail of interest" as he explores the information-space on his desk. Surfers, as a rule, *follow* trails of interest, through links that have been assembled in advance by other folks: designers, writers, editors, and so on. (Johnson, 121)

Moreover, there are many other features of the Web that define knowledge in ways that erode the freedom of users. There are filters, indicies, portals, search engines, and frequency indicators that restrict and shape the intertextuality of the Web. The Web is also a response to powerful commercial and state interests. Increasingly, it is also the site of legal debates concerning ownership and censorship.

Perhaps one crucial way to claim agency in the contested territory of the Internet is to first recognize, on the background of its material conditions of production and consumption (Lister, et al, 139), its relational and associative nature.[27] The crucial feature of Web communication is the link, which is, in other words, a process of arrangement, of *dispositio*: "The link, then, is the elemental structure that represents a hypertext as a [...] web of meaningful relations" (Burbules, "Rhetorics of the Web" 105). In an age where quantity, availability, and speed of delivery have grown exponentially, knowing pertains more to assessing than accessing (Bell, 190; Lévy, 158). Assessing consists in comparing and ordering, that is, studying and defining relations. Or, in other words, from the modernist procedures of induction and deduction, knowing has shifted to organizing. This was the great insight of Jean-François Lyotard's *La condition postmoderne*.

What we need then is a critical literacy of the Web that would consist of the skills necessary to evaluate the links that are proposed on the Web, to give one example. In two remarkable articles, Nicholas Burbules articulates the rhetorical terms that such critical literacy could use in interpreting and creating such links as signs (see also Gurak). As we have seen, Internet links are not created by the browser, but are authored, and as such they bear meaning.[28] If, as Pierre Lévy suggests, teachers must now be concerned with organizing skills as much as with dispensing information (158), the tasks of pedagogy consist in devising activities which foster a critical understanding of discursive arrangements. The work of George Landow is here groundbreaking, notably when it proposes smart hypertext exercises (233).

Such rhetorical literacy would not only prove to be useful to understand the Web, but would also be pertinent to many other facets of contemporary cultural productions. The process of *remediation* itself must be understood in the perspective of the link, thus calling for a critical literacy of the link. Much of what seems new in new information modes is actually a recycling of older forms: "The 'new' in the new media is the manner in which the digital technologies that they employ 'refashions older media' and then these older media refashion themselves to answer the challenges of new media" (Lister, et al, 40, quoting Bolter and Grusin).[29] Fragmentation has been for a long time a feature of television's promotional aesthetics, which constructs sequences, or "flows," of segments of fiction, advertisements, and various jingles to retain audience attention (Burnett and Marshall, 88). In the end though, fiction seems created to facilitate the reach of advertisers. In the age of the Web, a media which fosters even more a culture of the clip and sound bite, this aesthetics is ever more present on television, with political meanings that are as powerful as they are subtle.[30]

The vital role played by interfaces is also pertinent to this interpretation of contemporary modes of information as belonging to a culture of the link. In a clearly written and highly suggestive book titled *Interface Culture*, Steven Johnson describes the interface as:

> A new cultural form hovering somewhere between medium and message, a metaform that lives in the nether land between information producer and consumer. The interface is a way of mapping that strange new territory, a way for us to get our bearings in a bewildering environment. (Johnson, 38)[31]

Such a device is necessary when the quantity of information available to a subject surpasses his/her natural skills. The desktop icons displayed on the computer used to write this very paper constitute an interface. Of course, it does not take much effort to understand the meaning of the icon "scissors," "folder," and "trash can," but it is most likely that we will use more and more sophisticated interfaces in everyday life. Also, the sheer size and complexity of interfaces will lead them to proportions that will extend beyond the capacity of the average human memory. The consequence is that interface users will need to make circumstantial judgments about the interfaces that they will encounter. Some of these judgments will seem based on logic and common sense, but it is quite likely, as Johnson points out, that these same judgments will involve aesthetic choices as well: "We will come to think of the interface design as a kind of art form" (213, see also 79-80). There have been elaborate projects of interfaces that have tried to go beyond the desktop paradigm, to organize information under the tropes of a galaxy, for example. Interfaces are bound to rely more and more on synaesthesia, that is, the correspondence between various sensory data (Kress, 76). A critical literacy of the Web based on rhetorical education can teach how to manage this new information to make it a *knowledge*.

The Internet provides us with an information mode that is based on visuality, a feature that Ong has characterized as pertaining to literacy. But can we actually speak of a literacy when we are concerned with Internet-based knowledge? Pierre Lévy writes:

> Cyberspace dissolves the pragmatics of communication, which, since the invention of writing, has conjoined the universal and totality. It brings us back to a preliterate situation—but on another level and in another orbit—to the extent that the real-time interconnection and dynamism of on-line memory once again create a shared context, the same immense living hypertext for the participants in a communication. (98-99)

This is where our inquiry into the Post-Reformation mode of production proves to be useful. First, our findings in the field of the Post-Reformation information mode show how transitional information modes can pertain to the sphere of visual cognition characteristic of literacy, while retaining features of orality. Gunther R. Kress observes that "*arrangement* and *display* are the essential features of the logic of the visual" (69). But it is precisely this aspect of *dispositio* that places the process of linking in the sphere of orality. Internet speech, as many have observed, has struggled to keep the immediacy of person-to-person discourse, notably by using emoticons (Burnett and Marshall, 53). But "on the whole, Netspeak is better seen as written language which has been pulled some way in the direction of speech than as spoken language which has been written down" (Crystal, 47). I argue that it is the very discursive *dispositio* of the Internet, and of interface culture at large, that places it in the sphere of orality.

Thus much like in the Baroque, the truth criteria of contemporary information pertains to *ethics*, and not to *science*, because it is characterized by a performative nature. We live in times when "depth, narrative, and meaning are being replaced with the pleasures of sensuous experience and spectacular effects" (Lister, et al, 97). Our criteria of truth is verisimilitude, as in oral-aural cultures.

> As the true instrument of consensus, social memory does not embody an authorized version of the past, fixed for all time. Instead, the activity of commemoration continually reinterprets the past in light of an ever-changing present. In so doing, commemoration enables the community both to cohere in the present and to (re)define its aspirations for the future: memory working forward, the White Queen might have said. (Hobart and Schiffman, 27)

The historical comparison with Baroque information suggests that critical skills in an interface culture must be chiefly concerned with "counteracting the apparent naturalness of signs" (Burbules). These are the challenges faced by teachers nowadays.

Conclusion: History of Rhetoric and the Performance of Story-telling

History is a primary concern when evaluating the methods pertinent in an interface culture. A discursive *épistémè* founded on a performative idea of discursive arrangement, as Landow notes, bears also on our capacity to narrate: "Hypertext systems, which insert every text into a web of relations, produce a very different effect, for they allow non-sequential reading and thinking" (82). Johnson, in the same vein, writes hypothetically: "The links would transform our most fundamental expectations about traditional narrative. We'd come to value environment over argument, shape-shifting over consistency" (128). Walter Ong himself grasped the challenges that historical inquiry faces in our age of technological innovation.

Certainly Ong's work has limitations. As we have seen, he does not recognize that a logic of discursive arrangement can participate in the performative nature of oral statements. Visual communication is necessarily related to script, which places Ong at odds with his Jesuit peers of the French seventeenth century. Secondary orality remains for him a trait of oral communication. Also, his very faith leads him to essentialize the performance of meaning in oral cultures. Let us not forget that the title of one of his works on literacy and orality is *The Presence of the Word*. In his view, the performance of statements participates in a metaphysical continuum, a "timelessness, a supra-temporal existence." It is the living word of God, and Ong sees the general decline in religiosity of the 1960s as bound with the advent of script culture.

Nevertheless, what he criticizes as a failed relation with the past turns out to be, in my opinion, exactly what our own times demand. In the essay titled "Crisis and Understanding in the Humanities" (*Rhetoric*, chap. 13), he elaborates on how we have come to practice history in the sphere of probability and verisimilitude with a search for sameness and difference:

> Once knowledge of the past achieved a certain size or density, the present began to take on a distinctive face of its own. It now is seen to differ from the past, but does so in terms out of the past. In earlier ages when there was not enough historical background to project the present against, the present appeared largely inevitable, not something positively determined to be this rather than that, but a rather neutral circumambient medium, non-isolable, like water for a fish. Now, however, with knowledge of the past brought to the state it has reached in recent generations, the present can be examined for Renaissance, medieval, classical, preclassical, Christian, Hebrew, and countless other elements, or for its lack of one or another of these. (*Rhetoric*, 326)

These texts respond to the questions that were raised at the beginning of this essay. How can we have a modern perspective of the early modern? What is at stake when we attach that adjective, *early*, to what designates our own times? Pedagogy is a genealogy insofar as it responds to the injunctions of politics and ethics, of concerns belonging to the present. It is practiced in the sphere of probability and verisimilitude with a search for sameness and difference. This does not necessarily make it guilty of *presentism*. The question raised for this issue of EMF is particularly pertinent in these times of change in the information mode.

Finally, let us note that Ong went on to practice the type of history that he rejected in the texts previously cited. The challenge of critical discourse consists in avoiding the very rationality that it seeks to denounce. Because of philosophy's long-standing bind with technological rationality, rhetoric can then be considered the privileged object of a critical inquiry.

> It is in the rhetorical quality that culture, society, and tradition animate the thought; a stern hostility to it is leagued with barbarism, in which bourgeois thinking ends. The vilification of Cicero and even Hegel's aversion to Diderot bear witness to the resentment of those whom the trials of life have robbed of the freedom to stand tall, and who regard the body of language as sinful. (Adorno, 56)

Curiously, in this negative definition of what history has become, Ong found the principle of such a critical inquiry into technology. By practicing a history of rhetoric in the late Renaissance, Ong operated a powerful displacement of what was consensually defined as the present media mode, in the kind of *agonistic* gesture that he appreciated in oral cultures. His history of rhetoric was a rhetoric of history.

Notes

[1] Struever writes: "I use 'rhetoric' as I use 'philosophy,' a rubric designating an enduring, homogeneous discipline. Rhetoric most certainly is an art that teaches mastery of the techniques of persuasion, but rhetoric is as well, most certainly, a mode of inquiry committed to understanding the psychology and sociology of its appeal and its effects in action" (32). "There has been an intimate connection between the history of philosophy and intellectual history. I am arguing that the history of rhetoric offers a different approach to a different range of problems and solutions. The canons of inclusiveness, suppleness, and sophistication distinguish the well-founded rhetorical theory and practice—which includes the writing of instructional manuals—from a philosophical practice. However, we must accept that the distinctions operate within an integrated field of intellectual work" (35).

[2] Welch's own historical focus is on Isocratic classical Greek rhetoric.

[3] Walter Ong (1912-2003), a Jesuit priest, taught throughout most of his career at Washington University in St. Louis and was president of the MLA in 1978. See *The Life and Scholarship of Walter J. Ong, S. J.; A Digital Archive at Saint Louis University*, http://www.slu.edu/colleges/AS/ENG/ong/index.html. Accessed June 4, 2004.

[4] As Nelly Bruyère's work in *Méthode et dialectique dans l'oeuvre de La Ramée. Renaissance et âge classique* shows, Ramus's thought evolved throughout his career. We will focus here on his commentaries on Cicero and Quintilian, as well as on his 1555 *Dialectique*. This last text is considered to be a mature expression of his system and, decades before the publication of Descartes's *Discourse on the Method* (1637), arguably the first important philosophical text to be written in French.

[5] Agricola's thought was disseminated in Paris by Humanists, notably by Johannes Sturm between 1529 and 1536 (Vasoli, *Dialettica*, 311). Ramus's system proved to be very influential in northern Europe, even in the English colony of North America, and the changes in methodology that he brought about prepared the emergence of scientific and philosophical modernism.

[6] A method is a body of principles that show the right path to truth. It needs to first define a truth criterion. In a positivist scientific mindset, pleasure and discomfort, good and evil, are seldom considered to be criteria of truth. There are few who would judge the truth of a discourse on its rhetorical merits. Yet, as we will see, this is exactly what the Humanist revolution in methodology was about.

The Aristotelian definition of discourse can be found chiefly in Aristotle's *Organon*, but also in his *Rhetoric*, and in other texts as well, such as the *Physics*. Theoretical and contemplative sciences such as mathematics, natural philosophy, and metaphysics sought necessary and self-referential truths. They attained a degree of ontological certainty that was out of the reach of practical sciences, which dealt with particular and contingent matters. Practical sciences sought to produce things or, like ethics, had action as their goal.

[7] For example, see Aristotle's *Topics* 2: 2: "Now one commonplace rule is to look and see if a man has ascribed as an accident what belongs in some other way. This mistake is most commonly made in regard to the genera of things, e.g., if one were to say that being a colour is an accident of white—for being a colour does not happen by accident to white, but colour is its genus."

[8] McNally, "*Dux*," 343: "Not only was rhetoric despoiled of invention, persuasion, and the non-verbal sources of pleasure; most of the conceptual and terminological materials of classical rhetoric—among them the "states," the enthymeme and example, and ethical and pathetic proof—were pressed into the service of Agricola's expanded dialectic."

[9] See also: "He separates dialecticians from orators not according to practical use but according to the false fabrications of Aristotle, who taught that the former use syllogism, whereas the latter more freely use loose-knit speech. This man does not realize that, like grammar, dialectic through all its parts of invention and arrangement has common use in every speech; and that dialogues, lectures, debates, poems, and finally speeches—of whatever kind they may be—are all more dialectical than oratorical" (*Brut. Quaest.*, 123-24).

[10] Bruyère, *Méthode*, 233: "C'est une induction révélatrice, et non pas constitutive: c'est une expérience de la raison à l'oeuvre, non pas de la formation du rationnel."

[11] Lullism, which was well known also to Agricola, was taught in Paris by Bernard de Lavinheta in 1515.

[12] One can judge here how Ramus's thought can be seen as having played a key role in the emergence of Cartesianism; see Bruyère on this matter, *Méthode*, 385-94.

[13] The following is a condensed version of the first chapter of my book *L'optique du discours au XVIIe siècle. De la rhétorique des jésuites au style de la raison moderne (Descartes, Pascal)*. (2005).

[14] Let us remember that the founding fathers of the Society studied in Paris at the time when Ramus or others such as Vives were spreading their ideas.

[15] The book was a bestseller and was printed many times in France, until at least 1622.

[16] After many excesses, probabilistic morals were definitely condemned by the Pope in

1679.

[17] Space lacks here to elaborate on the rise of philosophical skepticism in the late Renaissance, notably in the wake of Henri Estienne and Gentian Hervet's translation of Sextus Empiricus' work (1562 and 1569).

[18] This bestseller of the Renaissance was published many times and translated twice into the French language, by Gabriel Chappuys (1598) and Charles de Vion d'Alibray (1634).

[19] Aristotle himself pointed indirectly to such a logical understanding of figures, by stating the role of *acumen* in reasoning (*Post. Anal.* 1: 34), by warning against the use of similes in arguing dialectically (*Post. Anal.* 2: 13; *Topics* 6: 2; see also Cicero, *De orat.* 2: 39, 168). In the same vein, one could read the *Sophistical Refutations* as a treatise on witticisms.

[20] *Inst. dial.* 1: 4-5; cf. Aristotle, *Post. Anal.* 2: 3.

[21] I am concerned here, then, with quite a technical view of rhetoric. Its notion of the sublime runs contrary to the letter of Longinus, who defined the sublime as the simplest means possible to express the grandest things.

[22] "The weight of a casuistical opinion came from the accumulation of reasons rather than from the logical validity of the arguments or the coherence of any single proof" (Jonsen and Toulmin, 256).

[23] Roger Paultre presents the following chronology in examining this trend: 1531-1571: formation and codification of the emblem genre; 1571-1607: the Humanistic emblem flourishes; 1606-1650: success with the Jesuits; 1650-1720: brief renewal and decline.

[24] There are many other factors that explain this French trend, including the relative proximity of the country to the Spanish Low Countries, an important production center of religious images, and the fact that French Jesuits concentrated their efforts on the aristocratic elite who, contrary to the *bourgeoisie parlementaire*, was less literate and was drawn to easy and entertaining effects.

[25] Among many texts, one could consult the narration of Lyon's festivities for the Treaty of the Pyrenees and the royal wedding: *Les Réjouissances de la paix* (1660); *Histoire du Roy Louis le Grand, par les médailles, emblèmes, devises, jettons, inscriptions, armoiries et autres monumens publics* (1693).

[26] This is where the idea of the Internet as a Deleuzian and rhizomatic text becomes relevant (Bell, 78; Landow, 38).

[27] "I would argue that the production of knowledge and information takes place within the framework of capitalism, and that while knowledge and information play significantly more central roles within techno-capitalism, they are still subject to processes of commodification, exchanges, profitability and control by capital and should therefore be conceptualized within the framework of a theory of contemporary techno-capitalism" (Kellner, *Critical Theory*, 186).

[28] "Moving from a page about IQ and intelligence to a page about the ideas of leading figures in eugenics may make users think about the implications of "innate" theories of intelligence for selective breeding; moving from a page about the ideas of leading figures of eugenics to a page about IQ may make users wonder how intelligent those thinkers actually were" (Burbules, "Web," 76).

[29] Such theoretical argument could even find support in the recent work of Jay David Bolter and Richard Grusin, who have recently proposed the concept of *remediation* (for a critique: Lister, et al, 155-154; Fagersjord). For them, the history of information modes cannot be thought in terms of progress and "technological Darwinism." Media history does consist in technological advances. The new media modes do not replace previous ones, but recuperate and recycle previous modes. For example, much of the Web's design is shaped by the design of tabloid newspapers, and in return cable news programs are increasingly presented as screens loaded with various windows of information, much like the Internet has come to be

(Crystal, 200). In Bolter and Grusin's analysis, the process of remediation is characterized by the twin logic of immediacy and hypermediacy. On one hand, information is presented as a whole, and pertains to the realm of certainty in invention. On the other hand, it stresses its composite nature, and hence its performative and circumstantial nature in arrangement. "The appeal to authenticity of experience is what brings the logic of immediacy and hypermediacy together" (71).

[30] Take the representation of the 2003 war in Iraq on cable news channels. Sequences of information footage were shown with a background of martial music, then followed by patriotic animated jingles to frame the information, and finished with U.S. Army commercials featuring virtually the same drum beating music, all in quick sequence. This mixing of real images and fictional images, together with soundtrack and visual stimuli, transformed reporting into epic narrating. It replaced ethos with pathos in the exercise of journalism.

[31] "An interface is any device that enables interaction between the universe of digitalized information and the ordinary world" (Lévy, 19).

Works cited

Adorno, Theodor W. *Negative Dialectics*. Trans. E. B. Ashton. New York: Seabury Press, 1973.

Aristotle. *The Complete Works of Aristotle: The Revised Oxford Edition*. 2 vols. Ed. J. Barnes. Princeton: Princeton University Press, 1984.

Baffetti, Giovanni. *Retorica e scienza. Cultura gesuitica e Seicento italiano*. Bologna: CLUEB, 1997.

Bell, David. *An Introduction to Cybercultures*. London and New York: Routledge, 2001.

Blanchard, Jean-Vincent. *L'optique du discours au XVIIe siècle. De la rhétorique des jésuites au style de la raison moderne (Descartes, Pascal)*. Sainte-Foy: Presses de L'Université Laval, 2005.

Bolland, Jean. *Imago primi saeculi Societatis Iesu*. Antwerp: B. Moretus, 1641.

Bolter, Jay David, and Richard Grusin. *Remediation: Understanding New Media*. Cambridge and London: MIT Press, 2000.

Bolzoni, Lina. *The Gallery of Memory: Literary and Iconographic Models in the Age of the Printing Press*. Toronto: University of Toronto Press, 2001.

Brody, Florian. "The Medium is the Memory." In *The Digital Dialectic: New Essays on New Media*, ed. P. Lunenfeld, 135-49. Cambridge: MIT Press, 1999.

Bruyère, Nelly. *Méthode et dialectique dans l'œuvre de La Ramée. Renaissance et âge classique*. Paris: J. Vrin, 1984.

———. "Le statut de l'invention dans l'oeuvre de La Ramée." *Revue des sciences philosophiques et théologiques* 70 (1986): 15-24.

Burbules, Nicholas C. "Rhetorics of the Web: Hyperreading and Critical Literacy." In *Page to Screen: Taking Literacy into the Electronic Era*, ed. I. Snyder, 102-22. London and New York: Routledge, 1998.

———. "The Web as a Rhetorical Place." In *Silicon Literacies: Communication, Innovation, and Education in the Electronic Age*, ed. I. Snyder, 75-84. London and New York: Routledge, 2002.

Burnett, Robert, and P. David Marshall. *Web Theory: An Introduction*. London and New York: Routledge, 2003.

Calabrese, Omar. *Neo-Baroque: A Sign of the Times*. Trans. C. Lambert. Princeton: Princeton University Press, 1992.

Cardano, Girolamo. *De la subtilité, et subtiles inventions, ensemble les causes occultes, et raisons d'icelles*. Trans. R. Le Blanc. Paris: P. Cavelat, 1584.

Caussin, Nicolas. *Electorum symbolorum et parabolarum historicarum stromata XII libris complectens*. Paris: R. de Beauvais, 1618.

———. *De eloquentia sacra et humana libri XVI*. 1619. Paris: N. de La Coste, 1630.

Chartier, Roger. *Culture écrite et société. L'ordre des livres (XIVe – XVIIIe siècles)*. Paris: A. Michel, 1996.

Chatelain, Jean-Marc. *Livres d'emblèmes et de devises*. Paris: Klincksieck, 1993.

Cicero. *De oratore*. 2 vols. Trans. E. W. Sutton. Cambridge: Harvard University Press, 1988.

Commentariorum Collegii Conimbricensis e Societatis Iesu in universam dialecticam Aristotelis Stagiritae. Cologne: B. Galthier, 1607.

Crystal, David. *Language and the Internet*. Cambridge: Cambridge University Press, 2001.

Dear, Peter. *Mersenne and the Learning of the Schools*. Ithaca: Cornell University Press, 1988.

Eisenstein, Elizabeth. *The Printing Press as an Agent of Change: Communications and Cultural Transformations in Early Modern Europe*. Cambridge and New York: Cambridge University Press, 1979.

Fagersjord, Anders. "Rhetorical Convergence: Studying Web Media." In *Digital Media Revisited: Theoretical and Conceptual Innovation in Digital Domains*. Cambridge and London: MIT Press, 2003.

Farrell, Thomas J. "An Overview of Walter J. Ong's Work" In *Media, Consciousness, and Culture: Explorations of Walter Ong's Thought*, ed. B. E. Gronbeck, T. J. Farrell, and P. A. Soukup, 25-49. Newbury Park: Sage, 1991.

Feldhay, Rivka. "Knowledge and Salvation in Jesuit Culture." *Science in Context* 2, no. 1 (1987): 195-213.

Fonseca, Pedro da. *Instituições Dialécticas. Institutionum dialectarum libri octo*. 1564. Trans. J. Ferreira Gomes. Coïmbra: Universidade de Coïmbra, 1964.

Frare, Pierantonio. "Contro la metafora. Antitesi e metafora nella prassi e nella teoria letteraria del Seicento." *Studi Secenteschi* 33 (1992): 3-20.

Fumaroli, Marc. *L'âge de l'éloquence. Rhétorique et res literaria de la Renaissance au seuil de l'époque classique*. Geneva: Droz, 1980.

———. "Définition et description. Scolastique et rhétorique chez les jésuites des

XVIᵉ et XVIIᵉ siècles." *Travaux de linguistique et de littérature* 18, no. 2 (1980): 37-48.

———. "The Fertility and Shortcomings of Renaissance Rhetoric: The Jesuit Case." In *The Jesuits: Cultures, Sciences, and the Arts, 1540-1773*, ed. J. W. O'Malley et al., 90-106. Toronto: University of Toronto Press, 1999.

Gilbert, Neal W. *Renaissance Concepts of Method*. New York: Columbia University Press, 1960.

Gombrich, Ernst. "Icones Symbolicae: Philosophies of Symbolism and Their Bearing on Art." *Journal of the Warburg and Courtauld Institute* 11 (1948): 163-92.

Graziani, Françoise. "L'art comme vertu intellectuelle. L'aristotélisme du Tasse et de Tesauro." *Littératures classiques* 11 (1989): 25-41.

Gronbeck, Bruce E. "The Rhetorical Studies Tradition and Walter J. Ong: Oral-Literacy Theories of Mediation, Culture, and Consciousness." In *Media, Consciousness, and Culture: Explorations of Walter Ong's Thought*, ed. B. E. Gronbeck, T. J. Farrell, and P. A. Soukup, 5-24. Newbury Park: Sage, 1991.

Gurak, Laura J. *Navigating the Internet with Awareness*. New Haven and London: Yale University Press, 2001.

Hobart, Michael E, and Zachary S. Schiffman. *Information Ages: Literacy, Numeracy, and the Computer Revolution*. Baltimore and London: Johns Hopkins University Press, 1998.

Huarte, Juan. *L'examen des esprits pour les sciences*. Trans. C. de Vion d'Alibray. Paris: J. le Bouc, 1645.

Ignatius of Loyola. *Exercices spirituels*. Paris: Éditions du Seuil, 1982.

Johnson, Steven. *Interface Culture: How New Technology Transforms the Way We Create and Communicate*. New York: Basic Books, 1997.

Jonsen, Albert R., and Stephen Toulmin. *The Abuse of Casuistry: A History of Moral Reasoning*. Berkeley: University of California Press, 1988.

Kellner, Douglas M. *Critical Theory, Marxism, and Modernity*. Cambridge: Polity Press, 1989.

———. "Technological Revolution, Multiple Literacies, and the Restructuring of Education." In *Silicon Literacies: Communication, Innovation, and Education in the Electronic Age*, ed. I. Snyder, 154-69. London and New York: Routledge, 2002.

Kress, Gunther. "Visual and Verbal Modes of Representation in Electronically Mediated Communication: The Potential of New Forms of Texts." In *Page to Screen: Taking Literacy into the Electronic Era*, ed. I. Snyder, 53-79. London and New York: Routledge, 1998.

Landow, George P. *Hypertext 2.0: The Convergence of Contemporary Critical Theory and Technology*. Baltimore and London: Johns Hopkins University Press, 1997.

Leith, Philip. "Postmedieval Information Processing and Contemporary Computer Science." In *Media, Consciousness, and Culture: Explorations of Walter Ong's Thought*, ed. B. E. Gronbeck, T. J. Farrell, and P. A. Soukup, 160-76. Newbury Park: Sage, 1991.

Le Moyne, Pierre. *Les peintures morales*. Paris: S. Cramoisy, 1640.

Lévy, Pierre. *Cyberculture*. Trans. R. Bononno. Minneapolis and London: University of Minnesota Press, 2001.

Lister, Martin, and Jon Dovey, Seth Giddings, Iain Grant, and Kieran Killey. *New Media: A Critical Introduction*. London and New York: Routledge, 2003.

Lyotard, Jean-François. *La condition postmoderne*. Paris: Minuit, 1979.

McNally, James R. "*Dux illa Directrixque Artium*: Rudolph Agricola's Dialectical System." *Quarterly Journal of Speech* 52 (1966): 337-47.

———. "Rudolph Agricola's De Inventione *Dialectica Libri Tres*: A Translation of Selected Chapters." *Speech Monographs* 34, no. 4 (1967): 393-422.

Meerhoff, Kees. "Ramus et Cicéron." *Revue des sciences philosophiques et théologiques* 70 (1986): 25-35.

———. *Rhétorique et poétique au XVIe siècle. Du Bellay, Ramus et les autres*. Leiden: J. Brill, 1986.

Menestrier, Claude-François. *L'art des emblèmes*. Lyon: B. Coral, 1662.

———. *Histoire du Roy Louis le Grand, par les médailles, emblèmes, devises, jettons, inscriptions, armoiries et autres monumens publics*. Paris: R. Pepie and J.-B. Nolin, 1693.

———. *Les réjouissances de la paix*. Lyon: B. Coral, 1660.

Michel, Alain. *Rhétorique et philosophie chez Cicéron. Essai sur les fondements de l'art de persuader*. Paris: PUF, 1960.

Montagu, Jennifer. "The Painted Enigma in Seventeenth-Century Art" *Journal of the Warburg and Courtauld Institute* 31 (1968): 207-35.

Ong, Walter J. (S. J.) *Interfaces of the Word: Studies in the Evolution of Consciousness and Culture*. Ithaca and London: Cornell University Press, 1977.

———. *Orality and Literacy: The Technologizing of the Word*. London and New York: Methuen, 1982.

———. *The Presence of the Word: Some Prolegomena for Cultural and Religious History*. New Haven and London: Yale University Press, 1967.

———. *Ramus, Method, and the Decay of Dialogue: From the Art of Discourse to the Art of Reason*. 1958. New York: Octagon Books, 1974.

———. *Rhetoric, Romance, and Technology: Studies in the Interaction of Expression and Culture*. Ithaca and London: Cornell University Press, 1971.

Paleotti, Gabriele. *De imaginibus sacris et profanis*. Ingolstadt: D. Sartori, 1594.

Palmieri, Anthony J. "Ramism, Ong, and Modern Rhetoric." In *Media, Consciousness, and Culture: Explorations of Walter Ong's Thought*, ed. B. E. Gronbeck,

T. J. Farrell, and P. A. Soukup, 50-63. Newbury Park: Sage, 1991.
Pascal, Blaise. *Œuvres complètes*. Ed. J. Chevalier. Paris: Gallimard, 1954.
Paultre, Roger. *Les images du livre*. Paris: Hermann, 1991.
Pelletier, Gérard. *Palatium reginae eloquentiae*. Paris: N. Buon and J. Camusat, 1641.
Pietrasancta, Silvestro. *De symbolis heroicis libri IX*. Antwerp: B. Moretus, 1634.
Possevino, Antonio. *Bibliotheca selecta de ratione studiorum*. Rome: Typ. Apost. Vat., 1593.
——. *Coltura degl'ingegni*. Vicenza: G. Gerco, 1608.
——. *Cultura ingeniorum*. Venice: J. B. Ciotti, 1604.
"Probabilisme." *Dictionnaire de théologie catholique*. Ed. A. Vancant, et al. 16 vols. Paris: Letouzay et Ané, 1908-1950.
Quintilian. *Institutio oratoria*. 4 vols. Trans. H. E. Butler. Cambridge: Harvard University Press, 1985.
Ramus, Petrus. *Arguments in Rhetoric Against Quintilian. Translation and text of Peter Ramus's Rhetoricae Distinctiones in Quintilianum (1549)*. Trans. C. Newlands. DeKalb: Northern Illinois University Press, 1986.
——. *Dialectique 1555. Un manifeste de la Pléiade*. Paris: Vrin, 1996.
——. *Ciceronianus*. Paris: A. Wechelius, 1557.
——. *Peter Ramus's Attack on Cicero. Text and Translation of Ramus's Brutinae Quaestiones*. Ed. J. J. Murphy. Trans. C. Newlands. Davis: Hermagoras Press, 1992.
Redondi, Pietro. "Teologia e epistemologia nella rivoluzione scientifica." *Belfagor* 45, no. 1 (1990): 613-36.
Résurgences baroques. Ed. W. Moser and N. Goyer. Brussels: La lettre volée, 2001.
Richeome, Louis. *La peinture spirituelle, ou L'art d'admirer et louer Dieu en toutes ses œuvres et tirer de toutes profit salutère*. Lyon: P. Rigaud, 1611.
——. *Tableaux sacrés des figures mystiques du très auguste sacrifice et sacrement de l'Eucharistie*. Paris: L. Sonnius, 1601.
Rossi, Paolo. *Logic and the Art of Memory: The Quest for a Universal Language*. Chicago: University of Chicago Press, 2000.
Slevin, James. *The Internet and Society*. Cambridge: Polity Press, 2000.
Struever, Nancy S. "The Place of Rhetoric in Intellectual History: The Early Modern Example." *Intellectual News* (1998): 32-43.
Tagliabue, Guido M. "Aristotelismo e barocco." In *Retorica e barocco*, ed. E. Castelli, 119-95. Rome: Bocca, 1955.
Tesauro, Emanuele. *Il cannocchiale aristotelico*. Turin: Zapatta, 1670.
Thomas, Gunther. "Secondary Ritualization in a Postliterate Culture: Reconsidering

and Expanding Walter Ong's Contribution on 'Secondary Orality.'" *Soundings* 83, no. 2 (2000): 385-409.

Toledo, Francisco de. *Opera omnia philosophica*. 2 vols. Cologne: Off. Birckmann, 1615-1616.

Vasoli, Cesare. *La dialettica e la retorica dell'Umanesimo. "Invenzione" e "metodo" nella cultura del XV e XVI secolo*. Milano: Feltrinelli, 1968.

———. "Topica ed enciclopedia nel XVI secolo." In *Acta conventus neo-latini turonensis. Troisième congrès international d'études néo-latines* 1: 721-28. Paris: Vrin, 1976.

Vigenère, Blaise de. *Les images, ou Tableaux de platte-peinture*. 2 vols. Ed. F. Graziani. Paris: Champion, 1995.

Voellus, Jean. *Usus rationis humanae studiosae iuventutis et theorice et practice*. Friburg: T. Meyer, 1630.

Welch, Kathleen E. *Electric Rhetoric: Classical Rhetoric, Oralism, and a New Literacy*. Cambridge and London: MIT Press, 1999.

Yates, Dame Frances. *The Art of Memory*. Chicago: The University of Chicago Press, 1966.

INDEX

Agricola, Rodolphus 152–54, 156
Allard, Sebastien 60, 69
Almquist, Katherine 2
Althusser, Louis 7–8
anxiety of influence 3, 71, 73; and *clinamen* 71–72; and *kenosis* 71, 73; and *tessera* 71, 74. *See also* Bloom
Archives Historiques de la Gironde 40, 51–53. *See also* Brunet and Delpit
Aristotle 23, 152, 165
Aron, Jean-Paul 80
Aron, Raymond 78
Austin, J. L. 7
Bakhtin, Mikhail 18–19, 25
Barthes, Roland 3, 92, 103, 126–43: "Plaisir aux Classiques" 126–27, 139, 142; "Qu'est-ce que l'ecriture" 132, 136; "Reflexions sur un manuel" 130, 134; "Responsabilité de la grammaire" 128, 132; *Le Degré zéro de l'écriture* 126–32, 134–35, 137, 139–43; *Critique et vérité* 139, 141; *Fragments d'un discour amoureux* 143; *Le Plaisir du texte* 143; *Sur Racine* 139; *S/Z* 140
Bataille, Georges 2
Beaumarchais, Pierre-Augustin Caron de 3, 91
Beaumarchais 90
Bensmaïa, Réda 140
Bergerac, Cyrano de 3, 108, 111, 113, 117–23

Blanchard, Jean-Vincent 3
Bloom, Harold 70–73: *The Anxiety of Influence* 65, 70
Bolzoni, Lina 150, 167
Bourdieu, Pierre 40
Brunet, Gustave 2, 39–44, 46–47, 49–53, 55
Bruyère, Nelly 155, 160
Bulletin du bibliophile 40–47. *See also* Techener
Burbules, Nicholas 170
Burnett, Robert 168–69
Bush, Vannevar 169
Butler, Judith 7–8
Calabrese, Omar 150
Camillo, Giulio 167
Camus, Albert 127, 142
Caprices d'un fleuve, les 90, 93–94, 100–1. *See also* philosopher
Cardano, Girolamo 163
Caussin, Nicolas 163, 166
Cave, Terence 11–12, 14, 18
Chartier, Roger 158
Chatelain, Jean-Marc 168
Chouans! 90–91, 97, 99. *See also* philospher
Christ: figure of 64–65, 67–68, 71. *See also* Michelangelo
Cicero 152–53, 157
classicism 131–34, 138; and *les Classiques* 126. *See also* Barthes

Index

Cloonan, William 3
Corneille, Pierre 135: *Le Cid* 80
Couperin, François 111, 115, 117, 123
culinary tradition; and cookbooks 79; and French excellence 78–79, 83–85. *See also* Vatel
Cusset, Catherine 110
Dagron, Tristan 7–8, 16, 21–24, 26
Dante, Alighieri 63, 72, 74; *The Divine Comedy* 64-65, 70, 72
deconstruction 9
Defaux, Gérard 6–7, 9–14, 16, 19
Delacroix, Eugene 60–74; *The Barque of Dante* 3, 60, 62–66, 69–74; *The Death of Sardanapalus* 60; *Liberty Leading the People* 69; *Michelangelo in His Studio* 66; *Scenes from the Massacre of Chios* 60, 73–74; *Journal 1822–1863* 66–68, 73; and Romanticism 70
Delpit, Jules 2, 39–40, 47–55
Denissel, Christophe 66
Derrida, Jacques 10, 14, 17, 19–20
Detcheverry, Arnaud 49
Deux Fragonard, les 90–91, 93–95, 99, 101. *See also* philosopher
Deyrolle, François-Marie 66
Diderot, Denis 3, 91
Dionne, Ugo 3
dispositio 153, 156, 164, 168, 170, 172
Dixon, John 65
Duval, Edwin 7, 11–12, 17–22, 29
early modern 1–3, 129, 133, 150, 169
écriture 3, 126–35, 137–39, 141–43. *See also* Barthes
écriture blanche 127, 142. *See also* Camus
Eisenstein, Elizabeth 158
emblem 165, 167–68; and book 166

Erasmus, Desiderius 6, 10–11, 13–14, 20
Foucault, Michel 7, 137; *Les Mots et les choses* 137; *La Volonté de savoir* 20
Fouquet, Nicolas 77–78
Fragonard, Cyprien 3, 91
Fragonard, Honoré 3, 91
Frame, Donald 41
Freud, Sigmund 2
Fronsac, Grégoire de 3, 89–90
Fronseca, Pedro de 161, 165
Fukuyama, Francis 85
Fumaroli, Marc 114, 150, 161, 165–66
Genieys-Kirk, Séverine 3
Gide, André 127
Gombrich, Ernst 165
Gray, Floyd 12
Grün, Alphonse 40–41, 53
Guizot, François 44–45
Habermas, Jürgen 169
Hannoosh, Michele 66
Hazard, Paul 103
Heidegger, Martin 2
Himmelfarb, Hélène 83, 86
Homer 11, 28
Huarte, Juan 163
Huchon, Mireille 24–25, 27, 29–30
Hugo, Victor 133
Internet 151, 168–72. *See also* World Wide Web
Jeanneret, Michel 11–12
Jobert, Berthléméy 66, 69–70
Joffé, Roland 82–85; *Vatel* 3, 77–78, 81, 83–87
Johnson, Lee 63
Johnson, Steven 151, 171, 173
Jonsen, Albert R. 166
Kress, Gunther R. 172

La Fontaine, Jean de 42, 127
LaGuardia, David 2
Landow, George 151, 170, 173
langue 135, 137–38. *See also écriture*
Lanson, Gustave 130, 136; "La Méthode de l'historie littéraire"136
Lévy, Pierre 170–71
Libertin, le 91, 96–97, 100. *See also* philosopher
littérarité 3
Loiseau, Bernard 79
Louis XIV 77–78, 80–82, 84–87; and court, 82–85; and *Louis, enfant roi* 86; and *Le Roi danse* 86, 167
Louis XV 89
Louis XVI 90
Lurine, Louis 81
Lyra, Nicholas de 6, 10–11, 16; *Postillae super totam bibliam* 13–14
Lyotard, Jean-Francois 170
Mallarmé, Stephen 141
Malvezin, Théophile 54
de Man, Paul 10
Marais, Martin 111, 115, 117, 123
Marot, Clémont 42
Marx, Karl 129
McGann, Jerome 39
McLuhan, Marshall 169
McNally, James R. 156
Michelangelo 63–68, 70–74, 85; *The Dying Slave* 68; *The Last Judgment* 3, 61, 64–67, 70–72; *Night* 63; *Pietà* 68; *Rachel* 63
Michelet, Jules 86, 103
Ministry of the Interior 45–46, 50
Ministry of Public Instruction, 44–45, 47, 49, 53–54. *See also Bulletin*
modern 1–3, 5; and modernity 2; and modernism 129, 134

Molière [Jean-Baptiste Poquelin] 111; *Le Bourgeois gentilhomme* 80
Montaigne, Michel de 2–3, 39–55, 127, 134–35, 138, 140–41; *Essais* 40–42, 45, 47, 54; and biography 39; and elite 39–40, 43
Mora, Stephanie 70
More, Thomas, *Utopia* 46
New Criticism 39
Nodier, Charles 41–44
Ong, Walter 3, 150–61, 164, 168–69, 171, 173–74; *The Presence of the Word* 158, 173; *Ramus, Method, and the Decay of Dialogue* 151–52
orality 158–60, 168, 172
Ory, Pascal 79
Ovid 11, 27
Pacte des loups 89, 91, 93–94, 97–98, 100–1. *See also* philosopher
Pascal, Blaise 138, 161, 166
Payen, Jean François 3, 39–44, 47, 52–53
Pelletier, Gérard 161, 166
performance theory 12
Persels, Jeffrey 32
Peters, Jeffrey 3
philology 5–7, 9, 11–13, 16, 20, 29; and philologists 5, 9, 12
philosopher: and characteristics 92–97; figure of 90–91, 98–99, 101–3; and French cinema 90–99, 102
Picard, Raymond 139
Plato 8–9, 16, 20, 27, 29: *Republic* 15–16; *Symposium* 6–9, 16, 20–21, 31
Possevino, Antonio 162–64, 168
postmodern 5, 102
poststructuralism 9
Poulet, Georges 10
preclassical 134–39

Prince de Condé [Louis II de Bourbon] 77–78, 82–84
Proust 1–2, 79, 127, 138
Rabanis, Joseph François 49–50, 54
Rabelais, François 10–12, 14, 17–25, 28–32, 42, 135–36, 140; *Gargantua* 2, 6–7, 9, 11, 13, 18; *Pantagruel* 26; *Tiers Livre* 31
Ramus, Petrus [Pierre de la Ramé] 3, 152–57, 160–61, 164
Raymond, Paul 54
Reeser, Todd 3
Regosin, Richard 16, 18–20
rhetoric 151; history of 150
Richou, Gabriel 39
Ridicule 90, 93–94, 98, 101. See also philosopher
Rigolot, François 12
Rimbaud, Arthur 121–23, 141
Romantic manifesto 69
Rossi, Paolo 150, 167
Rostand, Edmond 118
Rubin, James 60, 65, 69
Sade, Donatien Alphonse François, Marquis de 2, 103, 111, 113
Saint Paul 6, 15
Sartre, Jean Paul 129–32, 136–37, 141: *Qu'est-ce que la littérature* 129, 131–32, 136
Screech, Michael 12
Scribe, Eugene 79
Sévigné, Marie de Rabutin Chantal 1–2, 77–78, 127, 138
Shapiro, Stephen 3
Shrimplin, Valerie 64
Socrates 23–25, 31; figure of 8, 23
Sollers, Philippe 3, 108–23: *Le Débat* 114; *Éloge de l'infini* 120; *L'Étoile des amants* 109; *L'Évangile selon Philippe* 110; *La Fête à Venise* 108–9, 111, 115–16; *Les Folies Françaises* 111, 113; *La Gamme* 115; *La Guerre du goût* 123; *Passion fixe* 117; *Le Portrait du jouer* 109–10; and *illisible* 110–11
Sontag, Susan 130
Spitzer, Leo 9, 18
Steinberg, Leo 64
Stendhal [Henri Beyle] 68; *Histoire de la peinture en Italie* 67–68
Struever, Nancy 150–51
Tagliabue, Guido Morpurgo 164
Techener, Jacques 40–43, 47, 55
theory 5–7, 9, 16, 29
Thierry, Augustin 44–45, 48, 50, 55
Thomas, Gunther 160
Thompson, William 111
Toulmin, Stephen 166
Trinquet, Roger 39
Valéry, Paul 127
Vatel, François 78–81, 83–84, 86
Vaugelas, Claude Favre, seigneur de 128
Villemain, Abel-François 40, 47–49, 55
Villon, François 3, 108, 111, 113–17, 123
Virgil: figure of 64–65, 71–72, 74. See also Delacroix
Watteau, Antoine 111–13
Welch, Kathleen E. 150
Wimsatt, W. K. 11
World Wide Web 160, 168–71. See also Internet
Yates, Frances 167

Printed in the United States
35713LVS00004B/346-354